The Final Debacle

By Greg Cayea

Printed in the United States of America

First Printing, 2021

ISBN: 978-0-9970921-1-0

Black Apple Publishing

*Dedicated to my grandma, the deadliest bingo player
the world has ever known...
Ruth Greenfield - August 3, 1922 – October 19, 2021*

CHAPTER 0: THE WOLF

We were at a beautiful lodge in Vail, Colorado in a room that cost a million times the amount that I wanted to pay, and it sure looked pretty low-quality for the three hundred dollars per night I was shelling out for it. It was right on the slopes. I had to bribe Chloe with a fancy vacation to get her to be okay with all this. I even bought her those little bottles of wine from the liquor store, even though I was newly sober at her behest, to keep her not miserable and somewhat enjoyable; not an easy task to accomplish.

The TV was on. She wasn't even drinking her wine—probably to show me how "normal people" don't have to drink, even if there's alcohol in the room, even though she asked me to get her the damn wine to begin with. But I didn't give a shit how normal people drank, I don't give a shit about that right now. My head is spinning and my whole life is on the line. And here I am watching goddam reality TV shows, though I actually *do* enjoy the fuckin Bachelor.

But I had a million things on my mind: Will the last deal go through? How ironic and perfect of a story it would be for the DEA if the last time was the *only* time I got caught... How would I stay sober through this all? Am I beating myself up? Could I take a few Xanax just to keep from panicking and going to prison? Will the wolf attack me? Will my Harlem Guy and Joey Landlord get the packages? Will I get the money? Will this *really all end up as planned?* Do I even deserve to live happily ever after? The chances of this working *again*, me getting away with this *again,* well, it was just too hard to believe.

The Cotto fight came on. He was fighting Antonio Margarito. I had made sure we would get the pay-per-view fight in our room. It was the only thing that made me happy. It was the second fight in my life that I had watched without scotch. It was hard. Chloe and I weren't having sex, even though we always tried. We had known each other for too long and even though she looked like an Instagram model, I couldn't get my dick hard for the life of me to fuck her. That was embarrassing. It made me depressed. How could I not fuck her after all these years? What will people think if they find out? I had known her since I was like ten... Maybe that's why I got so nervous before every attempt?

Cotto beat Margarito, but not in the way I wanted him to. I wanted him to smash his face in, not win by decision after a twelve-round bout. I wanted that fuckin prick Margarito to go down on his neck—head smashed; life ruined—but that didn't happen. It should have, but shit isn't always fair.

Chloe took a shower. She looked like the definition of a girl that every guy in the world wanted to demolish, and here I was paying three hundred goddam dollars per night and giving her a fucking ski vacation with the little money I had left and *not fucking her.* I was the laughing stock of manhood. Still, somehow, she hadn't abandoned me after what happened, and that's seriously important. I would never forget her loyalty.

She got out of the shower. This is my chance. Do something, Greg. Make your inner sex child proud. I got outa bed to kiss her. Should I try again? If I try again and I can't get hard again—well, I couldn't take that type of emasculation to be honest. I wasn't sure if I had thick enough skin for rejection like that, not right now. So, we went to bed without trying to fuck.

I had to wake up at a little after four in the morning to get to the small town that My Grower lived in. I won't say where it was cause it's real, and it exists, and this was all very illegal. It was 2011 and weed was still a drug back then. For the protection of everyone involved, I'll never give you too much info, but I'll share just enough for you to understand. Where I was going wasn't the grow house, it was simply a house that he rented in a rural area many miles east. Chloe told me she didn't want to hear about it—not one word. She didn't want to be involved. After this was all done, we would never again speak of it. And after what happened, I had to respect her wishes.

I woke her up the next morning and said, "I'll be back in about twelve hours." I told her that cause she wanted to go skiing, which meant I had to pay for a half-day pass for us both, even though we'd only have one hour, but she didn't care. It was her way of saying: you're lucky I'm even here. And I'll give her that, I *was* lucky she was there. After all, I almost killed her a few weeks ago.

Her eyes opened with vigor and her words were sharp, without a morning crackle in her throat, as if she had been up all night doing vocal exercises to yell at me. With a disgusted tone, she said, "I told you NOT TO BRING IT UP!" And then she went back to bed. My heart beat hard, but I had no time to be anxious about *her,* not today. I thought of The Wolf. I hated that goddam Wolf. I'll tell you about The Wolf in a moment.

I brushed the snow off my rental car—luxury rental car—that was parked outside our hotel lodge. I spent more money than I wanted to on that damn car too to remind Chloe she hadn't settled too low. She was driving me nuts, but she believed in me, and she was all I had. So, I had to keep her happy. Then I drove four hours to a small house—not the grow house—another house where he lived after harvest—or before—or I don't know how that shit worked to be honest, I just sold the shit.

I parked outside around eight in the morning—that's when I told him I'd be there. He was always up early cause he loved to go snowboarding every day and snowboarders are always up early because of that. He opened the door and The Wolf stared at me, she was about seven feet tall on her hind legs and weighed close to two million pounds. She guarded the pot. He tried to calm her growl by saying her name in a calm voice: *Bianca*. He said Bianca many times in a soothing tone. She seemed to chill out. He told me to stay there, to not come in yet until she relaxed a bit more. I waited for a few moments before he told me to come in. And then:

CHOMP!

Her predator teeth sunk into my pants—right where my dick was. She missed me by a centimeter and tore a small hole right next to my cock. I had a mini panic attack, but I had to hide it. If I showed fear, she would surely attack. My grower just said to her in another calm voice to stop it. That wasn't the protection I was hoping for. "Just be cool, don't look at her," he told me.

We made cheap conversation about whatever. I couldn't think: The Wolf, Chloe, the lies, my life, everything; I couldn't think. Conversation was useless. I tried not to be scared, but The Wolf was very scary. Eventually, she laid down in her bed. Thank god. I didn't tell him that this would be my last package. I said no when he offered me his bong. I said I was sober. His look read: *sober?* "Since when?" he asked.

"Since like… a few weeks," I told him. I wasn't sure if that would affect business. My thoughts were loud. I pretended like all was kosher, that I'd be back in a few weeks like usual.

We packaged the weed together in the usual format. He asked me why I only wanted ten pounds. I told him cause it was a slow month, that I still had leftovers back east. That was a lie. I wasn't even living back east anymore. I kept all this a secret. When the weed was safely packaged, he told me I couldn't mail the boxes from his town, and that I had to drive fifty miles away to the next town and use that post office. He said that the feds had been cracking down around there. That made me very uneasy. If god wanted to punish me for this, now would be the opportune time. I had never had a problem in six years, but now that I was sober and had made a promise to stop, now that I had promised Chloe and myself that this would be it, it would make perfect sense for the problems to begin.

I drove fifty miles with two boxes in my backseat. It was a very nerve-racking ride. I went five below the speed limit. There were cornfields to my right, and cornfields to my left. In the distance, the Rocky Mountains could vaguely be seen. I wasn't so close to them anymore. That's where Chloe still was, waiting for my return: in the Rocky Mountains. I was in a completely new land since this morning. Colorado changes very quickly like that, especially when there're many years of prison laughing at you in your mind.

I got to the post office and got in line. I rehearsed my story in the car. It was the same story as always. *What are you shipping?* Art. *What's the value of the content?* Art is priceless. *What are the contents?* Art. *The value?* A million dollars. If I lose these packages, my life is over. Art is priceless. What's the fastest I can get them to Jersey and New York? *Why are you sending them to two different places?* My parents live in New York, I live in Jersey. *Why are they so weirdly weighted?* It's abstract art—I don't quite know how to answer that sir. I kept repeating all those sentences to myself as the line got shorter and the clerk approached. There was only one clerk in the no-name town post office.

Then something happened that had never happened before: The box wasn't sealed properly. The scent was fragrant—very distinct. I bent my neck forward to get a better whiff. It smelled—reeked— fuck. Weed was everywhere. People behind me formed a barrier to the escape route. Should I just leave? I can't—I need this money. It's like twenty-five-fucking-thousand dollars. I need this money to get sober. I can't get a real job. I have no skills. I need this. Stay calm.

The woman in front of me went to the clerk. I could hear everything she said. That meant they would all hear me too— everything. My entire bullshit story would be on blast. I rethought my entire existence. It ran like a short film behind my eyelids every time I blinked. The woman in front of me finished up. I had no idea what to do. I was about to get caught. My life was about to be over. Chloe will wonder why I never came back—and be mad about it too. She won't even feel bad about whichever prison I end up at. She won't come visit me or try to get me out. *It's your fault, of course you're in prison,* she'd tell me. They'd want my grower. I'd have to turn down the plea deal. I'd never snitch—ever. And once they found out how much I had moved this year alone, well, then I'd be fucked.

"Next," the clerk said.

I froze. Then unfroze.

I approached the counter. I felt faint, like I might collapse. I put the box on the scale. The clerk looked at it, then at me. *Breathe,* I told myself. *Breathe. Release. Breathe. Exhale.* I accomplished many great things these last six years, I thought to myself...

But this is the last deal I'll ever do, and it was. It all started six years ago, right when KC and I had broken up and I was rebuilding my life. My goal was to become the most famous theatre producer in the world, and to do that required capital. It all started when I was a barista...

PART 1: SHADY ENTREPRENEUR

CHAPTER 1: BOLZANO'S

The restaurant was called Bolzano's and it had just opened. All the employees were new, especially me, at least that's what it felt like. I boasted to my then-girlfriend, KC, how I miraculously pulled off the pizza-boy at some dipshit delicatessen in Long Island making dick money to the barista at the trendiest restaurant in Manhattan. But I probably had the shittiest job in the restaurant—worse than the busboys even, and they were treated like shit. At least they were needed. I was like that powdered cinnamon they put on your cappuccino that you could totally live without. I was treated like trash, like they treated all the Latinos. That's why I started learning Spanish, to fit in. I was around it all day and thought it would make me more accomplished if I spoke another language. It's all about looking good to the public, and looking good requires combinations of unlikely pairings, like tough tattoos and theatre, or being white and speaking Spanish, many others too, but so that's why becoming bilingual was so important. But all I was *really* concerned with at the time was making more money than KC, which I wasn't. I was only making a little more at the trendy restaurant than I was when I was making pizzas actually. All my ideas seemed to backtrack my life. So that's how it all started: not making the money I thought

I'd be making at a trendy restaurant—in fact, making *less money than anyone else who worked there out of all hundred employees.* That shit really got to me, and so that's why I started selling weed. I had no idea where this path would lead, but certainly not where I ended up.

One day I was standing by my barista station waiting for tickets to pop up, making whatever order that was on that ticket, even though I wasn't very good at making any of the drinks, but still got all erratic whenever someone questioned my competence and waiting for the overpaid and ungrateful waiters to come by with their black trays and pick up their lattes and shit. Why my life was so goddam frustrating is beyond me. Was I defective? I mean, it's terrible that the white people got the better jobs, and I suppose it's not fair—not like life was ever fair, but like—*I'm white.* Why was I at the fuckin barista station? Was I not white enough? Must be that goddam tribal tattoo I got in Colorado. Fuckin tattoo. Anyway, I started fuckin up the drinks on purpose. Self-sabotage was always my thing… not cause I was an idiot, it was all well-calculated to encourage myself—challenge even—to get myself outa whatever situation I didn't wanna be in. I was really upset about it all—my social standing and whatnot, but so I carried the weed on me in the beginning, hoping to sell at least some of it. It had been nearly three weeks and *still* I hadn't sold my first fucking ounce, the ounce I told The Gak would be sold in no more than a week. The Gak was my first supplier. I graduated to more sophisticated business partners later on, but for now I just thought: What a failure I am, can't even sell weed for The Gak. But that all changed and changed fast.

First, I met Handsome Arturo. I'll call him Handsome Arturo cause in real life that's what he looked like he might be named. He was an off-duty model that looked like what every man wanted to look like—I think, not me though, I was confident in my appearance. Anyway, he was also some kinda Italian or whatever, and Arturo is an Italian type name, I think—I don't know shit about Italy. But I'm Italian—and Jewish. I'm a Jewtalian. Anyway, that's why I'm gonna call him Handsome Arturo. Meeting dudes like him made me feel queasy cause *I was usually the pretty one*; the one that got all the attention. Now I just felt short when I was with him, but I got over it.

He was handsome, but his maturity level was a bit below average—like second grade maybe. Sometimes it bothered me, like his bathroom jokes—those are never funny—but he told them all the time so I kinda *had* to laugh. What was I gonna do? Tell the guy he wasn't funny? I could've told him that, but he was the first person to become a pseudo-friend at that place, so I didn't wanna upset him. The point is, he became a regular client, and soon I saw him often.

The first time I went over to his brownstone in Brooklyn Heights, we played video games and joked about girls; nothing out of the ordinary. The second time I went over, I met his roommate, Nate, and sold him some weed too. It was around that time that I finally sold my first ounce and made a goddam extra fifty bucks. The third time I went over he showed me his paintings. He was an artist too, a genuine Ken-of-all-trades. But by the time Bolzano's had shut down—I'll get to that—my visits to his brownstone slowed down and it had been quite a while since my last visit when he sent me a note one day on my Blackberry a buncha months later tellin me to swing by.

At that point, he had a girlfriend—a chick version of him—and she was pregnant and had moved in with him. He sent me a text one day and told me about it like it was some random fortune cookie that came with a cheap Chinese dinner. Like *whoaaa trippy! Pregnant?*

He and his girlfriend had met at the highly elite restaurant he had easily scored a job at as top waiter right after Bolzano's shut down and laid off all the employees—not me though, nope. I got fired like a champ. More on that later. Anyway, I remember thinking: if I were as tall as him, I could get those jobs too. What a prick that this guy never had a problem in his life, except for maybe his newly pregnant girlfriend that didn't seem to like him all that much from what I could tell, at least. And the beef jerky, that mighta been a problem too.

Oh right, when I showed up on that day, there was beef jerky everywhere; beef jerky hanging like laundry in the kitchen, in the living room, up and down the hallways. I mean, it was all over—disgusting, actually—but interesting. That's how Nate (his roommate) was paying rent. He was always on another hustle—Nate was—which is maybe why we got along so well. But anyway, it reeked like jerky in that damn place, a bit more toxicity to the already tense household. I didn't mind the smell, but Jacqueline did. I'll call his girlfriend Jacqueline cause that's a hot chick name, and she was a hot fuckin chick who seemed completely indifferent to the relationship with Handsome Arturo. Kinda like any dude with good genes woulda been fine with her. I don't think she woulda dated me, but I'm not sure. I probably had to be taller—and I'm not like a midget or whatever. I know that's some kinda bad word now, so sorry or whatever, but he was like six-foot-something, and girls like that shit, I think. But I don't wanna get tied up on that, I mean, not like it's his fault he's tall. Back to the bad energy I felt immediately upon entering that day. It was clear it was disrupting the household: The beef jerky had become a thing.

"Duuuuude!" He said to me after opening the door to his apartment. He was kinda dumb but always so excited to see me. That sounds bad, but what am I gonna do, lie to you? And the way he talked, his inflections went all over the place, so you gotta imagine that as he's talking, all his questions ended in these high-pitched surfer tones. "What's up bro?" Like that bro that he just said ended with a high inflection. "I haven't seen you in forever!" He said to me at the door and gave me a hug. "I'm gonna be a *dad*. Crazy, right?" But he said that like the tiny person growing inside Jacqueline was nothing more than a science experiment that was going just swell.

"It's def crazy," I assured him as I walked in, sniffing my way to the jerky. "You're like an adult." It was goddam wretched in there. Finally, I was like: "Dude, what in the fuck?"

"Oh, I know." He was frustrated, I could tell. I couldn't fathom how he and Jacqueline were keeping civil in that abomination of an apartment. That smell, jeez, it was rancid. There were dried cows hanging from clotheslines in the kitchen.

"What the *fuck is that?*" I asked.

"It's Nate's new thing. He's making beef jerky." And for the first time, Handsome Arturo was serious. "It's terrible, but we're moving into our own place soon, so, only a little bit longer. Is it bothering you?" I had never seen him so concerned.

"Nah man. All good." And you know what? After I got over the smell, I thought it was awesome. "It's actually pretty cool," I said. He didn't think so.

"I don't know…" he said.

As we walked into the living room, I saw that it was all over, in every room. Everywhere we walked: more jerky, fuckin everywhere. I stopped thinking it was so cool. It was horrible. "Sooo—what? He's selling it?" I asked.

"I don't fucking know. I guess so. *Jacqueline hates it.*" As if anyone would *not* hate it. *THIS IS DISGUSTING DUDE.* That's what I was thinking, but he seemed to have a good handle on it, maybe. Anyway, I could tell that he was stressed out. It was the first time I realized that I wasn't even there for the weed, I was there to rescue him from his life, to be his friend. That type of thing became common. I sat down on his couch and asked:

"How's it all goin? You guys happy still?"

He hushed me. "She's in the other room." Then he upped the volume of his voice, presumably so that she didn't think we were talkin about her. "You wanna play Xbox?" he asked like a teenager. And I got no beef with gamers, it's just… I never understood how to work those damn things. It's like, ever since I made it back to civilization, after boot camp and all the other juvenile institutions I was accustomed to, and after living on the road all grungy and whatnot, all that technology was dizzying. The damn controllers made no sense—too many buttons. And what's the deal with having to code my driver before the race starts? Can't I just choose between the black or white guy or hot chick or whatever and hop in either the Mercedes or Thunderbird and get on with it? I don't give a fuck what color hair the guy has, just make him fast and efficient, am I wrong?

But I said yes anyway. "Sure, but I don't know how to play." That's when Jacqueline walked out, wiping the crud from her sleepy eyes. She was gorgeous, but moody. She was pregnant—of course—but I got the feeling it was more Handsome Arturo that put her in a mood than the pregnancy. Or maybe it was the beef jerky.

"Hi Greg." And she *never* said hi to me, usually. "What are you playing babe?" She asked Handsome Arturo, in between heavy sighs. I was beginning to think that maybe I should just sell him the weed and get out, cause when she sat down, she sat down with a heavy presence. A presence that said: *Stop selling my boyfriend weed. He's supposed to be practicing how to become a fucking father. You're not helping you scumbag.* Maybe she was thinking something else, but probably not. Yeah, I should definitely leave. I forget that weed is a drug, that some people abuse it. I never understood people who smoked so much, but maybe that's because I was always drunk. Well, not always, not yet at least.

I tried to speed the visit up by saying: "You want an eighth, right?" I was feeling guiltier by the second. I thought to myself: how could you buy weed at a time like this? You're gonna be a damn father, what kinda dad are you gonna be? It was getting more uncomfortable with each heavy sigh Jacqueline let out. But he didn't seem to notice—or care—that she was the most upset human in the world.

He set up my character in the video game then said, "Actually, give me two." And although I felt bad about this whole scenario, I was determined to keep the clients I had, find more clients, and sell more damn weed. I was determined to make this goddam career a success. I had to *first* make some damn money so I could quit my fucking job. That was step one. Step two wasn't so clear just yet. I was still battling breakup fatigue from the horrendous breakup with KC, so I only had the capacity to think one move ahead. Right now it was: *make money.* There's no hope for you if you aren't wealthy. Sell more weed or bigger quantities. I figured out soon that if I just told people to buy more, they usually did. Then I learned that if I told them they had no other option—that all I had was a quarter ounce, they still bought it. And so that's what I did. But Handsome Arturo was one of my first clients, so I still went over to his place, even though he usually only wanted an eighth, except for that day when the problems in his life outweighed his desire to keep frugal with his weed-intake. I took out a quarter ounce—double his usual order, and Jacqueline looked double as pissed.

"It smells horrible, babe. Can you talk to him? Is he home?"

"So you're not a beef jerky fan?" I asked her, trying to make light of a shitty stench and redeem myself for selling too much weed to her unresponsive father-of-her-child-to-be.

"Every week, Greg… *Every week*, it's something else." She looked at Handsome Arturo, "Babe." But he was still busy setting up the game, even though I made it abundantly clear that I had changed my mind about playing and that I was going to leave. "Baby." She said again. But nothing. "BABE!"

"Yeah?"

"Can you talk to Nate?"

"It's just a phase baby, he'll be out of it soon. And we're moving. Just—I know. It sucks."

"But it smells like fucking shit babe. I'm like, throwing up in my throat right now. Aren't you?" And she looked at me. Don't fuckin get *me* involved, I thought. "Don't you just want to jump out the fucking window? Isn't that the most…" And she looked for the right word, the word that would most accurately capture her unhappiness, "*Revolting* smell you've ever smelt?"

"Well…" I quickly probed my brain for words. "I mean. It's not my favorite smell—I don't know, I kinda like the idea though. Entrepreneurial-spirited I guess, right? Is he making money from it?" But there was no happy ending to this conversation. She didn't like me, and the reason I was there was absolutely no help.

"It's fucking ridiculous—really—*ridiculous*. I hate it." She said to me, about to let it all out. I could see it resting below her eyeshadow: fumes. She hated me and everything I stood for. She wanted Nate dead and for her boyfriend to finally stop fucking with that goddam video game. Her eyes spoke death to all. *LET ME OUTA HERE*, I was thinking. But Handsome Arturo—in his oblivious state of being—just let me fend for myself. And she didn't stop, she kept going: "It's disgusting. *DIS-GUS-TING*. Ugh. I wish he would fucking stop."

Oh jeez, I had never thought to myself: Thank god this isn't my life, but at that particular moment, that's exactly what I was thinking. Get out, Greg. "So… Here's the weed dude." I motioned to him that the quarter was on the table, then made a break for it:

"I'm actually heading over to Scotty Gun's house in Jersey." Scotty Guns was another model-waiter that I had met at Bolzano's—before they shut the entire place down and laid off all the workers, like I said. But I didn't realize they weren't friends. I figured all model-waiters were friends with each other. I mean, they looked the same, kinda.

"He's a fucking asshole," Handsome Arturo said immediately. Ah, so he *is paying* attention. Jacqueline is right. Then he told me, "the guy's got problems—tell him I say hi." And before I left, he told me to: "Wait—I want to show you a painting I've been working on." He walked right past Jacqueline, not paying her much attention. I could see how that musta been frustrating for her, and he took me into the other room. He unveiled a big painting; it made no sense. Maybe I'm wrong, but I'm fairly certain it was fucking atrocious. "Crazy right?" He said. He always used the word *crazy* to describe everything. I rarely lied—just exaggerated. I preferred to twist the conversation to something that I could stand behind, you know... that wasn't mean or too deceitful. So, I just said something along the lines of: "I definitely couldn't do that." Which is true, I doubt I could replicate that monstrosity.

"Are you showing him your painting?" Jacqueline said from the other room, like *don't think you can run away from your child you piece of shit*. Handsome Arturo rolled his eyes like I would understand his irritation. But I didn't. She seemed right about everything, but what was I gonna do? Tell my almost-friend that he was wrong? I just knew that I had to get the hell outa there.

Finally, he paid me and I busted out. Jacqueline couldn'ta been happier to rid her jerky-infused apartment of me. But not every client was easy to handle. Some frightened me, like Scotty Guns. He was a goddamn lunatic. Every time I saw him, I hoped to leave his place alive.

Later that day was no exception…

CHAPTER 2: SCOTTY GUNS

Scotty Guns was a volatile southern dude—big in size, mid-thirties, from Jackson, Mississippi. His has-been modeling career had left him hungry for fame and it didn't seem to be fading with age. He auditioned every week for some shit and never booked a damn thing. Just some background work and bullshit model gig every now and then. The whole situation gave him a wild temper; it was bad. He frightened everybody that was around him.

I remember one day after a long night of coke and booze, he came into Bolzano's on his day off cause someone called out sick. He was cleaning off the table that he had just been serving cause the busboy hadn't been quick enough to get the glasses off, which agitated him. The poor, newly immigrated kid from Bangladesh had no clue what he had done wrong. Scotty Guns started screaming about how *sand niggers* were taking over the country and how they couldn't even speak English and how the fuck was he supposed to serve *Americans* when his son-of-a-bitch busboy couldn't even comprehend his *simple English directions.*

The entire restaurant was full of people. His girlfriend at the time was one of the floor managers, her name was Martina—she was humiliated. Her dark Italian skin turned flush red and she ducked out of sight. When he came over to me at the barista station to pick up some coffee, I was sure he'd exclude me from his rampage—he always liked me, I think—but no. "Where in tha fuck is the gadang coffee—motherfucking sand nigger motherfucker—WHY THA FUCK'M AH HERE OHN MA DAY OFF!" And he gripped the cup of coffee hard onto his black tray and went off to another table.

Martina told him to go home. She transferred herself to another restaurant a week later when she tried to break up with him and he threatened to break her neck. But the thing that pissed me off was nobody ever spoke about that day ever again. I mean, I'm all for second chances—wait, am I? I don't know, but screaming about *sand niggers* and calling all the food runners *spics?* That kinda thing really got to me. It was the first time I realized how goddam racist the restaurant industry was. How could they let that slide?

But the reason I went all the way to Jersey to see him after I left Handsome Arturo's house is cause I told The Gak (not only my local wholesaler, but also some kid I went to middle school with before I was shipped off) that I would have his money ready on a certain day, and I was a man of my word. I never broke my word—not really. That's why I was goin all the way out to New Jersey to see that fuckin sociopath. I only had a handful of clients, and they weren't buyin weed from me every week, so I had to make these trips, but I was motherfucking determined to make a name for myself: First as a drug-dealer, then as a movie star. Sometimes I didn't even care if it was in weed or theatre, a name is a name—unlike what Scotty Guns had. He may not be able to achieve prominence, the old fuck, but I sure as hell wasn't gonna turn into what he turned into: A goddam prick with no skillsets other than balancing three entrees and five appetizers at the same time, which he didn't even do cause the food runners did that shit. No way. I was gonna make enough to produce a movie or Broadway play and go to all those fancy meetings and be goddam important; be known. A fucking legend. I had to do *something.* I had to be more than a fucked-up dropout with a minor juvenile record. No, I'm not some moron. I had to fucking make the most of life. Maybe I really failed up until that point, but I wasn't about to lose again. I'll win at *something.*

I hopped on the New Jersey Transit to Princeton, which was like more than a fuckin hour train ride and got to his shitty apartment. It was like the bottom of some house, a basement sorta. All this time acting and still the dickhead lived in a basement. What a pathetic fuck this guy is. He thinks he's gonna be famous? Famous *for what?* Livin in basements? I don't understand how anyone could devote their life to such a risky endeavor just to *get famous.* I wasn't in this game to be famous—I don't think—I was in this game cause my destiny was to be a legend, so that all my cousins and uncles and family friends would see that I was right all along: I don't need a damn full-time job. I was a movie star in the making—but not cause I thought fame was *cool*, like I said, cause it was all I had to offer the world: my story. All those institutions were gonna make great late-night TV show snippets. Jimmy Fallon was gonna love me. And I was right.

I walked onto his set and he asked me just like I thought he would:

"So how did you become the most interesting person alive?"

I knew he had to flatter all his guests, that it was partly his job, but I also knew that there was a hint of truth behind every compliment he gave. I told him all about how I was treated as a kid, how I overcame my shit, how I took revenge on the system, how I got caught, how I ran away, how I escaped, how I ended up livin as a beatnik, how I got into acting, all that, and he was dumbfounded. He had never met anyone like me. I was—

—"Motherfucker shit! Come in! Shit"

I snapped out of it. Scotty Guns was at the door. I get lost in my head sometimes, but I'm back now. I'm okay, don't worry. I walked in—still thinking about what a failure he had become. How long you really gonna chase such a fantastical dream? It's time to do something productive dude, like get into real estate and buy a house—not that I would ever buy a house, that sounds horrible, so does real estate. How normal. But anyway, his basement was somewhere in the middle of the suburbs. I wondered if that famous college Princeton was nearby. Where all the white guys with plaid ties go. I imagine that's probably what it looks like: a buncha bros in plaid ties seeking a boring life that they're certain will entertain the world, but none of us even care. We all think you're boring. Try hitchhiking the wrong direction on 9/11 dickfuck. I bet they all got their driver's license at the same time too; typical. I thought of my childhood friends that were now in some fucking university probably probing potential jobs on Wall Street. I bet they think *I'm the fuckup*. Whatever guys.

There was some really young and overly hot chick at his place. She was still in his bed, which was probably on purpose. He probably told her to stay there. The bed was nestled in the wall in the back of the room in this little enclave that you couldn't even sit up fully in cause the ceiling was a foot away from the top of the queen-sized mattress she was laying on. She looked at me from her cage and I wondered: How could this chick fuck him? Where did he find her anyway?

"She's the hostess at the other restaurant," he told me. Oh right—he worked in, not one fancy restaurant, but two fancy restaurants. Meanwhile, I couldn't even get outa the barista station—couldn't even land a job as a bar back. That's why one day I went up to Salvatore and quit.

"Sal. I'm leaving. I can't be a barista forever, I'm making sixty bucks a day," I said to him after four or five months.

"Craig we fuhkkin need you." He always called me Craig... fuckin Italian goombah. I stopped even correcting him. "How can I get you stay? Name a price."

I told him to make me a bartender. He laughed. "You don't know how ta fwuckin bahrtend, do yaz? I'll tell you dis, I'll make ya bahrback, good?"

So that's how I finally got a job as a barback, but I was a bit too lazy for that. My coworker, the other barback of the restaurant, this Mexican guy who worked way too hard, he kept yelling at me. But eventually, we started drinkin beers in the walk-in freezer together and bonded over that—but yeah, I was pretty bad at it. I asked the bartender to show me how to bartend. He was a tiny forty-year-old guy with a bald head from the Lower East Side. You wouldn't pick a fight with this dude, even though he was a hundred pounds.

"So look, de only ting you really gotta know is to get da colah right. You get da colah right an da customahz think it's them fault. I been doin dis twenty yeahrs." So I started memorizing the colors of all the drinks. Then he told me, "And de Jews—dey don't like ta taste de alcohol. Okay? So you just put in extra juice, got dat?" He looked over repeatedly to see if I was paying attention, as if he wasn't explaining the shit just to be talkin to thin air.

But anyway, the hostess in Scotty Guns basement, he tried to get her to leave by sayin all sortsa rude remarks. And I had to pretend like we were friends. It was horrible. He wasn't even trying to be cool or impress me, I think he was just straight up a prick, mad about all kinds of whatever, you know? Life just hadn't panned out the way he wanted it to. Serves you right asshole. All those years with the moms of the guys on the football team tellin him he was handsome enough for Hollywood, charismatic enough for New York—all those cheerleaders that probably asked him out to prom, tellin him he would be famous one day, well, that shit just didn't cut it up here. He was a penny a million in this city, and he was ass-angry about that shit. I would be too if I were him.

I wasn't planning on hanging out with him, but he was too much of a loose bullet to just leave like that. He was like a biology experiment gone wrong if that even makes sense. Who cares if it doesn't? And I'm not sour about it, I'm just sayin this guy coulda done so much, but instead he blew lines of coke with me in the bathroom and got called in to serve tables on his day off. Chump.

When the teenage hostess finally left—well, maybe she was twenty… jeez she was hot. Anyway, when she left, he told me we were meeting his friend Sarge at a bar in town. I didn't wanna go to town, no way. Buy the weed and drive me to the station—or I'll walk, just like I did to get here. Why didn't he pick me up if he had a car? But then when we started walking over to town, I realized he didn't even have a car. You don't even have a car? Man, I really better work harder than he did. The bar was only like twenty feet from his house, but still.

So we met that guy Sarge—no idea who or where he came from, he was just there. He was a blue-collar dude: bald, thick, muscular, and very Jersey. He was a bit scary actually. He practically ignored me the whole time we were there. He laughed without looking away from the TV whenever Scotty Guns made some idiotic remark that demanded some kinda chuckle.

About an hour into our aggressive hangout—we were on our third drink and Scotty Guns was gettin loud and makin me uncomfortable—I told him to buy the damn half-ounce, the whole reason I came all the way out there. He still hadn't paid me. Sarge looked over at me like I was an amateur.

"So you want this weed or what dude?" I asked him.

"Whut kyna nig-nug ya got?" I hated the way he talked. He was a racist motherfucker, but still talked like a black dude. What a psychological mess he was. And he was always makin up words, and those words always sounded a bit like the *n word*... Like *nig-nug*—am I wrong? Doesn't that sound a bit racist? I mean, hadn't he ever seen a black person before New York? Isn't the whole state of Mississippi black? Maybe that's why he hated them. But why? Did he think they took all his acting jobs?

I looked at him. "Why you so anti-black man? You think they're all stealing your modeling gigs that you used to get when you were younger?" That mighta been mean, but still—it had to be said. Sarge finally took notice and gave me a pound. Scotty Guns got pretty upset but I handled the situation by saying: "Don't get all mad dude, come on. I've seen some shit, you don't scare me man. You're just tall and southern—nothing else. Nothing special dude. I promise you that." He was surprised I was talkin to him like that and stood up to fight me. That's when Sarge got up and got right in the middle of us.

"Don't fuckin touch him," he told Scotty Guns.

I felt powerful.

"Sup dog? You lost in yer head er sumthing?"

I snapped out of it. Sarge hadn't moved. I was really tired I guess. Anyway, like I was tellin you, it made me sick to associate myself with a racist like that, but what am I supposed to do?

Defend all black people while I'm basically alone with this big southern redneck fuck? Better to not stir his hick pot. His anger always simmered below a boil. I didn't want him to lose his dumb southern fuckin temper. He was always ready to pounce for no fuckin reason like someone had challenged him to a duel in front of his non-existent mistress—like an overgrown bully with no adult coping mechanisms. So I just let him be all ignorant and shit. I even used his lingo back to him so the redneck fuck would understand he was winning the conversation, even though no competition had been formed.

I told him: "My *nig-nug* is called Alaskan Thunderfuck, and it's the best weed in the goddam city." I had started to tell everyone I had the best weed in the city. I thought I did, but then I realized how much better I could get if I was only willing to hop on a plane and go directly to the source, but at the time I was still buying locally—like an amateur. That would change.

"Damn nigga! You makin them strayns up boy? Alayskain WHA?" Ugh, he *always* said that word. Who does that? The guy was havin a serious identity crisis. Whatever, not my problem. "Gimme em both son! I want em all! You want some bruh?" He was talkin to Sarge at that point. "It's ohn me—I got you!" But Sarge gave him a shake of the head, then went back to lookin at the TV on the wall and sipping his beer. Actually, I don't know what Sarge did, but he wasn't very responsive the entire time we were there, and he definitely turned down the weed. That much I remember.

We were the only people in the damn place. The sports bar was big enough to host the Olympics but it was only like 2PM. Sarge really didn't seem to like Scotty Guns—who the hell *was he anyway?* The guy definitely did not work in a restaurant. I have no idea where the two even met. To be honest, I didn't really know too much about Scotty Guns either, just that he truly believed he was some rising star that would make it later in age, like Morgan Freeman. He used to always tell me shit like: "Know how old Morgan Freeman wuz when he broke?"

"No." I would tell him.

"Nigga bartended teel he wuz damn near forty or sum shit." He was full of justifications for his failures. I didn't realize how much I really hated him till that day. Scotty Guns ordered another drink—angrily—and started to get even more loud: "DAMN NIGRO! I WANT IT'ALL! THAYT ALAYASKAN BUMBLEFUCK! How much son? GIMME A NUMBER BRAH!" His temper was startin to bubble. Fuck, I wanted to go home. He scared me when he was half-drunk like that. He was an insecure son of a bitch too, I tell you. He was all trying to impress Sarge I guess.

"You still want a half ounce?" I asked.

"Mayn I wunt it all! How much you got?"

I told him I had a bit over an ounce. Then he told me: "Just put it up here nigga." He was talkin about the bar. He wanted me to put the weed on the bar. "ALL OF IT!" he told me. "Ain't nobody in here cahyr! We got ma boy Sarge! My *boy* here is a cop!"

That's when I froze. A what?

"But he's layke, you know—the good kyna cop. The movie kyna cop! A *Departed*-typa cop!"

Was he kidding? Sarge didn't move, not even his head. He watched TV still, or whatever he did. He didn't give a reaction really. That's when I figured out he wasn't kiddin around, he *was* a cop. Then all kindsa shit ran through my nervous system. I was thinkin: if I looked scared that Sarge might actually arrest me, that would make me look like a goddamn idiot cause maybe cops smoked weed too. Maybe they don't smoke weed, maybe *he doesn't smoke weed.* Maybe he's a cop with integrity that takes his job serious as fuck. But what if he *did* smoke weed? Then he obviously wasn't about to hassle some small-time drug-dealer like me. Then the very idea of me thinkin that he might arrest me could offend him within itself. I was really confused. This had never happened, but maybe it might help to have some cop friends? "Brah he don't care! Raight?" And he turned to Sarge—Sarge shrugged. "See?!"

"Dude, I'm not scared about that," I told him. "I'll be right back." I went to the bathroom and ate a Xanax. Then I thought fuck, the Xanax won't kick in for forty minutes and I had been drinkin on an empty stomach and didn't have a way to get to food. I might pass out on the train ride back. I started panicking.

I came to later that night when we were all laughing and drinking at some *other* bar—I have no recollection of how we got there. But even though the cop and I built a close comradery that day, even though he told me if I ever ran into any problems to let him know, by the time I was sellin pounds a week, I knew my petty weed sales had grown into potential felonies and distanced myself from Scotty Guns and his cop friends. I wasn't sure if maybe it was a ploy to get me to come clean or whatever—give up my connections maybe. Maybe they were building a case against me. I never saw Sarge ever again and began to eat a bit more Xanax to calm my paranoia. It didn't always work. Anyway, it was around that time when I approached my first celebrity...

CHAPTER 3: THE WEATHER MAN

First, let me tell you how I got booted from Bolzano's, cause that's really where this tale begins. Sal never followed through with his promise, cause actually I was working half the week as a barback, and the other half as a barista. That was the deal Sal came back to me with. Somehow, I was always getting 50% more screwed than anticipated.

One day I was at the barista station and Sofia, my relief, she *never* showed up. Sure, maybe she was runnin late, but no way was I gonna stay late for such a shitty job. I packed up my shit and left. But before I got out the door, my manager, Seth, asked me where I was goin. I told him Sofia was late and it wasn't my problem.

"We'll talk to her when she gets here but you're not leaving right now when we've got a full restaurant."

What a liar. Only half the tables were seated. Still a lot of people though, I guess.

"Dude, it's not my problem—tell her to show up on time then."

"Greg, you're not leaving, not right now."

"Fuck you Seth," I said holding the door open. I was already outa the building.

He looked at me gracefully and smiled and said: "You know what? Thank you very much for your service here. Have a nice day." And he shut the door on me. What an asshole. I'll just get another job, but this time as a waiter, you know, just till my weed business gets off the ground. I grabbed the Village Voice and looked at the classified section and walked across town to a fancy Italian restaurant on the east side and told the hostess I was there to see the manager—her name isn't important.

"Is she expecting you?" the uninterested-in-her-job but seriously hot hostess asked me—why are they *always so hot*? You know what? Before I go on, speaking of hot hostesses, I forgot to tell you a story. I was at Bolzano's a while back, and the hostesses were Tanya and Liza. Tanya asked me if I wanted to hang out with them later. I asked her, "And do what?"

She said: "I don't know, dance?"

I said: "You both wanna go dancing with me?"

"Doesn't that sound like fun?" she asked.

"Am I gonna dance with both of you?" I flirtatiously replied.

"Until you take us home…" Yes. She invited me to have a threesome. I said I couldn't; that I had a girlfriend. I never lived that down. I still think about what that night mighta been like. But when I'm famous, I guess that shit'll happen all the time. Whatever—not important.

So anyway, the lazy hostess asked me if the manager was expecting me and I told her of course she was expecting me, so she called down to her office and said I was there to see her. The manager asked her a question—I don't know what. The hostess looked me up and down and said "yeah." Then she hung up the phone and said, "Okay. It's downstairs. Through the kitchen."

So I walked past the waiters to the kitchen and said hola to the kitchen staff and went down the stairs and looked for the office. "You have experience?" she asked me as soon as I walked in. She was Moroccan-looking. Maybe Egyptian. She had a French accent and was like three years pregnant. Her hair was springy and her smile was upside down. She totally coulda lived without me, but she half-assed interviewed me as if she had nothing better to do for thirty seconds.

"A lot of experience," I told her. "Over three years."

"What kind of cuisine?"

Bolzano's was an Italian restaurant, so I just said, "Italian. Mostly."

"Then she asked me, "Northern or Southern Italian?" I looked for an answer, then I saw a menu on her cluttered desk—in fact, her desk seemed to be nothing but a heap of revised menus, like she couldn't make up her mind on the size of the font. It said *Northern Italian Cuisine.*

"Northern," I said. Then I waited. She looked at me, told me to come in the next day in a white button-down shirt for training and if I was good, I got the job. I was now making three-times as much as I was an hour ago. But none of that is the point. I finally had a job as good as KC's job, but it didn't fucking matter cause we broke up in a very bad way. It was the worst day of my life—one of them. I gobbled lots of Xanax and drank many dirty martinis and ended up at a random apartment in Bayside, Queens the next morning lying next to a girl I used to hang out with in eighth grade. God knows how in the fuck I even found her, or how I got into her bed—or if the sex was good or if it even happened.

Anyway, a few months later, I added many other weed clients to my rolodex. I was making good money but kept the waiting job to explain how I was able to afford trips to Argentina to my parents. That's another tale. I kept getting fired and rehired at the restaurant for leaving in the middle of shifts and going to auditions without tellin anyone. But one day my favorite manager, not the Moroccan chick, but another one, she was forced to fire me. Her boss made her do it cause I fucked up the lesbian chef's wine order when she came in with her wife and family. They all sat at my table. It was terrible. I couldn't remember the specials and totally forgot about their champagne. So that's why my manager was forced to fire me, cause the chef was part owner of the restaurant and she wanted me gone. But I didn't care so much, though I did negotiate my way back into employment when my manager—the good one—said she wouldn't fire me and that she'd figure out a way to keep me on but asked if I could stop by her place in Bensonhurst, Brooklyn later that night and bring her and her husband an ounce.

"No problem," I told her.

And so that's how I then began selling weed to everyone who worked at that joint. I tried to move onto coke later on but failed, more on that in a bit. I called up The Gak and placed my biggest order yet: an entire pound. It was expensive. He didn't really give me a good deal either. I had no idea how I would sell it. I was already having trouble with the half-pounds I had been ordering, but I knew I had to push myself. I showed up to work from that day forth with only one purpose: to sell the pound of weed I had been housing at my little brother's apartment for a week.

That's how I met The Weather Man.

The Weather Man was from a major news organization that worked right by the Italian Joint. They all used to come in after their late-night TV news show every night and we'd open back up the restaurant just for them, then lock it as soon as they walked in. They all had families in Connecticut and Westchester or wherever, so we'd put the curtains up so nobody could see into the joint and do a buncha blow and drink a ton of dirty martinis together until the last train outa Grand Central. That became routine.

One night The Weather Man and I were snorting many bumps of blow in the bathroom, blow that we had bought from the maître d' of the Italian Joint. That had become a thing too: dirty martinis from the bartender and cocaine from the maître d'. Anyway, The Weather Man and I were in the bathroom takin a piss when he asked me my name... again. I had already told him my name many times. Also I hate talkin to people at the urinal. Not my thing. "I'm Greg," I told him. "I sold you weed a month ago, in this very same bathroom."

"Oh that's right. Yes. I remember. So many faces. I didn't recognize you." But I didn't look any different than I did when I sold him the weed, he was just a phony typa guy like that. Saying shit just to say shit. "Well, I'd love some more," he told me.

"I've got a pre-packaged ounce right now," I told him.

"How about I just put you on the air?" he asked me.

"You mean on TV?" He said yes. I asked him when. He told me tomorrow. I showed up to his news station and I read the forecast for him. The entire news team thought it was hilarious. That's when they decided to offer me a job as the assistant weatherman. "You hired me as a meteorologist and I never even went to high school," I told them. They thought that was the funniest shit in the world. Jimmy Fallon found out about it, and that's when he called my publicist…

The urinal flushed. I snapped out of it.

"That's too much, but maybe a bit less? You working tomorrow? I'll stop by and we can—how should I say it nowadays, do the deal?"

"Yeah, 'do the deal' will do," I told him. And that was how I started selling weed to the late-night news crew for a major TV station. That was good business, but it got better when this new website was invented and changed life as we knew it…

CHAPTER 4: NEW WEBSITE

The new website was called Facebook—basically MySpace, but for college kids. I could finally sign up without an @edu email— pompous fucks. The first thing I did was find KC. I added her as a friend but had to wait for her to accept to talk to her. It was

2006 or some shit and I was twenty-one. It had been a year since KC left and moved back to Georgia. On the day she accepted my friend request or whatever it was called, I spent the day looking at her new boyfriend. He was a more muscular version of me. I had to work out. I got so mad all I said when she accepted my friend request was:

u guys haven't broken up yet?

She didn't reply. I sent another message, this time a bit later and bit more drunk:

Happy almost birthday!!

A few days later, after no response, I checked back and saw I had to request her as a friend again. Did she delete me already? I added her again and she accepted a few days after that, again.

u erased me as a friend? wtf?

Nothing. So again a couple days later just a simple:

ugh

Then after a week I got aggravated:

r u ever gonna say hi to me stranger? my dog is in ur profile pic after all...

Then I saw she removed me as a friend... again. So I repeated the process, and again she accepted. Or maybe she didn't. I don't remember if we had to be friends to send messages to be honest. But I wrote to her:

u DEFRIENDED ME alreadyy?!?!?!?!??!

And at last, a reply:

yeah couldn't take it

Then at my weakest, most zonked out moment on Xanax and vodka, I sent her a message that said:

you are so special and pretty. you are so different than anyone else.

Why I sent such a cheap message, who knows…but nothing. No reply. Then one day she says:

HEY! So I can't find my phone anywhere and I'm goin NUTTY will u PLEASE PLEASE PLEASE call my phone as soon as you get this message?? PLEASE!!!!!!

What in the—so, I did. And so that's how we began talking again. It actually happened on a family vacation in Aruba, which was always odd. Family vacation? Yeah right. Still, they invited me—my parents did, but there was an entire life happening on the other side of our relationship they had no idea about. Nothing was ever the same after Hidden Lake. We never fully recovered. Not until I was twenty-seven, which I'll tell you about later, but for now, I had two lives: One which I lived, and the other which I presented to my parents at dinner in Aruba. But I couldn't hold my poker face for very long. Like, for instance, right after dessert was served, I'd say:

"Gonna go get a drink at the bar next door."

I mean, what the fuck were they gonna do? Tell me not to drink? I was twenty-one years old. So, I'd head to the bar with my brother, Eric—some beach bar—and find the fat Aruban dude slanging blow and buy a gram off him and be snorting coke till the world came crashing down, then I'd head back to the room. Then I'd log onto Facebook and check to see if KC had written anything. Every time I saw her face I became obsessed all over again. I hated it. But loved to see her in any way I could. I couldn't help myself.

I had to write her something. I had to see her. In a coked out mess of a drunk, I scribbled:

babyyyyy can you pleassse download skype and talk to me??
I miss you so muchhh. have you gotten all my txts? I haven't gotten
any of yours ☹ que pasa con eso?

I tried to impress her with my Spanish, which I had learned at Kitchen Kabaret making pizza with Juanito. Anyway, KC never replied. So I went in for the kill:

Come up here and let's fuck...

I didn't want her to think I was the type of guy to still make rash decisions all on account of her and a wavering moment of lust. I mean, I had to show her I'd changed, which I had. Right? And so I let her know I'd been thinking about this for a very long time. A spur-of-the-moment relationship blossomed and soon she accepted my offer.

She came up from Georgia, now with a little southern accent and her fake tits settled a bit more than they were when we broke up, looking much better than the last time I had seen them. I wanted to fuck her so bad the second I saw her. No way this'll end well, I thought. Anyway, she walked into my studio apartment on 35th and Third in the Murray Hill section of Manhattan and looked at my bed on the floor and the furniture crammed into every little spot I could think of.

"Sooo… this is where you live, huh?"

Immediately I remembered why we broke up. What a fuckin cunt. We had sex, of course, but it wasn't romantic sex, it was hurt sex; the type of sex that makes me hurt. It hurts because her power over my hormones is demonic and unhealthy, and that makes me even hornier, and so we fuck—hard, but then the sex is over and all the dirty talk I asked her to say while we were fucking lingers in the room. During sex it was great. I'd always say to her, right in the middle of the act:

"Tell me about the guys you fucked."

"Why?"

"Did you blow them?"

"I guess."

"You did?"

"Yeah."

"How many at once?"

"One!"

"One?"

"Maybe two..."

She wasn't even into all the dirty talk to begin with, but I think I forced her into it.

"Did he like your fake tits? Did he squeeze em?" Just saying it all made my dick throb and thump inside her and pulsate with anger and frustration, and when she clenched her pussy hard around my cock as I put my hand over her throat to punish her and squeeze her till she felt how little she had become and what a whore she was, my tongue had a mind of its own: "Did you fuckin stick your pussy in his face?" I didn't want to say that shit, but it gave me a pleasure I hadn't found anywhere else on planet Earth. I always did whatever made me hard. That's how I lived life. And right as I said the most demeaning of sentences—whatever it mighta been at that particular time—right as I was about to launch into a whole other tirade of offensive and self-abusive demands, I'd cum. Then we'd fight about everything she said: "So you're off sucking dick in Marietta, huh?"

"Greg, you *told me* to say that."

"So you weren't?"

"Ugh, Greg. No."

"So you haven't fucked anyone."

"I didn't say that."

"And when you fucked them, you didn't blow them?"

"Why do you want to hear this?

"What a whore."

"Whatever, you love it."

And then we'd have sex again. Jeez, it really was no good. No good at all. She had to leave. She stayed up there, in my bed in Manhattan, for a few more days then went back to Georgia just as we were nearly about to strangle each other all over again, and as soon as she left, the pain rushed right back to me as if it had never left. All that hard work for nothing. I was hung up on Xanax and whisky again for like a month. It was a horrible idea having her up. I had to get back to work.

And I was about to make it BIG…

CHAPTER 5: THE TRAIN

But I wouldn't have made it big without The Train. Without him, I had no connections. He was my boss when I lived in Boulder. He owned a coffee house in a town, where I used to work. This was about three years ago when I was eighteen. Once I was rated the worst employee there but most fun to work with. That about describes my entire work existence, even till today. And now I'm 37. Anyway, he hired me for pennies and I worked for him till I moved away from Boulder right before my twentieth birthday. But the thing is… The Train and I had a couple misunderstandings in the beginning.

One day, my coworker at the coffee shop, Alisa, says to me:

"So, I don't want to—never mind."

"What?"

"It's probably none of my business."

"Just say it."

Alisa's face was dark-featured and picturesque. She had black hair with blue eyes, so blue they scared you if you looked at em for too long, and hairy arms, which was quite distracting. She was small and dated a handsome tough guy who came to pick her up after work. She was nineteen at that time, but still felt like "an older woman." I always wondered if her boyfriend was better looking than me. What a shallow fuck I am. Anyway, she says to me this one day: "Train told me about your P.O."

I was flabbergasted. "P.O.? What P.O.?"

"She apparently called here. What were you in prison for?"

"What? What the fuck are you saying? I've never been to prison. I don't have a probation officer."

"He said it was your parole officer."

"What the FUCK are you talking about?"

So apparently this fuckin guy—The Train—my boss, told this hot-ass chick that I was in prison and that my fuckin parole officer was calling to check up on me. So I confronted him:

"Hey man, can I come in?" He was in his office at the back of the café.

"Sure, what's up?"

"You told Alisa my parole officer called?"

He blushed. "It's no big deal."

"No, you don't get it. I don't have a parole officer."

"Well I'm just repeating what she told me."

"So you're saying a woman called and said she was my parole officer?"

"She was checking up on you."

"Are you nuts? I never went to prison. Why in the fuck would I have a parole officer?"

"I don't know man, but it's not my business."

"Are you suggesting a strange woman has been pranking me?"

He shrugged and we left it at that. I left his office completely dumbfounded. What in the FUCK was that about? Did he wanna fuck Alisa and did he think that she wanted to fuck me even though she had a boyfriend and so he was trying to push her away from me by telling her lies that I was bad news? Anyway, doesn't matter. Cause he became my partner in crime three years later and the topic never arose again.

This is all very important cause if I was gonna sell weed professionally, I couldn't depend on The Gak. He was third in line. By the time the weed got to him, it was already so marked up there was practically no way for even him to make money, let alone me. No, he won't work. I need a connection. That's when I hit up Train and asked if he could help. He told me he'd introduce me to a guy who knew a guy. So he set up a meet-n-greet and I flew out to Denver.

I got to the airport and hopped on the bus to Boulder, where Train picked me up. He took me to some white trash house with three grimy dudes in it. They looked like they were wasting their life away in front of a bong. We joined their huddle on the couch in the living room. The air was odd and a bit too quiet. One of burnouts was playing a video game. I could see they were evaluating whether I was legit or not. Every eye-glance and uncomfortable side-whisper I took notice of made me a bit more uncomfortable. Finally, I had to bring the topic of weed up since it didn't seem like anyone was ever gonna acknowledge the whole reason I was there.

"So uh, who can I buy some weed from?"

The room went blank. All I could hear were the buttons being pushed on the Nintendo 64. Was that not right? Was there a different way to ask? Then:

"How much do you want?" the least likely guy to be selling weed asked me. He had curly hair, massive legs, a fat ass, and probably stood well over six feet tall when standing. But he looked like a nerd.

"Well," I said… I actually hadn't thought that through just yet. That's bizarre. Seems like I should know that. So I just said, "can I start with two pounds?"

There was a chuckle, as if two pounds was either too much or too little.

The nerd looked at me and said, "I'll sell you four pounds, and give you two strains. Two of each."

I didn't think I could sell four. I mean, I could barely sell one, and already I was asking for two. So I casually said, "Four is a bit too much for this month."

For this month? Why would I say that?

"Yeah thing is, two is more than a bit too low. It's not even worth it. Four is low, but I'll do it once, if the next time you take at least five."

Holy shit. What'd I get myself into? FIVE? That'll take me a year! But I played it cool... "Hmm, well, how much for four?"

"How about... 38 each."

I was always good at doing math in my head. Not like autistic good, but good, nonetheless.

"So $15,200?"

"We can do an even 15."

Was that a joke? Taking $200 off? Was he serious? I'm not sure what's goin on. I looked at The Train, who was looking away, I guess so he wouldn't have to see me strike out if that's in fact what I was doing. But without thinkin this through I just said:

"Okay deal."

"Can you come back in two weeks?"

Is this prick serious? Come *back* to Colorado? Does this dipshit know I live in NY? But I didn't say that. I just said: "Come back to this house?"

"Well, you'll have to go a bit further. I live four hours away, so you'll have to come to my house. This was just to meet you."

"Oh."

I agreed and left the house. I got in the car with The Train thinking about how I was gonna do all this. Still I thought about that day, years prior, when he lied about my "parole officer" calling to "check up" on me. What a load of horse shit. Whatever, no time to get distracted. "How should I send it you think?" I asked him in the car, trying to forgive him in my head.

"No idea. Post office? I don't think anybody is paying attention. Mail is probably fine."

"What if they get x-rayed. Is that a thing?"

"The coffee bags we use are x-ray proof. You can use them. Just leave me an ounce and we'll call it even."

And so that's how The Train and I entered into our arrangement.

First I had to get fifteen grand. I was shy two thousand so I took out a cash advance on my credit card. I stuffed it all in my underwear to see if that'd be the best way to get it through the airport, but it made me look like I a dick tumor. It was too much money. I need these twenty-dollar bills and fifty-dollar bills to be hundreds. That'll thin it out. But to do that, I had to go to the bank, and how would that look? And someone at some point in my life, someone—no idea who—told me that banks will "mark it down" if you bring in over nine thousand dollars. Not sure what "mark it down" means, or if that's true, but I didn't wanna find out. So I had to split the bank trips into two.

The first bank I went to was by my apartment. I walked in, nervous that I would be arrested for having so much cash, and stood in line with sweat dripping down my rib cage. The teller opened up. I approached. I gave her, some recent college graduate she looked like, $7,500 all scattered in twenties and fifties.

"Can I actually just trade these in for all hundreds?"

Did that sound drug-dealer-y? I stood in silence and anticipation, trying to figure out whether the look on her face was one of suspicion or normalcy. She took her time rearranging all the bills so that they were face up and in the same direction while a line built up behind me.

Fuck. I should do that myself next time so I'm not standing here for so fuckin long.

"The entire amount in hundreds?" she asked me loud enough so that everyone behind me could hear. Why would she do that? She tryin to get me robbed?

I tried to act normal, like no biggie. So I shakily said: "Yeah, hundreds, thanks." Then she handed me all the cash through the window. "Oh, do you have like, an envelope?" I couldn't believe she didn't put it in an envelope herself. Everyone must be looking at all this money. FUCK!

"Have a nice day," she told me as she handed me an envelope with the cash.

I shoved the cash in the envelope and high-tailed it outa there. I still had to do one more bank trip. After it was all done, I got home and rolled up the money as tight as possible, wrapped a rubber band around it and put the roll in my underwear. It *still* made me look like I had an overgrown penis, but it'll have to do, I thought. I pulled the roll of money out—

OUCH!

I tore out like fifty pubes doing it. Now it was a hairy roll of money. Gross. I woke up the next morning, the morning of the flight, and again put the money in my underwear and walked in circles around my apartment to make sure it wouldn't come loose and fall down my pants leg. I seriously looked shady. This won't work. Fuck. But I went outside and hailed a cab to JFK anyway.

When I got to the airport, I had no luggage to check, just my backpack filled with my journal, a book I wasn't reading, and my screenplay, you know, in case I met anyone of importance on this business trip. Is that weird I have no luggage? I had some Xanax hidden in my wallet.

Anyway I grabbed my ticket from the self-serve machine and went to the security line. Fuck fuck fuck. I looked down. My cock seemed huge. It's okay, this is normal. Just a white dude with an oversized ballsack. I need a Xanax. No, if I take it now it won't kick in in time, not even close. I can leave the line and wait for it to kick in. Do I have time? Plane leaves in an hour. I have time. Do I? Yeah.

So I left the line and took a Xanax, now all white and powdery from my wallet. Then I waited on the floor of the airport for thirty minutes waiting for it to kick in. Okay. This should be good now. As soon as I felt the slightest bit of relief, I got back on line. Hey, if I get caught with the money and anyone asks, I just wanted to keep a good eye on fifteen grand, okay? Fuck you if you don't get that. Why do I have so much cash? I'm buying art in Denver. Art has to be paid with in cash. What do you care? I didn't make the rules. This is the way life is, okay?

I watch the people go through the metal detector without a worry in the world. I wish that was me. There's no metal on me, right? No. My nose ring is gone—whatever happened to that thing? My ear piercings are… yeah, no. Gone. Eyebrow ring gone. No change in wallet. No plates in head. I'm good.

I put my backpack on the conveyor belt. I was sweating bad, fuck is wrong with this Xanax? I held my breath as I walked through the metal detector, cock first. Everything was good.

Phew.

I grabbed my backpack and ran to the bathroom. I pulled the money outa my—

AHHH!!! FUCK!

Another hundred pubes came ripping out. FUCK! I threw it in my backpack and just made the flight.

I landed in Denver and happily walked to the Boulder bus stop and got on the bus. I was a bit buzzed from the scotch on the plane. I got off downtown and waited on 14th and Walnut. The Grower was picking me up on this first go-around. I spotted his Subaru—the whole state of Colorado has a Subaru—and got in. It wasn't that nice of a car, but probably cause he's the type of guy who doesn't spend any money even though he has a ton. He was a survivalist and was prepping for doomsday as I found out. He was saving up to buy some cabin with cash in the middle of nowhere, totally off the grid.

We got to his house four hours later after weird talk about nothing since neither of us wanted the other to know too much about who we actually were. This was before he got the wolf. His house was so peaceful back then. We cooked food from his garden, and he showed me around his regular house, not so special, just a middle-class home in a ski town, and then I was introduced to his grow operation, which was spectacular. The ventilation system alone probably cost a hundred grand. That was the first time I realized: I'm *way* over my head here. What am I doing?

I had to rent a car since he wasn't willing to drive me back, so I rented a car in his town of ten and drove for *four fucking hours* with four pounds of weed in the trunk. I drove ten below the speed limit. Is that too slow?

It was nighttime by the time I got to Boulder. I drove to Train's house and under his mat was the key to the café. I got to the café at like 2am and ducked below the opaquely painted part of the glass windows so nobody would see me. I crawled around the counter to where the scale, bags, and vacuum sealer was. I packaged everything, including Train's ounce, and crawled back outa there, not before leaving his ounce in his back office, where he accused me of having a parole officer.

I drove back to his house and snuck in quietly so as not to wake him. That was part of the deal: to act like he wasn't involved at all. I crashed out on his couch and woke up at 8am or thereabouts the next morning. I walked to Kinkos cause driving with weed in the car was giving me serious panic—and boxed up the coffee bags in the open in front of the entire store. Nobody would box up ten huge coffee bags of weed out in the open like that, so that's why I did it: cause I was smart. I brought the two massive boxes to the counter—big ass boxes that weighed four fucking pounds—fuck, I shoulda thought of that. I gotta throw a telephone book in these things. But then it'll be weighted weird.

"Next time you don't need to address it, just so you know," the Kinko's guy said.

"I don't?"

"Where's it going?"

He printed out a sticker and slammed it on each box and off I went back to New York so I could sign for them, since they'd be arriving at my building in less than twenty-four hours. I took a

Xanax after I dropped the car off at the airport and fell asleep on the plane, praying they wouldn't lose the packages while in transit, and that I didn't go to prison. In one swoop, I could lose all my money and freedom at once. That couldn't happen, so I had to be careful.

Good news people.

It arrived untouched. How long can I get away with this though?

I made so many mistakes so far that just worked out lucky. I can't get lucky all the time. I need practice. I opened the boxes like it was Christmas—not that I give a shit about Christmas, I'm a Jew, and tore open the weed bags and—

WOOF!

The entire building exploded with skunk. Whoa. I didn't even have enough jars. I ran to the Container Store to buy more but by the time I got everything in its respective jar, the whole building was drenched in weed stank. Whatever, point is, that was how my trips to Colorado started. When people find out about how good this goddam weed is, I thought, everyone will be my customer. I promised myself I would overcharge everyone but provide amazing customer service. That would be my business: high prices, high demand, incredible customer service. It's all about the customers. Luckily, Train introduced me to one of his famous friends in New York: The Survivor. We'll call him The Survivor because he was one of the winners of Survivor—the reality TV show. Which season, I won't say, but he started coming over frequently.

That's when business *really* took off. And for once, life was working out perfectly.

CHAPTER 6: THE SURVIVOR

The Survivor was very famous, especially at the time.

Not only that, but his referrals were also slightly famous. He never purchased a lot, which didn't so much matter, cause from him came many. Plus he was famous, which is the goal of life—I think. I could learn a thing or two from this dude.

Before my Colorado connect and The Survivor came into my life, I wasn't making tons of money. My career was tiny. And the money I did have, most of it went to silly purchases I believed might make me the legend I was destined to become, such as the DJ booth I put in my "one bedroom" of my apartment. Right, so my studio apartment in Murray Hill, which is a total bro-neighborhood in Manhattan mind you, but I can assure you I'm no bro, had been advertised as a one-bedroom apartment. Not true. That bedroom was a closet, no bigger than a DJ booth, so that's exactly what I made it: a DJ booth. I had never DJ'd before, but I bought the most expensive turntables I could find since better equipment might help make me a better DJ. Turns out I wasn't very good, but the important part is I knew I couldn't sell weed forever. Eventually, I'll get caught, so I need something real. My hunt for something real was furious and obsessive. But certainly being a DJ wasn't it…

I was never a music guy. I just listened to the same old Eminem and Doors songs over and over on repeat. So, I was missing a pretty necessary ingredient to becoming the DJ I envisioned I might be, that being enthusiasm for music. Whatever, I bought the damn things cause I thought becoming a DJ fit the persona I was trying to build.

I also went out on a lot of dates, expensive dates with girls I hardly knew. I invested in finding a girlfriend essentially. We'd go out to glamorous dinners—even glamorous lunches sometimes—all accompanied with pretentious wines and desserts, which often went untouched since I hate dessert, but I ordered them to prove that I was tasteful. So, I spent a lot of cash on that too—roughly all of it—but shied away from furnishing my apartment like an adult. I suppose I have time to figure it all out—my life, that is. But I didn't want to wait too much longer. After all, the kids I grew up with were already buying apartments and shit. Anyway, meeting The Survivor was glorious, and his visits thereafter were always inspirational. He was a really upbeat guy. Like this one day he came over and convinced me to be a public speaker…

My buzzer went off at about 11:35AM. Next to my bed were my valor sweatpants that everyone made fun of, but I liked the color: teal, and I didn't really know what was fashionable anyway, or what made something "cool" or "not cool." My choices were usually odd, as I later found out when people felt comfortable enough around me to address how ridiculous my current outfit was. But anyway, I liked those sweatpants. They made me feel liberated, but maybe that's because I wore them with no underwear. Sometimes that was a bit much for anyone to feel comfortable around, but life was uncomfortable, deal with it—*I have*. Anyway, I threw on the valor sweatpants and a sleeveless shirt, and this is basically what I wore 85% of my waking hours.

I bought the sleeveless shirt from my boxing gym, even though it had been nearly a year since I was actually there. I boxed for two months then had to stop when some Korean dude punched me in the solar plexus sparring one day. My boxing trainer, Daryl, used to always say to me, "DON'T THINK ABOUT IT, BE ABOUT IT!" I suppose it was an important lesson that I still hadn't learned, which might be why it still shines bright in my memory. I was a great puncher—and I could dance, but I was terrible at getting hit—probably a requirement I shoulda thought through before adding "boxing" to my personality kit. I left the ring that day, took my gloves off, unwrapped my hands and grabbed my bag. Daryl wasn't too happy. "Wussup Grayg? You not stayin—wussup!? We got fo fights ta watch!"

"I gotta get home, tomorrow. Yo, thanks for today." And I gave him a knuckle pound and left the gym and its sweaty and humid atmosphere and walked down the rickety stairs with posters of all the semi-famous boxers who went there pasted to the pasty walls and exited to 28th Street. I was short of breath—or gulping too much of it, dizzy, and the bottom of my stomach felt ill. I was only seven blocks from my apartment but stopped walking no more than ten feet from the bottom of the steps of the gym and bent over and puked all over the grates. I tried to move further—to make it far enough away from the gym so I wouldn't be seen. I couldn't fathom the embarrassment I might feel if any of the other guys walked by me like this; I had to get home.

But I couldn't. Instead, I collapsed on the cruddy sidewalk and didn't move for about an hour. I couldn't even hail a cab. It's not like I gave up the next day either, I gave up the day after the next day. I went back to the gym once more the next morning to prove that I was just fine, that I could handle losing a fight. But yeah, that was the last time I ever boxed. Maybe it wasn't for me anyway. I was a nice guy—not like those other angry fucks at the boxing gym. Those guys had problems. So yeah, I thought boxing might be a good look for my persona, like DJing, which is why I signed up, but that didn't work out either. Still I wore the shirt anyway to remind people that—at one point—I boxed. How people thought of me was all that mattered. I even made sure to buy the tee-shirt with *Kingsway Boxing* written in the biggest font, so nobody would miss it when talking to me. That's right motherfucker, I boxed— used to, at least. The sleeveless boxing shirt was also my way of showcasing the half-sleeve tribal tattoo I had gotten when I was nineteen; another idea I had to decorate my soul. I coulda sworn it was cool. Turns out it wasn't. Anyway, I got it to prove that those years I spent institutionalized as a kid weren't easy. It was my way of saying: this has been hard, fuck you. Life is all about angles.

Anyway, I buzzed The Survivor through the first set of doors and tried to time the *second* buzzer perfectly so that he wouldn't have to hit the buzzer again. See, my building was the back building. The first building you entered from the street, so I had to buzz people through those doors first, then they had to walk down a narrow hallway, which led them to a shitty outdoor courtyard: just a buncha crooked slabs of cement that tripped all who attempted its ten-foot walk. The courtyard also housed the dumpsters for both the front and back buildings, but all the tenants threw their trash from their window and always missed the dumpster—or maybe that was just me, so there was trash all over the place. Basically, it was a trashyard—not a courtyard. But so yeah, on the other side of the trashyard was my building, the back building.

It was roughly a fifteen-second walk from the time I buzzed people through the first set of doors to the time they got to my building in the back, but I got impatient and buzzed too early often. I could imagine everyone racing over the poorly constructed slabs of rock in the trashyard to get to the second building when they heard the second buzz. I imagined they were still too far to make it in time, just nearly missing the buzz, then feeling bad about having to buzz again, but that was all in my head. I have no idea what they really thought about me. I'm not so sure the courtyard floor was *that* crooked either, but I assure you, it was ugly. Just don't wanna mislead you. Lying isn't a good look.

The nice part about being in the back building was that it gave me an extra layer of security and made me feel safe, like an alarm system. I could also stick my head out my window by the fire escape that overlooked the dumpy courtyard after I buzzed people through the first building and spy on them to make sure it was who I thought it was, and not like, whatever, the damn FBI. But I didn't start getting that paranoid until later when it was necessary. In any case, I was sure that I had held the buzzer down long enough and timed it precisely, but the second I walked back over to my dresser, the fuckin buzzer went off again.

I could hear The Survivor's footsteps on the stairs as he climbed the tight squeeze of my four-story walk-up. The footsteps always sent echoes ricocheting against every flat surface of the stairwell and probably disturbed my neighbors—who surprisingly never said a thing about the amount of visitors I had, or the strong scent of fresh Cannabis that was impossible to ignore. I tried to clear out some space for him to sit, but ever since I started buying furniture there was nowhere to move. My new Crate & Barrel table that I just purchased didn't help—that's what an adult would buy, rather than Ikea, but it made it practically impossible to move. I never took measurements. I guess I just wanted to feel like I had a home, for once. That's why I sacrificed living space: to feel like I belonged. But now there was no place to really live anymore and definitely no place to walk. Anyway, I tried to make room for him to sit, but jeez, it was hard.

I had my screenplay laying out. I had just started writing it and wanted it to be known, especially to The Survivor, that I was gonna make a movie. So, of course, I left it laying around. Conversation bait.

"Come in dude," I shouted from my computer when he knocked on my door, pretending to be working on some dialogue. He walked in—handsome dude. I always wondered if he was better-looking than me, or if it mattered.

"Hey buddy," he said as he walked in, chipper as usual. He grabbed one of the four chairs that my Crate & Barrel table came with and sat down—even looked comfortable. He faced me and lent me his full attention. He hadn't noticed any inconvenience whatsoever in my dysfunctional and cramped living space. The thing I really liked about him was that he was always a good listener, super smooth and nothing phased him. I picked up those qualities later on in life.

"What's this? Writing a book?"

"A screenplay."

"About…?"

Here was my shot. Maybe he could introduce me to someone else who's famous that can help me get my career off the ground. So, I gave him my best pitch: "Well, I was in this rehab in Louisiana and—"

"You were in a rehab?"

"Well… I was in two rehabs, a wilderness program, and a boot camp actually, for three years—well two years at the boot camp and another year at the other places."

"When did you get out?"

"Well, I ran away. I was supposed to be there another ten months, but I escaped and was on the run for a buncha years—but anyway, this girl I met in rehab, I was in Louisiana and—"

"But wait, sorry—I'm very intrigued. Were you homeless? How old were you?"

"Uhh, yeah. I was homeless, but I always found places— usually, to sleep. I was sixteen when I ran away from that boot camp and hid till I turned eighteen. Then I didn't have to hide anymore—cause the cops were after me, I think. Actually I'm not sure if they were really looking for me—the cops, my parents and I never talk about it. But when I turned eighteen, I was in the clear."

"So, you talk to your family?"

"Yeah, we talk often now—not about that. But aside from that we're pretty close, I think."

I never wanted to talk about my entire life at once. I love talking about myself but thinking about myself is a whole other thing. But that was the day I realized that I had a real shot in show business, maybe on TV even. I always knew that I was worthy of TV, and if I'm able to pique the interest of the winner of Survivor, I must be right. It was all very exciting. An hour went by and still the subject of weed had not come up.

"Have you ever thought about public speaking?" He asked me. I thought that was pretty dumb.

"Speakin to who?"

"I travel the world speaking to students about how to combat poverty. I could put you in touch with my agent... if you want. They pay really well."

"But like, what would I talk about?"

"How you overcame, man!"

I dug his enthusiasm but wasn't sure about all this. "Yeah but... I mean, I'm a drug-dealer."

"But you're good now, man, you're... You're fixed! That struggle was real, and I think the world needs to hear about it."

I went from excited to confused to excited again. He was really pumped about this idea.

"It's just—I feel like I should have my life a bit more put together before telling other kids how to live."

"Well, think about it."

I really wanted to take him up on the opportunity, but if there's one thing I would hate to be, it's a fraud. I hate phony. "So, you wanna buy some weed I guess?"

"Yeah just gimme an eighth of something good—so, when you were homeless, how were you eating?"

"Umm, I stole a lot of sandwiches, met this girl from Brown University while I was sittin on the street one night... She took

care of me during the winter and gave me her meal card. Uhh…
I panhandled, told dirty jokes for a dollar and—"

"YOU TOLD DIRTY JOKES FOR A DOLLAR? LIKE
WHAT? Tell me one!"

"The thing about my dirty jokes was that I didn't really have
any. So, it was always awkward when someone actually took
me up on it and put a dollar on my blanket. Usually I'd just make
something up on the spot. It was never funny, or dirty. Usually
very uncomfortable, actually. I had no strategy other than make a
sign that would get me a dollar."

"This is an incredible story man, I see why you're writing a
screenplay! Is it about your life?"

"Oh it's actually about this girl that I met—"

"Man! You should be writing about *you*! Not someone else!
You should tell *this story—your story!*"

I had thought about that before, but never did anything about it.
Maybe The Survivor is right. Maybe *that's* my calling. My story!
"Well, I guess I should," I said to him, pondering about all the tales
I had to tell. I was paralyzed for a moment. Was I living my life
wrong? I felt stumped. *Why was I writing about Robyn?* I should
write about *me*! He was right.

I sold him an eighth and he left.

I sat dumbfounded in my apartment and began writing my
life story down, event by event. Hmm… Public speaking. Maybe
a book. Anyway, The Survivor is the reason I started to believe
in myself. And from him came Tech Zach, who introduced me
to all sortsa interesting people, like the couple I met at The
Ritz-Carlton.

CHAPTER 7: THE COUPLE AT THE RITZ–CARLTON

A world tour bender is a good thing, as I learned.

It was 10AM when the cab dropped us off at The Ritz-Carlton on 50 Central Park South. Jana and I took the elevator to the 26th floor. Jana was for sure impressed. She was a bit younger—a student at Columbia University—so I think she found it fun to run around with a high school dropout drug-dealer that lived life the way I did. I was exotic, that's why she liked me.

I was always excited to meet someone I had never met before, and the referrals were just starting to come in from The Survivor and Tech Zach—who you'll meet later. Point is I was just starting to meet a lot of strange characters, and I loved that early on in my career when it was all still fresh—before the paranoia set in; before the girls stopped; before I had to move to south Brooklyn, when I was still young in spirit. Yeah, I loved all the stories I got to hear from people, they were all so interesting, they were all from such different walks of life—I loved my job.

I knocked politely on the door, like a respectable guest. I was wearing a collared shirt with a V-cut cashmere sweater over it and baggy jeans—my version of a good outfit. I always wore good outfits on my runs—especially runs to the Ritz-Carlton, not that I'd ever been on a run to the Ritz-Carlton before that day, but anytime I was going to meet someone fancy—by that I mean rich—I tried my best to fit in. I told people that I dressed up because I was less likely to be stopped by the cops when in costume as an intellectual, rather than if I were in my Tony Soprano valor-sweatpants, which the entire world despised. But that's not the real reason. The real reason was I wanted to appear professional and I made sure Jana knew that I was strategic with my risk-adversity skills—not that I even know what that really means: risk-adversity. But Jana was a college student, so I knew I had to say shit like that, even if I was using the word improperly; at least I knew it existed. In any case, I was certain this would all lead to me getting my movie made and becoming the show business mogul I was determined to become. All this was only to fund my lifestyle as an aspiring famous— well, filmmaker, or actor—whichever came first. I wasn't selling too much just yet, so it was still a healthy side job with room for improvement. Anyway, I knocked on the hotel room.

A Wall-Street type opened the door. He mighta been in his mid-forties, which meant wherever he was in life, I had twenty years to get there. I wasn't sure why he was in town, who he was, where he came from, or in general, what the fuck was goin on.

"Hello, welcome, welcome—please, come in, come in, please—come in!" Jana and I entered. "Oh, and hello!" He looked at her as if he thought I might be alone—no way dude. I was popular. Why would I be alone? She wasn't my girlfriend or anything. I don't think I wanted her to be my girlfriend anyway. It wouldn'ta worked out. I was just for sex, and I knew it. It didn't bother me either. Really, it didn't. I don't think.

We entered an immaculate suite with multiple rooms and exquisite furniture that I never expected a hotel to have. These guys are all the same, I thought. All these finance guys. They just, I don't know, make money and that's it, but they don't have a story to tell, and if you make money without a story, what's the point?

"Wow." Jana gazed around.

"Please, sit—wherever you'd like! Make yourself at home! Nice pad, huh?" The rich guy said.

"It's not ugly, that's for sure," I said—it just came out.

A cozy comforter on the California king-sized bed was the first detail I noticed. That and the hot middle-aged woman in the corner. She was… Well, she looked expensive. She was in a cushy chair looking at us, smiling, as if life had just gone down on her. She was snug in a tight dress from probably the night before. I don't think they had gone to sleep.

"So welcome to our abode. I'm Mark, this is Larissa."

Larissa smiled like all this was just too much for her—too much. "Hi," she said, observing her husband trying to be young again.

"Larissa this is—I'm so sorry, I don't think Matt gave me your name!"

Who the fuck was Matt, I was thinking. "You mean Zach?"

"ZACH! Yes, *that's* his name. I couldn't remember—it's been one of those—well, you know how it is, I'm sure. And you are?"

"My name is Jana. I'm a friend."

Wait, why did she feel the need to say 'friend'?

"What can I get for you? A glass of water? Soda? Fruit? Scotch? Cocaine? We've got chocolate-covered strawberries, take a look at this—Larissa, can you get the—where are they?"

Larissa didn't move as if this *must* be a joke. Me? *Move?* So funny.

"What's your name again dude? Mark?" I asked.

I always called people dude. Nobody was special just cause they made money or acted on TV or ran a business. That's why all my clients—and everyone in my life—was reduced to dude. My way of reminding them—and me—that nobody was any better than anyone else.

"Yes, Mark, that's right. So nice to meet you two. And I'm sorry, your name is—wait, did you say you wanted a drink? Something to eat?"

"Maybe some of those chocolate-covered strawberries?" Jana said shyly.

That made Mark really happy. "YES! Great, excellent— SUPERB choice. Larissa, would you mind bringing over the strawberries?" Then he looked at me. "And for you?"

"Oh, I'll have a scotch I guess—if you're offering it."

"Oh I'm offering it all right… Anything you want. Give me just a moment…"

It was early—10AM, but I mean, why turn down a glass of good scotch? Assuming it was good—it must be, this guy is rich.

"Ice?"

"Three cubes, please. Thank you."

Any more than three cubes and it diluted the taste, and that's no good. I had just switched over from dirty martinis to scotch. I didn't drink that much, not as much as some, at least. I guess it was picking up a bit though. Maybe I should chill out on it. But for now, it's okay.

Larissa brought over the chocolate-covered strawberries then took a seat next to the couch where Jana and I were sitting. Mark brought over a glass of scotch for me and a water for Jana.

"Sooo… Are you guys traveling?" I asked.

"Well—kind of, sorry—do you mind?" Mark put a bit of cocaine on the glass table next to the chocolate-covered strawberries and scotch. This is exactly how I thought rich people woke up in the morning. I saw Jana get excited—then upset about the coke all at once. We had done a lot the night before and she looked at me this morning and said, "No more coke for a while." But whatever, sometimes things just happen. I didn't want to make a client feel uncomfortable, plus I kinda wanted a line.

"Not at all. Snort all the cocaine in the world." And he did.

"Want some?"

"Sure," Jana said.

"Yeah, I'll have one too," I said. He cut up some cocaine for us. I really liked my job. "So are you on vacation?"

"We're celebrating," he said as he cut the coke on the expensive glass hotel table in front of us.

"What're you celebrating?"

"We just sold a company."

I didn't really know what that meant, but I pretended to be in the know. "What kind of company did you sell?"

He and Larissa kept exchanging smiles and inside-joke type of glances. In a calculated tone, he looked at me, then Larissa, then back at the table to continue cutting the blow and said: "We're on a world tour bender."

I had never heard that term before, but it sounded like everything I wanted in life.

"A world tour bender? That sounds… serious."

"Oh, it is."

"These strawberries are delicious," Jana said, smiling bigger than ever.

Mark agreed, "They're *incredible*."

Larissa smiled, "Eat as many as you want."

I knew it was a good idea to bring Jana; she loved dessert. She was a good chick. I liked her. I especially found it cute when she was enjoying herself. Plus, this all made me look really legit, and that's what girls like: A guy with status. I think. I was trying to figure it out and then do whatever it actually was they indeed liked. I wasn't always right, but I always tried.

We snorted the cocaine. I sipped more scotch. Jana ate more strawberries. Again, it was 10AM.

"So what's a world tour bender?" I said after realizing he wasn't going to explain himself any further till I inquired.

"I tell ya," and he thought for a moment. "I have *no idea*. But we're doing it."

"So, are you two, uhh—married? Vacationing together? What's goin on here?"

They looked at each other and exchanged a deep-rooted silent joke. These two, jeez. How silly they were. I liked them a lot.

"Not married, no… But vacationing together, yes. Something like that."

"Are you guys visiting—I mean, obviously—you're in a hotel. But where are you two from?"

"Well, I'm from Cleveland—but live in Berlin. And Larissa is from London—but lives in Shanghai."

What the fuck? I didn't even notice Larissa's accent till he said that. The cocaine was starting to drip down my throat, so I took another sip of scotch, more like a gulp, and let the whisky burn down to my stomach. I hadn't eaten anything yet, so it all hit me pretty hard.

"Can I do another line?" Jana asked.

"OF COURSE!" Mark said. That really seemed to make his day. He cut her another line. "So!" I knew the sound of that type of 'so'. That meant *Okay! Enough chit-chat! Where the fuck are my drugs?* People are all the same—but really different too. But what did I expect? I was a drug-dealer. What else did I come over for? So, I prepared for my presentation. Jana would be so impressed with my salesmanship. I really was great at what I did.

I had to ensure that from the second I walked through the door that I presented myself with the utmost professionalism. If I failed at that, I failed at my job, and my job was cool. And if I failed at being cool, I failed at all. That's how important my career was. One day I'd stop—as soon as my acting career could keep me afloat, or my movie was sold, whichever came first. Maybe the public speaking gigs. Anyway, I placed my backpack—expensive backpack—on the couch between me and Jana. I wouldn't want her to miss a second of this. I removed all three jars from my bag and gently placed them on the glass, cocaine-covered table and let Mark and Larissa soak in the splendor. They gawked—as they should.

I had just flown all the way to Colorado with twenty-thousand dollars wrapped around my cock to buy the best weed ever grown. My second trip out there. I had the best product in town—far superior to anyone else in the city doing what I was doing, though nobody did what I did. I was the best, and that made me special. That made me important, and important is, I think, the only thing that matters. I was now officially the most important drug-dealer in New York—well, just pot. Not like I'm sellin meth or anything. But then he gave me a dad comment:

"This looks way stronger than the shit I smoked in college!"

Better than the *shit he smoked in college?* Are you fucking serious? Do you have any idea what I had to go through to get these jars to this goddam five-star hotel room? Do you have any clue of the history that brought me—and now you—to these three strains of weed? I guess I got offended too easily. I've always been hypersensitive, and that's not manly, so I try to hide it.

"I got here"—and he counted his money— "about twelve-hundred dollars."

Holy shit. What? That was the first time I ever sold an order that large—but as I learned later, those are the most toxic orders of all. Those are the orders that keep your acting career on hold so that you can fly back out to Colorado for more. Those are the orders that fill up your safe with cash... And without a safe full of cash, what would I have?

I kept a straight face. "Not that I won't take your money, but you're buying all this for you two? How long you in town for? A month?" Maybe I was too polite to be a businessman. Why wouldn't I just take the damn money? I guess I just wanted to make sure they knew how much weed that was. But what do they care? They're on a world tour bender... Whatever that is.

"Well I wouldn't want to waste your time with a small order and Chad—I mean... Matt?"

"Zach."

"Right. He told me you were a busy guy."

I coulda given him anything. I coulda ripped him off real good and he wouldn'ta even known—or cared—but *of course* I would *never* do that. That would be an insult, not only to myself, but to my industry. I had a vision and I wouldn't compromise it for a quick buck. I guess I had conflicting beliefs. That was always a problem. I gave him the rundown:

"Here on my left is Chemdawg, in the middle, the best Mango Kush in the world—and I'm not exaggerating—it *is* the best." I took out my display nug—I always had a display nug, which I never sold. "Take a look at that. Have you ever seen a nug like that? It weighs almost an ounce. This one nug is about six-hundred dollars, but it's not for sale."

"Wait—why not?"

"I just can't—and this here to my right is White Widow." I grabbed the jars, undid the lids—filling the room to the brim with aromatic skunk—and tipped each one toward his nostrils so he could inhale a proper whiff. Then I aligned the jars perfectly together on the glass table. "I'm giving you an ounce of each. I would explain the benefits of the purchase, but in the interest of time—just trust me. This is the way to go."

"Oh this looks delicious, right honey?"

"Mmmm." Larissa was hilarious. So sexy. I want a woman like that when I'm forty. I better become famous soon. Jana watched me with allure. I was well on my way to being the guy I had to be. I think.

"Altogether, the price is $1,400. Do you want me to take out a few nugs to make it an even $1,200? Or do you want to just—well, spend a bit more to get the right amount?"

He happily took out a couple more hundreds—as I expected he would, *as I truly believed he should*, after all, the guy was newly rich, on a world tour bender. Goddammit that sounds fun. So yeah, why not get the best?

I never brought my vacuum sealer with me on runs. I had just bought it recently, ever since one guy yelled at me for not packaging it up well enough. He said his wife smelled it on him when he got home to Connecticut, so I made sure to never get another complaint like that again. But yeah, I couldn't bring that thing with me when I made house-calls. The vacuum sealer was only for when they came to me.

So, I took out the larger Ziploc bags, the ones that fit an ounce. I didn't normally sell ounces—not at that time in my early career, so this was very exciting. Then I took out my scale and my Tupperware and weighed out one ounce of Chemdawg ($400), an ounce of Mango Kush ($400) and an ounce of White Widow ($600).

I bid them farewell, "Congratulations on your world tour bender."

It was about 11AM by the time Jana and I left. The hour really flew by. I wasn't even quite sure what had just happened, but it was really intriguing and I wanted more of it. Maybe I should build a business and sell it? Is that a better use of my time? I was getting older and didn't have much to work with other than my checkered past, so I had to use it wisely, and fast while I was still pretty. And that's not in a cocky way of saying it. That's like, you know, how I was feeling. But at that moment, it felt like everything was coming together. I felt excited, but maybe that was the coke and scotch.

That was the start of what soon got way out of control… But man, what a guy he was—Mark. And I never even told him my name. They weren't the only insanely rich clients I had. I met another guy that invented a very popular website that everyone knows of. He was a fucking prick, and that's why I'll call him: The Website Prick.

CHAPTER 8: THE WEBSITE PRICK

The Website Prick was a big deal in the world of *who cares* types of people.

I met him through Sebastian, his marketing director, who I met through Tech Zach, who came from The Survivor, who originated from Train, the guy who lied about my "parole officer." Everyone was in my phone with another name in parenthesis next to them, and the name in parenthesis indicated who referred them. Sometimes there were two names in parenthesis, which meant the third name was referred by the second name, who in turn was referred by the first name. Nobody would be able to decipher what the hell the names meant if I ever got caught. Writing in code is key.

I also kept a notes section in my Blackberry to remember what all my clients had intimately told me on their last visit, cause some of those conversations were private and important.

"How was your dentist appointment last week?" I asked Motion Graphics Dmitri once. "You find out about the mole on your leg?" I asked Lawyer Aaron another time. "Sell that piece of art yet?" I asked Gay Jason on another occasion. "Still training that asshole sous chef?" I'd say to Chef Danny, and so forth. Like I said, my business was built with high prices and propagated with great customer service. It's all about connection. Anyway, I had no notes for The Website Prick, cause I didn't care if this was his last call or not. He truly sucked. By the time I got to his office in Tribeca, I was already mad about putting in the amount of work I'd already put in to even get downtown. I walked into his Silicon Valley-esque boiler room and all his employees stared at me, especially Sebastian, who like I told you was the one who introduced me to this prick—his boss.

I walked to the back desk—the big desk, and sat down, glancing over my shoulder at his army of interns. "Don't worry about them," The Website Prick told me with the NYC city line towering in the window behind him. "Just make it fast, okay?"

"What do you want?"

"Just something better than last time."

Everyone always complained about "last time," even though "last time" was always full of fantastic product. Customers always want more. "You like the Sour Diesel, right?"

"I don't remember the fucking names—just give me good shit, okay?" Then he mumbled something to himself as he was counting his cash in full view of his employees. There were about twenty of them. I wonder if they thought he was a bit of a prick the way I thought he was a bit of a prick... He was—for sure—a bit of a prick.

"Okay, well—here," and slid him a prepackaged ounce, vacuum-sealed. That was the better way to make deliveries. "$450," I said conclusively.

He never wanted to spend more than $450, and even that was a hard sell *every time* I showed up.

"Are you fucking kidding me? $450? Is it plated in gold? I don't even charge that much for a year of my services." The Website Prick was *always* talking about his business, *always*.

"Dude, I told you—an extra fifty for when you want me to deliver. Just give me fucking $400." I didn't feel like arguing about this *again*.

"Here—is it at least good? What's it called?"

"I thought you didn't care about the names?"

"No, I don't fucking *remember* the names—that's what I said. What's the name of this? I've got a lot to do. I've got a business to run."

I glanced over at Sebastian, the marketing brain behind the company. He gave me a *I warned you he's a prick* kinda look.

"It's AK47."

"AK47? Where the fuck do you come up with these names?"

Man, I wanted to slap this idiot. "It's not my name dude, it's the name of the strain—the farmer gave it the goddamn name, I think." It was okay if I was a dick back to the prick, cause he was *such* a prick that if I didn't dick back some words at him, I'd lose my self-respect.

"Done, thank you for your time." And he handed me the money.

Anyway, people like that were just in the world and there's nothing to really do about it other than ignore their misery. Usually, Tech Zach hung out with cool dudes. Not sure why he knew this fuck. But yeah, let me tell you about Tech Zach for a moment, who, like you know, came from the Survivor, who came from Train, my ex-boss who lied about my "parole officer" to Alisa nearly four years ago.

Tech Zach did some shit tech-related, but I never remembered what it was, though he intimately described it every time I asked. He plays a major role in this story because he was the one who eventually introduced me to Mike Z, and I'll tell ya all about Mike Z later on (he deserves an entire book, perhaps more). But let me set the scene for you when I met Tech Zach.

It was a Brooklyn apartment I showed up to, somewhere in Williamsburg. Tech Zach had a boring work setup in the corner of his living room. It was the first time I'd ever met him. He was a curly-haired Jew, but not religious or anything, just happened to be born from a Jewish vagina. His life resembled a science experiment gone right. He was giddy, upbeat, and seemingly had his finances in place. That was something I admired about him: He could work from wherever and be a high-paid stoner.

The door opened and his curls were bouncing in the air.

"Yes! Come in, please, The Survivor speaks very highly of you," and he rubbed his hands together as if to keep warm, or in this case, because the severe excitement of fluffy weed was making his mouth water. He never waited to get acquainted. "So? Whattaya got? I hear this comes all the way from Colorado." That's one annoying part about The Survivor: he always told people too much. "I'm a huge Colorado fan," Tech Zach concluded as I walked in.

"It's a great state. I lived in Boulder."

"Boulder! Oh I *love it there.* My absolute favorite place. Have you been to…"

Here's the part of the introduction where he starts dropping names of obscure locations in Boulder that I, a former local, should clearly know about, of which I knew nothing of. It made me look pretty dumb. I can't remember where he said, but the answer was always:

"Nah, I don't think I know it. I might."

"What about…"

"Yeah, umm… I'm not sure I know that either."

"It's cool. I get it, lots of places. Too many to get to. I wish we lived to be three hundred. Huge fan of travel."

I could relate. I think. So I said: "Totally. That's why I'm in this game." He looked lost by that statement. I had to clarify. "To travel." But I traveled only when my drunken internet browsing led me to purchase a flight, which I guess is still traveling. But my hitchhiking days are over; I'm far more elegant now.

"Ah, yes. And it's a great product," Tech Zach said. "Good business. Everlasting demand. And I hear you have top quality shit. I just finished an Indica blend I got from a friend who was visiting from Norway. Scandinavian Fuckbomb. Isn't that a great name? I loved it. Excellent high. I was completely upset when the bag grew empty. I wasn't looking forward to calling my Williamsburg hack after that shit. I was sad. Truly. So my spirits are in super high shape now that you and I have met. Well? Sit down. Let's get to it. Whattaya got?"

Wow. He was seriously anxious about my visit. He was again rubbing his hands together, ready to buy a million dollars of anything I had so long as it lived up to the standards that The Survivor had planted in his hopes. I wasn't nervous. I knew my shit would be better than his Scandinavian Fuckbomb, which really was a wonderful name.

"I brought some variety," I said as I unzipped my backpack on his well-maintained couch.

"Oh yes. Excellent. I'll take it all."

"That'd be a lot. Big first bill."

"It's worth it. A sane mind is worth every dime."

He was full of these little one-liners that stuck with me for years after, even though I paid little attention to them when they were said at the time. Anyway, I showed him the weed. He bought some of the weed. It's not really so important. The point of the matter is he never bought that much, just like all the other connector clients. There were big spenders with no friends, and small spenders with tons of friends. That was the way it generally worked.

So Tech Zach, after all the hype, after telling me how long he'd been waiting for my arrival, after telling me how bad he needed this, how ready he was to "kick back and code in slacks," and how insanely irritable he'd been since his last bowl, he asked for a goddam eighth.

An eighth?

What are we in fuckin middle school? But whatever, I gave it to him without any resistance or upselling, which was a good call cause he became my main source of high-income referrals. I mean, The Survivor was just a cog on Tech Zach's wheel of human interaction. Tech Zach was the engine that powered my business full throttle, which in the end ran my life into the ground. That comes later though. Point is he was an untapped oil field of Manhattan's entire ecosystem, all sprouting from one little oil rig in Williamsburg. From him I met lawyers, motion graphics designers, software engineers, photographers, real estate moguls, actors, and eventually… Mike Z, the man who gave me my first big shot. Even The Chicken Farming Jew came from Tech Zach. I mean, the guy truly knew everyone. The Chicken Farming Jew was my introduction to the niche world of Chicken Farmers in Brooklyn. He was actually the first referral I got from Tech Zach, and he lived just a few neighborhoods away…

CHAPTER 9: CHICKEN-FARMING JEW

The Chicken-Farming Jew might sound offensive, but it's not. That's just what he was.

I got outa the cab by his brownstone in Crown Heights, a neighborhood I detested. It's the only part of the country where rap-blasting black dudes on street corners intersect with Hasidic Jews smoking far too many cigarettes in their dirty deli aprons outside shithole bagel shops, and look, I'm a Jewtalian, so as you know, I can say these things. Maybe you can't. But that's not the only reason I hated the neighborhood, it's just one of them. I just hate shitty neighborhoods, period. Hate them.

Plus, the hassle to get there was like a bonus *fuck you*. And the hecklers that clowned me walking down the street were like a *PS: still, fuck you*. But that never happened to me, so I don't know why I even brought it up. Anyway, I called The Chicken-Farming Jew when I got to his house—brownstone actually—to let him know I was outside. But he told me the address was a bit further down, to keep walking, and that he'd come meet me outside. I was upset about that, or nervous. I really didn't wanna walk too far with pot and money on me. Usually, I would never do that. This was the first time that *I* ever went to *him*. Usually he came to me, so I wanted to be respectful this first go-around.

He stood outside his door with his kippah on—that's Hebrew for yarmulke—the Jewish hats that Jews wear. I'm Jewish, so I know these types of things.

"Chalm in, chalm in! Welcome!"

He was a nice dude—straightforward and to the point, but nice. When I walked inside his house, his wife was busy being busy. I'm not sure what kind of busy she was being, but she was doing shit, that's for sure. Women like that don't just sit around, and I don't mean Jewish women, just the type of woman that doesn't waste time. But I had never met her, so what the fuck do I know? I was unsure if she'd talk to me—her being all super Jewish and whatnot—but she offered me something—something to eat maybe, peanuts could be, but I'm not sure. It's still worth bringing up.

I followed The Chicken-Farming Jew to another room, somewhere a bit more private. It was in the back of his home. The furniture in his brownstone was well put together and seemed to match, but it wasn't a particularly nice brownstone, just as nice as it coulda been. After all, we were in goddam Crown Heights.

He spoke intently about his chicken business. I listened. He failed to mention that just below where we stood, outside the window and behind the weed-filled grass of his ten square-foot backyard, was the fucking chicken coop he had been referring to the entire time I knew him.

A chicken coop.

In the middle of Brooklyn.

Chickens.

I couldn't believe it. Who woulda thought there'd be a damn chicken coop in the middle of Crown Heights? I swear I thought that was the funniest shit in the world, not to mention how he neglected to even bring it up, to even—I don't know, let it register how odd it might seem to someone who wasn't an orthodox Jew—not that all orthodox Jews had chickens—all I'm saying is I don't know anyone else with chickens in Brooklyn who *isn't* an orthodox Jew. You know what I hate? How Jewish people are always asking me: "Are you Jewish?"

And when I say: "Yeah, my mom is Jewish, and my dad is Italian and French."

They say: "So you're Jewish. If your mom is Jewish—you're Jewish."

And I'm like: "I just fucking said that."

Whatever, I was lookin outside his window for a bit before I could comprehend in my head that the chicken coop was real. I finally interrupted his business spiel, which he was always on. "Wait—are *those* the chickens?"

"That's them. There's ch'about… Mmm, twenty or so in the ch'oop right now."

"Wait. Sorry—Those are real chickens? Just… Living there?"

"Twenty."

I couldn't wrap my brain around it, and I'm not the sheltered type, I've seen a thing or two, that's for sure. But chickens? In fuckin Brooklyn? Maybe his Jewish accent wasn't as thick as I remember it being, but it was still there, so that's that. Anyway, the chickens…

There was a fence enclosing his miniscule backyard, which was nothing *but* chickens, and to his right and left were other backyards that you could see into without straining your eyes or even turning your neck. Everyone lived on top of each other. Behind *those* backyards were three *other* backyards, all engulfed in a patch of land that was no more than fifty feet by fifty feet. Point is, there were five other backyards from where I stood in his living room that I could clearly see. That meant *they* could also clearly see into his backyard, which meant they could also see his chickens the way I could clearly see his chickens, and I imagine that musta been pretty damn entertaining to watch. I'd be watching those chickens all day if I were them. *Let's smoke a joint and watch the chickens!* That's what I'd say probably. I don't know to who, but if there was anyone over, I'd say that to them. Maybe I was making too big of a deal of it.

"That's fucking crazy dude. You've got chickens in Brooklyn!"

His wife came by again. She was in the other room during the chicken talk. She offered me something. I swear I wanna tell you what she kept offering me, but I simply can't say for sure. But the point is, she was overly helpful, cleanly, and hospitable, like *oh my, better have some food prepared and clean up for the drug-dealer!* It's more than most people did for me. They mighta been the second-best hosts. I had another client—he was a photographer. He did similar shit, like was all hospitable and whatnot, maybe the best, but The Chicken-Farming Jew was nearly as good. I liked his place, even though the location was not ideal.

"We've got a warech'ouse in Red Ch'ook too, that's where we process."

I coulda talked about his chickens all day. A traveling chicken salesman—I loved it. Is he smarter than me? I just wanted to dive into his whole business. Maybe I should farm some kinda animal? But, as with all the relationships in my life, I was there for a reason: Pot. Pot is one of those dad-words, but I always said it. I liked the way it sounds. Better than *weed,* which was for like… I don't know… Santa Cruz skater-types with no vocabulary.

Here's another thing I liked about The Chicken-Farming Jew: he was a low-quality ounce-buyer, and by that I mean he always bought my cheapest shit, which was sometimes hard to sell since everyone wanted the better shit. So this was a good thing. He *never* bought the good shit, even though he knew it was available. That was what mattered to me: that he knew he *could* buy better weed if he wanted to, but he never did. He never took more than what he needed, and never took less than what he needed. He was precise. That's why I took a cab all the way to Crown Heights. And an ounce isn't a bad sale. It's not like I was cashing out my entire inventory, but still, not a bad sale.

"I love this. Man, I love it. I want a chicken coop now."

"You should! I show you ch'how!"

I just thought of another reason I hate Crown Heights… Years later, my ex-employee Ronny moved there—he worked for me when I was running my music business, which you'll hear about when you meet Mike Z. But yeah, I had a business promoting concerts, a great way to launder my money.

Anyway, Ronny was my A&R guy—talent recruiter basically. He had a good ear for music. I paid him to find bands in the city that could draw a crowd of fifty people or over, bands with no agent, and a decent social media following. Social media was this new thing that had just come out. I already told you about that new website, Facebook. It was a great resource to find out who was liked and who had no friends. Anyway, Ronny would find the bands that had friends and insert their numbers into a spreadsheet. Then we'd assign them a score—one number—that would represent their importance. Then we'd know how much money to offer them. So, that's what he did, and he moved to Crown Heights not long after we split ways. And you know what happened to *him?*

He came back to his apartment one day, and a bomb exploded. Boom.

Someone from the block tried to *bomb that motherfucker* outa the neighborhood. That's how bad Crown Heights was. I really disliked it there—always will, no matter how many times some hipster-fuck tries to tell me it's a "cool" neighborhood. So sick of all these phony New Yorkers that leave their families to pursue a life in the projects.

"So… What do you ch'ave today?"

"The best pot in the city," I told him. I put my bag down to begin my presentation, but The Chicken-Farming Jew switched topics fast. Good business people do that sometimes. That's also the trait of a horrible friend—I think—not that all great business people are shitty friends, but they might be. He also hated my stories. "You're gonna like this right here cause I just got back from Colorado, where my—"

"Yes, yes, I don't need all the story—just ch'what is the best price?"

He was the type of dude who *never* wanted to pay more than what he had to, like I said. I used to think that was dumb, now I know that's not the case. "The Lemon Kush is the cheapest, but—"

"Ch'ow much?"

"$400." I never *ever* sold any weed for less than $400, and usually there was an extra fee for delivery—but I let it slide with The Chicken-Farming Jew. Maybe he just intimidated me. Yes—he did. Anyway, I charged at least $400 for even my shittiest weed, even though the going rate at the time for good New York weed was about $350 - $375. And some of the ounces I had—my best shit—I sold for $600 *and* never even had a problem selling it. It sold easily. It was always worth every dime, and I *loved* to tell people why it was worth so much. I didn't get much of a chance to give my full sales pitch anymore, most people knew my deal, they knew I was legit, safe, had quality product, and was trustworthy. That's the most valuable invisible asset of all: Trustworthiness. Nobody wants a shady drug-dealer, not that I was really a *drug-dealer*, I just sold pot.

"It's not shit like last time?"

"Oh stop," I told him. He always complained. He *always* tried his best to make me feel as if he was doing *me* a favor for buying my weed. Of course I had to defend myself—can't just let it slide completely. "You know damn well I've *never* sold you shit, not once. Some strains are better than others, but you never want—"

"Fine, not *shit*, but not *great*."

"Well if you want the good shit, I have it—but it costs more."

"Just give to me the Lemon Kush."

It was the same bullshit negotiation technique every time I saw him: He would tell me my weed wasn't as good as I thought it was, then I would tell him that of course it was, then he would agree half-heartedly and buy the damn weed. But I was happy to engage.

And I liked his chickens—hated his terrifying neighborhood, but the chicken coop was on point.

Now I just had to somehow find a cab, and there weren't many of them in this part of town. But I thanked his wife for the peanuts—or pickles—or whatever she kept offering me, before I left like a gentleman. As I was leaving, I thought about what it might be like to sell something *other* than weed—like chickens, which weren't illegal. Sometimes I forgot that what I was doing *wasn't* legal. At some point, I'd have to stop.

As soon as I have $80,000 in my safe, I'll stop.

And at the rate I was going, it wouldn't be too much longer. My clientele list was up to many by then. Tech Zach sent me so many versatile customers it made it really hard to leave the excitement. I mean, I was meeting people who truly appreciated me—not just as a drug-dealer, but as a human. That's a priceless benefit most businesses don't provide.

Anyway… It's time for you to meet the most hospitable client on my roster. I mean hey, while things are going well, why not ride it out, right?

CHAPTER 10: THE PHOTOGRAPHER

The Photographer always sat a bit too close to me.

I was never sure if he was gay. It's okay if he was, obviously. Just wasn't sure. I was over his East Village apartment, which had been completely converted into a photography studio, and I sat on his brown leather couch as he prepared one of the many drinks he always offered me. As he was serving me the drink, he sat right beside me, even though the couch was big enough for some privacy. He was a bit too close, but I never said anything. I mean, how the fuck do you bring a thing like that up? *Yo dude, back the fuck up, your dick is too close to my scotch.* That'd just be offensive. I could swear he was hitting on me. Maybe he was just lonely, but do lonely people sit closer than non-lonely people? Did he not even like the weed I had? Was I only called over for conversation and potential ass-fucking? That's what made me nervous. I didn't want to get into that type of situation. I thought about what I might say if he moved in for a kiss. *Sorry man, that's not my thing.* Nah, that wasn't good. *Not my thing?* What's that even mean? It means I'm not gay for starters, I guess. *Dude—what the fuck are you doing?* But that's too mean. Is it? I mean, I don't go over to some chick's house and sit on her couch and suffocate her with close-talk conversation then try and kiss her without approval. I've never done that—I don't think. Probably not—nah, definitely not. That's not my style. So why would it be okay for *him* to do that to me? *Whoa, dude. No.* I could say something like that, I guess. That'll for sure embarrass him, but it's not so easy of a situation for me either. Point is, if he tried to kiss me, I wouldn't know how to respond.

"And in all different sectors of the industry," he said, then stopped talking to look at me, waiting for a response.

"Sorry, what? Say that one more time?"

"Long day?—another scotch?"

Another one? Was this guy nuts? "Sure, yeah. Three ice cubes please." Whatever, it was free, and present, but the only thing that bothered me about the way he poured his scotch was that he poured it in these rocks-glasses that were a bit too big for scotch, and so what ended up happening is the ice melted too quickly because the ratio of scotch to ice was off. There's nothing worse than watery scotch—nothing. But it was free—not that money was an issue, I had over four grand in my pocket. But like I said, it was there—the scotch—good, expensive, aged scotch at that, and so I drank it.

"Thanks again man. I appreciate it."

"Oh, absolutely sir! You're always welcome to whatever you'd like!"

Was that a gay thing? Was that like: You wanna fuck? Is that what the fuck that meant? I didn't say any of this out loud, of course, I just thought of things like that often.

He had a nice apartment, so he musta made a good living at it—photography, you know, to have this apartment and all. That's impressive. It's not so easy to make a living off that sorta job. Maybe I could learn a thing about how he did it. He wasn't too old, either—maybe late thirties or early forties—though everyone in that age-range looked either much older or much younger than they really were. Some were bald with motorcycles, others were gray with full heads of hair, some overweight with thinning hair and—I felt my head. I'd been feeling my head ever since I realized my hair was thinning on the top when I went to Argentina to visit a girl I was sure I was in love with who I met in Hawaii. Turns out we had nothing in common, but I didn't know that till I learned more Spanish and could actually communicate with her. But anyway, while I was there she told me she liked my hair better shaved—or buzzed or whatever. So, I did it—why not? That's when I looked in the mirror in her apartment in Buenos Aires and I realized my hair wasn't as thick as it used to be; that there were lighter spots on my scalp. I flipped my goddamn shit and made three appointments with hair restoration doctors, and from that day forth, my life had been a mess. My looks were all I had—and money. I'll just get a hair transplant if I need to.

"So how's takin pictures goin? Snapping up a storm?"

"Oh yeah, I spent all day today with a client shooting a video."

I didn't want to bring attention to the fact that I had no idea he shot video too. I'm sure he's told me that a million times. I felt my hair all over my head as he put another glass of scotch down in front of me. I swear, he never wanted me to leave. He *must* be gay. I was more interested in knowing the truth about his life than the preference—or state of being—of his sexuality. I mean, what the fuck do I care? *Do I care?* No. I just—how do we have truthful communication if we don't talk about sex? Or his love life? All my other clients talked about sex with me—that was my specialty—but he always talked about other shit, like industry parties that he threw, which he *always* asked me to attend. But I'm his drug-dealer. Why would I go to some photographer party? The fact that we never talked about sex made it that much more apparent that we *weren't* talking about sex. Am *I gay?* Whoa. Why do I even ask myself that—of course I'm not. But why am I obsessed with *this guy* being gay?

"It'll be next Friday," he told me.

Goddammit, I completely missed what he said again. Fuck. I can't let him know that I wasn't paying attention *again.* He's *gotta* be talking about those damn parties that he's always inviting me to though. I hope he wasn't talkin about some surgery that his mother was having next Friday. Nah, it was definitely about those damn parties he always throws. "The party?" I asked him, unsure if I was anywhere close to the matter at hand.

"All types will be there. I think you'd really enjoy it. Great contacts for you to make as well, for your movie."

I told everyone about the damn screenplay I just finished. Have I even told you what it was about? It was about this girl I met in rehab—Robyn Smith, crazy chick that I had crazy sexual escapades with—still do actually. Flyin to Houston to see her soon. She's from Lake Charles. Houston is just the closest airport. Anyway, she told me she witnessed a murder when she was a little girl, and that it was the Sheriff's son who did it—and got away with it, and that her now-boyfriend was the gay lover of the Sheriff's son, and that he had been with her for two years only to find out how much she remembered about that day, and that now he was trying to kill her, and in fact already *had* tried to kill her, but she escaped. And I was trying to get to the bottom of it. Anyway, that's the gist.

"Well, it's just a screenplay for now, not a movie yet," I told him.

"Not until you come to the party on Friday!"

Well-played, I thought to myself. This guy's sharp. I wonder if he *does* know some movie producers... Then it'd be worth showing up. I hate parties though, too many people, which is weird since I love to talk. Anyway, I *did* have a completed screenplay. That's not nothing—that's something. But what a horrible reason to attend. I'm not some fame-hungry, ladder-climbing, socialite dickhead. I'm a real dude with authentic values. I dismissed the thought.

He *really was* sitting close to me. Fuck dude, it's a big enough couch, back up. Maybe I should move over. But I didn't.

There was this white-screen in front of me with a large tripod—two screens actually—one to my right, and another straight ahead next to his kitchen. His apartment made an L shape. There were two different screens with two different tripods. I think they were there for... goddammit. I couldn't remember why. *I know I asked him that a billion times*, but I couldn't remember what he told me. I was always in my head—never listening, not to him, at least. I couldn't ask that question again. I'll just have to wonder.

"Okay, yeah—I think I might come. When is it again?"

"Friday. You'll have a blast. We all do."

I sipped the scotch without making any change of expression when it ran down my throat. The burn felt relaxing and the taste was rich. I was a bit buzzed. I usually got buzzed from the first glass, especially *his* glasses, but I generally maintained the same buzz until glass number three or four. I plateaued with a steady buzz till I turned lightly drunk. That's why I never turned him down for a third glass if he offered, which he always did if I drank fast enough.

"How many people show up?"

"Oh, a lot. Lots of great contacts."

"When is it again?"

"The first Friday of every month."

"Oh you do it every month?"

"Yup, every month."

He took a sip of his scotch. He always drank with me, which was better than drinking alone. I hated drinking alone. Well, alone was fine, but if someone else was in the room, they had to drink too. He was a great host—better than most. Anyway, it was about 3PM and I had a full day ahead of me, I had to leave—always hard, especially with him. But I mean, I was his drug-dealer. Obviously I can't hang out all day.

"Aright dude. This has been an absolute pleasure, as per usual. But… I gotta get on with it—would love to stay, but I can't. Work, work, work."

"Oh, I hear ya! Yes, absolutely."

That's when he usually retorted by offering me one more glass before I left.

"One more glass for the road?"

"I'll be fuckin drunk dude. I wish, but I can't." If he asks again, I'll have one, I thought.

"Well, free scotch is free scotch, right? Do you want to smoke a quick bowl for the road?"

I had to smoke with most of my clients; that's just the way it was. If I didn't stick around and listen to a few more of their problems, I wasn't providing the service a drug-dealer—especially a weed dealer—had to provide. Listening to people's random problems is just part of the job, like a shrink, or barber. I really *did* want to leave, but I took out a small nug for him to pack in his bowl anyway, you know, customer service.

"Oh no, please. Use my weed, it's the least I can do."

The least he can do? The guy already gave me two glasses of forty-dollar scotch. He didn't owe me anything. Why did he think he did? But I let him pack his weed anyway, not cause I didn't want to use my weed—I had over two pounds in my backpack—I just didn't want to decline his hospitality.

"What do you want anyway? And I guess I'll have one more glass, that cool?"

"As many as you'd like, my friend."

I took out three pre-packaged half-ounces. He always bought ounces, and to sell someone an ounce of the *same weed* would be a disservice. Variety was key. We all get bored with the same shit, at least I do.

"Aright, well, I got Sour Diesel, Blueberry Kush, and OG."

It was really called *OG Kush*, but to have *two different kushes?* That's no good. So, I changed the name and left out the Kush part—just called it *OG*. The OG was probably the worst weed I had, but it was still insanely great fucking weed. There's just always one cheaper strain that offsets the cost of the pricier strains.

That day, it was the OG. Anyway, you always have one slightly shittier strain. It's just business.

"Well, what do you recommend?"

That was the golden question. I could package up the perfect amount of cheaper weed and expensive weed whenever a client asked me that. Of course, I never sold a bad package—not once. That's what made me so damn good at my job.

"Take a half of the OG and a half of the Sour Diesel. That's what I would do." And that's the truth, by the way—that *is* what I'd do.

"Great, I'll take it."

He put the third glass of scotch in front of me. I drank that one quickly, not cause I wanted to leave, which I did, but because my throat was numb by that point and I could drink it faster. "The OG is $200 and the Sour is $225." I was way drunker than I had planned on getting—not that I planned anything, ever. My life was a mess.

He gave me the cash like a newbie—faces all over the place. He didn't know how to deliver clean bills, so I had to organize them—the bills—in front of him while counting them out. And that's not to be a dick, just out of habit. Why not just flip the bills in the proper direction now as opposed to later?

"Oh, I'm so sorry. I must look so messy! You like all the dollars to be facing one direction, right? I forgot, so sorry."

"Oh—not at all dude. Yeah, so the reason is because when I go to the bank to swap out all the twenties and whatnot for hundreds, you know, to keep the amount of paper to a minimum, if I don't make the bills all facing the same direction, the bank teller has to do it, and that takes time, especially when you've got a lot of cash. Then you got the whole line of people starin at you like: Yo, this dude *must* be a drug-dealer, which is never a good feeling. But if you show up and hand them face-up bills, the deposit goes much quicker."

"Oh wow, that makes a lot of sense, you really know your trade. That's great."

"But yeah, don't worry a damn fiber in your brain. You're all good. I like flipping bills, it's fun. And thank you by the way, for the scotch, for the conversation, and for the generosity."

"Absolutely. You should one-hundred percent come by on Friday."

"I think I might."

I swayed down the hallway as I left his building. I was definitely drunk, which is fine. I liked being drunk on the job. And I was well on my way to saving the perfect amount of money: $80,000. After that I'll stop living such a dangerous life. Till then, I had to keep working on my screenplay—finishing touches and all. And once it was good to go, I booked a ticket to see Robyn to show her the movie I was about to make about her fucked up life.

But whenever I saw Robyn, she completely disoriented me…

CHAPTER 11: ROBYN SMITH

Robyn picked me up in Houston, which was the closest airport to her home in Lake Charles. Lake Charles had an airport but a small one, and it cost double the amount to fly there. So, she picked me up in Houston and we drove to her townhouse in the suburbs of Lake Charles. I couldn't believe where she lived. It looked like an adult's house, but yet she was one step away from a straitjacket, which I loved.

"Wanna hear the script so far?"

"Graigh, it ain't safe to be talkin bout that round here. Yew know I sayd it ain't right."

"Look, I'm making the movie. It's coming out. I just wanna make sure it's right."

"Oh maigh god are yew gonna be een it?"

"Maybe."

"Sexy layts go to the casino. Yew wanna go to a casino? There a good one close t'here."

She took off her shirt to get changed. Her fake tits matched her press-on nails, glued-on eyelashes, caked on makeup, and shiny plump lips. There wasn't a girl sexier, even in the movies. That's why I had to always remind people she was with me whenever we went out, like when we got to the casino.

The hotel lobby was filled with outdoor plants and Vegas-style couches. The public dropped their conversation to a whisper as soon as we entered. Nobody drew attention like Robyn, and she goddam loved it; she was an expert attention-getter. I kept grabbin her hand so everybody would know she was with me. I got nervous when we sat down at the bar cause I had to go pee and the bartender was staring at her—a good looking guy, possibly better looking than me, and that made me nervous. She was staring at him the way he was staring at her, and the thing about Robyn was as easy as she came was as fast as she went, so I had to keep an eye on her, at least for the time I was in Louisiana. And I couldn't say "stop staring at him," or whatever, cause it's not like we were dating or anything; that'd be controlling and weird, but I thought it. I was so mad at this fuckin bartender for being who he was, and I had to pee intensely but held it for as long as I could.

I was wearing this suede beige jacket and was nearly certain I was a solid nine. I was missing one point for being shorter than I wanted to be. It's not a proud declaration to write something like that, but I mean, that *is* how I felt, so whattaya want me to do, lie to you? Fuck no, I tell the truth. But that night I felt more like an eight than a nine with this fucking goddam bartender—

"STOP STARING AT HIM!" I finally snapped.

"GoooLLLLLLY! Yer paranoid Grayhg, yew know ah only luv yew."

Then she went back to staring at him. I couldn't hold it anymore. "I gotta go to the bathroom."

"It thayt way sexy."

So I left but kept checking over my shoulder to see if she was gonna call him over to talk to him while I was gone. I went and peed and was sweating for no other reason than I was anxious she might be a new relationship when I got back—not that we were dating, but I'd look like an asshole. Worst of all, this guy was gonna think he'd beaten me. I hated losing. I had to keep my damn jacket on cause my sweat was showing through the fucking purple button-down shirt I was wearing. So even though it's a million degrees everywhere in Louisiana, I was stuck in this goddam suede jacket on.

I got back to the bar and she was deeply engaged in pre-fuck convo with the damn bartender, just as I'd thought she'd be. She was hot, but seriously predictable. I goddam knew she'd be flirting with him, so I acted normal as I returned and talked loudly, cockblocking any further flirtation.

"Graigh this is… wuts yer name agayne? Ronald! Graigh this is Ronald.

"Hey, Ah'm Kyle," he said, fairly politely actually. Still, he'd crossed the line. I didn't wanna react in any sorta fashion that mighta shown too many of my insecurity cards, but that only made me ten times angrier. I was about to explode. Then… I did.

I grabbed a high-ball glass and smashed it into his pretty face and left shards of glass stickin out of his cheeks. It was fuckin gross. His flesh was so bloody. Some of the glass got caught in his eyelid and was sticking outa the white part of his eye. Chunks of skin were falling off and Robyn was disgusted, so mission accomplished.

I could see people at the other end of the bar calling the police. I didn't want to go to jail down here. They'd all call me yankee and make fun of my clothes, even though I was better dressed than they could ever be. Fucking southern pieces of shit. Who the fuck wears those high socks anyway? Everyone down here is always hiking their socks up to their knees like a goddam tool, and they think I'm dressed like a pussy? Fuck all of you. I'm a Jew and proud of it you anti-Semitic pieces of—

"What're you drinking?"

I came back.

"Oh, uhh…" I noticed he didn't have an accent. "Do you have Macallan 12?"

I coulda ordered Johnny Walker Black, which was much cheaper, but I had to show off a bit, so I ordered the more expensive one. She kept looking at Kyle and Kyle kept looking at her even with me standing right goddam there, so I had to do something to take the attention off him and get it back on me.

"So is Clyde still after you or what? You haven't brought him up at all."

"Baby yew look so sexy in thayt"—and she started rubbin my shoulder—"leather suede whatever jaycket."

"Thanks babe. Are you gonna answer me or what?"

She stopped abruptly and laughed at me, then at Kyle, then looked back at me and came in close. I thought she was gonna kiss me or suck my lip, but instead she whispered psychotically: "Yer gon git us keelt." But she said it without really seeming to care that much or taking her attention off my jacket. She said it kinda jovially, actually. I could never get a straight answer from her, but every time she said something like that I thought about it for a moment. Was she serious? Was I *really* gonna get us killed?

"No one even heard me. Whatever, just… I need you to read it tonight cause there're still some holes."

Then in a sinister whisper, she says: "Yew wanna put yer big New York dick in ma hole?"

She was already drunk as she waved Kyle over, who had left us for other customers. "Sexy, can ah git another martini, dirty as fuck, yew know how I like you… I mean *it*." And she smiled at him while she was rubbing my shoulders and then moved her hand down to where my crouch was. "And kin we git the check?" I was so fuckin hard. This girl was such a fuckin whore it made me absolutely crazy and I couldn't stand it. I had to be inside her before I lost my mind. But first, I ordered another drink:

"—Me too, please. Another Macallan."

I said please to let him know he didn't faze me, that I was secure.

We drove back to her suburban house in suburban Lake Charles, drunk as fuck, or at least buzzed as fuck, and walked into her bachelorette pad. I couldn't believe *this girl* lived here. I mean, the living room was just so well decorated, and everything matched. There wasn't a speck of crazy in the house until she opened her mouth. It really was a conundrum.

"I want yer cock in ma mouth," she said immediately, right after we got through the door.

She took her shirt off, fake tits glowing in the light as if they were sent down from heaven to cure cancer. I couldn't believe how far I'd made it in life. I remember staring at her in rehab at New Beginnings thinking to myself: I'll never be able to fuck that girl. After all, she was almost nineteen and I was fourteen. Those two worlds don't collide. But now look at me. I'm the man. She took my jeans off and spit on her hand and spit on my dick like a wildcat and started blowing me from the side, sucking on me like a lollypop.

"Don't yew cum yew fuckin fuck yew."

"Aright just… Okay."

I tried to move us into her room but she didn't stop blowing me, so I grabbed her hair and stood her up and threw her into the bedroom and slammed her onto her bed, but not rapey-style, in like a soap opera fashion. Maybe more aggressive than that, but she loved it. I took her pants off and couldn't make it to her thong before I just grabbed the string with all my sexual angst and tore it off her ass and chucked it in the corner of the room. I put my dick as far inside her as it would go.

"Choke me yew fuckin—"

And she started grindin her teeth as she said that and—Look. I don't wanna make this book into a sex novel. Point is I fuckin fucked the goddam living shit outa her and we NEVER even talked about my screenplay. I left two days later and it was a very long time till I saw her again. In fact, I'd only see her once more before she went missing, which made the story that much more interesting. Is that selfish?

I started putting together a movie budget, but since the movie would cost far more than I could make selling weed, I decided to capture the attention of the world in a different way first before I took on outside money. I decided to begin with a play.

So, after returning from Colorado from yet another trip, I went to the Drama Book Shop on the west side of Manhattan and browsed through a million plays till I found one that me and Louie—who you'll hear more about in a second—could star in. The play was called *Manuscript*, and there was a make out scene I could perfectly cast myself into. The thing about theatre is once the lights go down, there're no more takes. Whatever happens on stage is happening and there's nothing anyone can do to stop it. I could shape the world however I wanted it to be. I could be the hero, the villain, or a character that makes out with an insanely hot actress. Not only that, but it was cheap. Way less money than a movie. This revelation: that theatre would be my savior… It was a revelation that totally destroyed my life—as with many of my epiphanies. But in the beginning, I swore it was full proof. And so I set out for stardom in the world of theatre.

It all started and ended with Louie…

PART 2: SHOWBIZ

CHAPTER 12: GODDAM LOUIE

Louie destroyed my life.

At the same time, he had revived me when I was dead, so it was an unhealthy dynamic to say the least. I met him two years ago when he cast me in a play called *You Are Here*. It was about a psycho who pretended to work at a rest stop—Louie played that psycho—and a visitor who just wanted to use the bathroom and leave. I played that visitor. Somehow, the plotline had become analogous to our actual lives. He was half Irish and half Native American from Rhode Island, but if you asked him his background, he'd just use whichever ethnicity or geographic location was most beneficial to the point he was trying to make at the time you asked. The bottom line is he was a piece of shit, and I loved him. But a piece of shit he was, and the longer I hung out with him, the bigger of a piece of shit I became... especially the way he treated women. Like the chick who came in this morning to audition for the female role in *Manuscript*.

"Why don't we run that one again sweethahrt, take it frahm tha tahp."

"Oh, okay, so, do you like, is there some direction or changes I should make?"

"Youh doin fine sweethahrt, let's just get this one in, eh?"

Nothing he said made sense. Then when she left, before the door was even closed on her way out he'd say something like, "Dime piece, eh Cayea? I wouldn't mind stickin your Jew dick in for me, just to get a whiff." Then he'd drop his register and look at me and say things like: "Who's your boy, eh? Me. You'hre my brutha, you know that? My brutha."

It was exhausting hanging out with him. He convinced me aggressively to come out drinking with him after everything we did, and eventually it became the only activity on our friend list. We drank nonstop after every audition and rehearsal, and every night, by the time he got plastered, which was always, at some point, he humiliated me in the worst possible way. And he was *always* ready to fight, raise his voice, and scream obscenities at anyone who got in his way.

Anyway, the audition studio was in a random building on Ninth Avenue, and like I said, Louie was saying questionable shit to every chick who walked in to audition. We hired a director from Harvard to make us feel legit, for the sake of this story, let's just call him Lip. He was there too. Louie said questionable shit to him just as often.

"She was smokin, right Lip? Not that you like that type of box, but even you'd slip one in her, am I right?"

"You know, just because I'm gay doesn't mean I'm constantly looking to have sex, nor does it mean that I can't find a woman attractive. Got that? I went to Yale, you graduated nowhere. Let me do the directing. Keep your homophobic comments to yourself."

Oh that's right, he was from Yale. Louie dropped his pants and pulled his dick out.

"This look like I'm homophobic to you? C'mere." And he started walkin over to Lip.

"Ew, you fucking creep, pull up your pants."

"Packin a pole, know what I mean?"

"Louie, why? I'm gonna fucking vomit," I told him.

"Listen to your partner," Lip said.

"Fuckin faggots, both of yaz."

Lip got up to leave. "I quit."

Louie stopped him and blocked the door. "I'm only kiddin, c'mon Lip. I love you. C'mere. Gimme a hug. Never again, I swear."

"One more thing and I quit."

"He won't do that shit anymore," I assured him.

There was a knock on the door. I opened up. A chick entered. She read the lines wonderfully. Truly great. Finally, we found a chick to play the role, I thought to myself. She was almost perfect.

"Ya like hehr?" Louie asked. "Or she not haht enough for ya?"

What a dipshit. Like I wouldn't wanna cast a chick just because she wasn't as hot as some of the other actresses. I wasn't him. No. I wouldn't do that. But I guess I could, I mean, if I wanted to. I suppose I *did* need someone to take my mind off KC. It's not like I was over her, even with Robyn and De'Ena keeping my scrotum empty. You remember De'Ena? The first girl I cheated on KC with? My old neighbor in Queens—the cocktail waitress from Alabama? I still saw her, pretty often actually, but I *never went* over to her place anymore. That was *way too close* to where KC and I used to live. No way. She always came to me. Anyway, KC was still a thing in my mind is what I'm trying to say here. That's why when Minnie showed up and gave a half-assed performance, I reconsidered.

"Maybe we should cast *her*," I said.

"You're fucking kidding. Are you? We already gave the role to Beth," Lip said.

"Well, but she's not right maybe, you know?" I said.

"Oh now she ain't right? Ya believe this shit Lip?"

"Can you *please* think for *once* with your brain instead of your insatiable dick?"

"That's not it at all, she just has the look and—"

"And you want her in your bed, which has NOTHING to do with the FUCKING play—why did I even *take* this job? Do you know I went to the Yale School of Drama? Whatever, do what you want. You're the producer... What the hell do I know, I just studied directing at one of the most prestigious universities in the world..."

"Cool, so do we fire Beth and cast Minnie?" I asked, sincerely curious.

Then he stormed out. Louie stood there and looked at me.

"You're my brother," and he came over and messed up my hair like he always did. "And I know you wanna bang this broad... But does it make sense?"

"Yes."

"It's your money."

"I know. It is. It's my fucking money."

All these actresses were fuckin with my head. Then I couldn't stop thinking of KC under ten million guys fucking her in the ass. Maybe she's just watching TV. Whatever, I'm firing Beth.

So the next day when she showed up for our scheduled rehearsal, I said: "Hey Beth. So, look. You're a great actress. There's no doubt about that."

She started to get worried. "Am I doing okay? Is there something you'd like me to work on? I can do better."

My heart was already starting to crumble. I'm not a cold man. I have feelings you know. Maybe this is a bad idea? I mean, she *was* perfect for the part. Lip walked out, like he may implode. Louie sat in the corner and watched me make a bad decision.

"No, you're doing great... It's just, I don't think you're right. For uhhh... You know, just, for this particular part, I just don't know if—I just think that maybe... maybe we can work together on a... another play."

"Wait, are you firing me?"

She started crying.

"Uhhh... Well, not *firing* you. Just, not for this play, you know?"

Then she ran out. Oh man. What a sick goddam person I am. So I left the rehearsal and went over to the pub. I called Minnie. I had no idea if she even still wanted the part.

"Hello?"

"Minnie?"

"Who is this?"

"It's Greg, the producer of Manuscript."

"Sorry, which project is that? I audition a lot, so... I'm sorry, who is this?"

"From the play about the college students. Manuscript."

"Sorry, but… where was the audition? That would be more helpful. I'm really sorry, I just go out a lot." Holy shit. This chick was driving me nuts. I gave her the address, whatever the hell it was, I don't remember, but finally: "Oh, yes. Sorry, right. Hi."

"We want you to play Elizabeth."

"Oh! That's great! Is this paid?"

"Uh, well, no, but… It might be. It's being produced on 42nd Street."

"Oh. Umm, yeah, sure."

It was a weird start, and she really wasn't that good. She was later cast in a big movie where she was naked the whole film, maybe I'll tell ya what it was later on, but for now that would blow her cover, but the point is she sucked. But she was fucking hot. And that's important, well, it was for me. I just needed a distraction, and isn't that what doing theatre is all about? Anyway, we had this make out scene, which I told you about, but it was rough. It wasn't going very well. Lip hated our performance. *He hated me.* But that's another story.

One day I asked Minnie if she wanted to get a drink after rehearsal. She said yes and we went to some restaurant. I knew the show was becoming a mess entirely because I was in love with her, or the way she looked at least, but still the make out scene *did need work,* I mean, it was horrendous, and I couldn't ignore that. We had to fix it. I'm the damn producer for fuck's sake. I had to act responsibly—in the best interest of the show. So I asked her at the restaurant:

"How are you feeling about everything?"

"The play?"

"Right."

"Good. I guess. Our scene together is a bit rusty."

"Well, do you wanna… And I mean, I'm totally not trying to be weird about this, but… do you wanna, well, practice it?"

"Sure."

"Okay, well, hmm… we could get audition space, but honestly I'm outa money. So, I'd like to *not* spend money if I can avoid it. Does it matter where we rehearse? Do you want to—in the most professional way possible—do you want to maybe, like, go back to my apartment and run the scene?"

"I guess."

"Cool, well, let's get the check and we can head over there."

So we went to my apartment and ran the scene. We got to the make out part. The scene called for a *hate make out* scene, cause in the play I *hate* her, but she tempts me into kissing her in this sexy scene, you know, in a manipulative and mind-fucking way. So anyway, we had to get that across to the audience, but when we got to the make out scene in my apartment, I never stopped kissing her.

I picked her up—she was this tall model girl—she modeled shoes for this famous reality TV star, and she had a size six foot and long beautiful brown hair with crystal-blue eyes and perfect thighs and a round Irish ass and perky lips and her nipples were always popping through her shirt… Or maybe they weren't, I don't know, but I picked her up and chucked her on my bed. She spread her legs and looked at me with a look that said: *You have NO control in this situation… I have you.* I just love that shit.

I ripped her pants off and grabbed her ass and slapped it ferociously and squeezed the sides of her thighs and... oh no... I started to get nervous.

Shit Greg don't get nervous. Oh no. I was losing it. Focus on her, focus on her! I always got so nervous, fuck! I looked at Minnie in the eyes. *Fuck me you piece of producer shit* is what she looked like she was thinking, but my dick was only half hard, so I kinda had to stuff it in her to get it fully in. She looked at me like *please don't tell me you're not hard anymore.*

Holy shit, what will rehearsal be like tomorrow if I can't get hard? DO IT GREG! I slowly held my dick in her, even though I wasn't fully erect, and I looked at her blue eyes. They were mesmerizing. I acted myself into serenity. Everything is okay, Greg. Breathe. Just... relax. Finally, I could feel myself growing inside her. I slipped it out a bit then thrust into her a bit, then her moan lifted my dick up even more and I got rock hard immediately and all at once, I fucking pummeled into her as hard as I could and grabbed her hair and slapped her face and choked her neck and sucked her lip and nibbled her nipples and pounded into her so that I had to grab the edge of my mattress cause it was starting to slide all over the floor since I had no bedframe.

She grabbed my back and squeezed me hard enough that I could feel the bruises coming in before she even stopped, and she scratched her nails into me as she let out a sigh of relaxation. So, I flipped her over on her stomach and looked at her perfect ass and went inside her so far that I couldn't last one second more. I pulled out and exploded all over her back and her hair and it went on my bed and the sheets were covered and I pulled out and turned over on my back and stared at the ceiling with the exposed brick wall nudging into my skull cause I was laying weird but didn't have the energy to move.

The next day at rehearsal we fucked in the green room while she was changing and later that evening we fucked in the bathroom of the theatre, which was right by a Tony award-winning producer's office. Our performance got weaker, my acting tanked, our relationship was blatant to anyone watching, and then, well, we were scheduled to open the next night.

And then, the most horrible phone call ever…

CHAPTER 13: SMASHED IN NOSE

I was sitting outside the theatre—still inside, at the top of the stairs, and my Blackberry starts buzzing. It was a Georgia phone number. Oh fuck. It was gonna be KC. Fuck, fuck, fuck.

"Hello?"

My whole life felt like it was on stilts any time a 912 number called—like any wrong move might send me in any myriad of downward directions. But the voice on the other end of the line was not KC.

"Grayg?"

It was her dad. Even worse. I *never* wanted to talk to him. He was a stern man with a poor sense of hillbilly humor that worshipped the civil war and believed the South had really won. He was also a faithful member of the NRA and owned a rifle for every day of the week, even though he lived in a wildlife preserve. But worry struck his vocal cords on that afternoon. I could tell he was all bent outa shape. This wasn't good.

"How are you sir," I said in a shaky voice, scared of whatever mighta brought him to my receiver.

"Have yew spok'n t'my daught'r, KC?" Like I don't know who the fuck his daughter was. Oh KC! Is *that* who your ex-wife gave birth to? But I didn't say that. I just said:

"No, I haven't talked to her since she left."

"Ah've just bin hearin all these rumors bout her all round town—"

"Sir—"

"Horrible stories Grayg. Stories bout'er sleepin with men she hardly knows—"

"SIR! I can't have this conversation right now. It's a big day for me—it's the opening night of my show. I'm at the theatre—"

"Ah know. Ah know, an ah hope yewl forgive me. But, if yew cud just help me find her, just call her maybe—I don want er wakin up with strange men—"

My stomach dropped. "I'M SORRY! I CAN'T TALK ABOUT THIS!"

And I hung up. I could feel my stomach swallow my heart. I could barely move I was so disoriented. Sleeping around? With strange men? Already? How could she do that to me? Why would her dad call me about that? What the fuck is wrong with everyone? Am I wrong? Am I doing something incorrect? My gut was throbbing with emotion. I felt like reality was caving in on me. Oh no, another panic attack—no no no, not now!

I went inside the theatre. Louie, Lip and Minnie were waiting for me. Louie got all mad, but Louie was *always* mad. Musta been cause most of his family was impoverished, dead, or in prison. We both wanted to win a Tony, but that shit seriously didn't happen. At the time, we *really* took ourselves overly serious, especially him:

"You ready to play producer now and care about our fahkin show?" His voice—no. Stop. I couldn't hear his chatterbox right now. He *never shut the fuck up.* Always was talkin. Serious talking problem this guy had. But he kept going, like usual. "Remember? The show? The show we been rehearsin fer a month? The one that opens in four fahkin hours?"

"DUDE SHUT UP! NOT NOW!"

"Then when? Eh? Is Greg Corleone ready to rehearse yet?"

His stupid fuckin Godfather jokes, just cause I learned how to earn money. Piece of shit. I remember thinking for a second: I swear you motherfucker, *you say one more fuckin word.* But then I just stopped. The air went black and nothing mattered. I grabbed the broom that was propped up against one of the chairs in the first row and squeezed it with all my strength. I was gonna ruin his face. I swung the stick part right for his head, with as much velocity as I could muster, but he ducked outa the way and the broom ricocheted off one of the theatre seats right back at me and slammed into my face and splattered my nose. Blood poured out from my face. Lip looked like he might faint. He hated Louie and I, but I was paying him, so shut the fuck up, okay? I didn't even look at Minnie—now my new girlfriend who, as I realized, resembled nearly every girl in every Old Navy commercial ever produced. I didn't wanna see her reaction. What I had done was crazy and I knew it. The last thing I wanted was to ruin *another* relationship. I was embarrassed. I walked right by her ignoring her presence.

"FUCK!!" I screamed. First the phone call, and now this? That's why I punched the fuckin wall, but it wasn't a real wall, it was the wall of our set and my fist went right through it. Now there was a big hole in the middle of the goddam set. What the fuck is wrong with the universe? "FUCKIN SHIT!" I walked straight back to the greenroom and sat down, not even touching my nose, just letting it bleed forever. The room looked like a murder scene within moments.

Lip ran up to me with paper towels, instructing everyone what to do. I paid no attention to the drama—the drama of everyone trying to help me. Louie came into the greenroom and put his arm around me. "I love you brutha. If something is ever wrong—evah, you hear me? You let me know, eh? I love you." And he hugged me and kissed my forehead. I cried in his arms and told him I had to make it to an audition for *As The World Turns*, which I wasn't even gonna tell him about it cause I never wanted to make it seem like my career was further along than his was. But *As The World Turns* was a pretty big deal to me. It was some soap opera that filmed in New York.

I walked over there with my nose all bandaged up, blood seeping through the bandages. I walked into the casting call and made the other actors jump. What's wrong? Never seen blood seeping through bandages before? Fuckin pussies. But I didn't say that shit, I just thought it. Then I sat down and waited for the damn audition. I thought maybe I'd say hi to everyone while I was there.

"What's up fellas?" I said to them, but they weren't too friendly.

Neither was the casting director. When she called me into the room, the first thing she said was: "Whoa, what happened to *you*?"

"Fight choreography," I told her.

I got word an hour later, after the audition, that the sheltered casting director said I was "too dark for the role." Loser.

Anyway, I ran back to the theatre. I sat down in one of the chairs in the audience, closed my eyes, and wondered how the hell I was gonna do this damn show. How did my life get like this?

I looked at the set and the dude we hired to do our set design, some dude we met at a pub near Times Square, he had already patched it back together. It was as if nothing ever happened. That's good, I guess. And all he wanted was a few beers for it.

I went into the greenroom and apologized to Minnie. She wasn't too impressed with my manic episode. Shit. Maybe I was bi-polar. The thought of that freaked me out, so I took a Xanax—maybe not the best move an hour before opening night.

"Yeah, that was pretty... insane," Minnie told me. I said I would never do it again. My family showed up for the first show. My nose was bleeding through every bandage we tried to cover up the gash with. It looked all disfigured in the mirror. I was supposed to be playing a preppy college kid who had never been in a fight in his life. Now I look like a character from *Casino*. That actually sounded nice. Maybe I should join a gang?

I couldn't remember my lines. The doors opened to let the footsteps fill out the theatre. I was bleeding all over the place. That might disorient the audience when the lights go down and the curtains go up. They'll gasp and ask their wives if that cut is real. *It looks real. Great costume makeup they've got for this show,* they'd think. But then they'd wonder what a bloody nose had to do with the content of the play after about twenty minutes, then they'd just be confused.

The curtains opened and the world was spinning. The audience was full. Audience? Where'd they come from? Oh wait, my parents are here! I'm on stage. Perform! Say your lines! The words came out. The lines were mostly right. I put on a new bandage in between scenes whenever I exited stage. Minnie's character entered. The kiss scene arrived. It was no good. The lights were hot on my head. I was sweating. Blood dripped on the stage. They'll think it's part of the show, don't worry. Part of the show? I'm playing an Ivy League college student. Why would there be blood leaking from my nostrils and onto the stage? Will people know it's real blood? Or will they think we have great props? The audience half-ass clapped. I saw my uncle. My uncle? The theatre emptied. I took a Xanax.

My mom asked me what the hell happened to my nose right after the show. By that time the bandages were completely soaked in blood and we had no more fresh ones. I said, "fight choreography." But there's no fuckin fights in the damn play that require *fight choreography.* I don't know why I kept saying that—it was the only thing I could think of. Goddammit. *You had to call at that moment didn't you?* This was all his fault: KC's dad.

Lip came up to me after the show: "Are you okay?"

"Yeah. Sorry about that," I told him. "I'm better now."

"Better day tomorrow?"

"Sure," I told him.

Minnie and I left the theatre together. She had spent every night with me since the kiss scene at my apartment. And so the month went. We performed over twenty mediocre shows, got mediocre reviews, and at the end of it all, I was down seven grand and in another broken relationship.

But before I left that night—opening night, Lip said: "Hey it was a good show." Then he paused. "I'm sorry if this is unprofessional— but fuck it, today was about the most unprofessional day of my entire life. Some guy I used to date wants to see you, can I give him your number?"

"See me? Whattaya mean, he wants to fuck?" I was always giving him a hard time about being gay. He never liked it.

"No you dick, he wants to buy some… you know, of the stuff you have. Now can I give him your number or what so you two can go do whatever it is you're going to do—even though you *should be hating* each other during the show and not looking like you're just waiting for the applause to stop so you can go leave to have *sex*. But what you do is entirely none of my business. What do I know? I only went to *Yale*."

He was pretty mad about us fucking. But I guess it was all true, the show was ruined. Our relationship had made our performances pretty lame—to say the least. We were supposed to hate each other, but she was so hot.

"He wants to come over now?" I asked Lip.

"Aren't you two going to be up for a while—doing… whatever you two do?"

"Why are you afraid to say sex?"

"Because I don't want to *think* about my two co-stars *fucking* when they *should be hating each other.*"

"Yeah, give him my number," I told him. "See you tomorrow at the theatre."

His ex came over later that night around midnight, or later even. He came up and couldn't even look me in the face. He was super anxious and couldn't focus. I later found out he was on meth, which is why he eventually got sober. But for many months at a time, he would come over every few days and buy a quarter ounce, then stop for months at a time. But the first time I met him was that night.

He walked in and said, "Sorry, I just got off work, ugh. It's so late, I know—oh my god. What happened to your nose?"

Oh yeah. My nose. I forgot about that. "Fight choreography," I told him. "It's fine. Don't worry about it. It'll heal." But it never did—it's still fucked up to this day, and I'm 37. Anyway, "Where do you work?" I tried to change topics.

"It looks bad," he said, which was awkward, but I played it off like it was no big deal. But he kept talking about my nose. "I'm so sorry. Are you sure you're okay?"

"Really man. I'm fine. Thank you though. Just been a long day. What can I get for you?"

"Long day—I hear you. I just got off work, ugh. It's so late." He kept saying how late it was.

"Where do you work?" I asked again.

"In the west village, at a perfume boutique. It's ugh, it's whatever—good I guess. We sell perfume—whatever, it's a good job, but I don't know." He searched all over his backpack for money, but when he couldn't find it, he got on his knees in the middle of the apartment to better search through his bag. He mumbled to himself about why his backpack was so cluttered and useless.

"This is Minnie," I told him. I loved introducing her to everyone. She was like a TV ad in person. I was so impressed with myself that I had a girlfriend so hot, even hotter than Robyn. Actually, no. Nobody was hotter than Robyn. I don't understand why I still thought about KC when I had all these wonderful women around, but I did.

Anyway, all Minnie said to him was: "Hi." She didn't say much.

"I'm so rude, so sorry. You're so incredibly beautiful. You're like, perfect looking. Wow," he said, but he wasn't really paying attention to her when he said it.

"Thank you," she replied.

"I'm Austin," he said, still not looking up from his disheveled backpack. "How is Lip? Tell him I say hi—actually don't. I'll text him later." And he emptied out everything from his bag onto my floor. What a crazy guy he was. "I'm so fucking sorry—just this BAG! I can't find ANYTHING in it!" Then he found his wallet and he was all upset about it. "So, can I have whatever, an eighth?"

"Can you do a quarter you think?"

"I only have fifty dollars—so just, give me whatever you can. Fuck it's so late." I wasn't about to tell him to give me more money—not after all that. What an episode. I took out a couple jars of weed. "I'm sorry. I'm being so rude, I just have to get home and, well, it's so late. I really don't care whatever it is, that's fine. It all looks good to me." And he gave me the fifty bucks.

We had the same conversation every time he came over: How is Lip? Lip is fine. He would say something about how they slept together once but whatever. Then I would say that's cool or something. I kept forgetting what he did for a living, so I'd ask that. I always forgot. He was the fucking Perfume Man, how could I forget that? He would constantly tell me it was late, then look for money, then get all stressed out when he couldn't find it. Eventually, he'd locate his wallet, pay me, and leave somewhere around one in the morning. I could never understand what perfume store was open so late that he always got there at like midnight. He was my last client, always.

But like I said, I later found out he was strung out on meth. He finally got sober and I never heard from him ever again. Doesn't matter so much cause he was a small-time customer. Not important. What's important is, after all that preparation, I destroyed the play and it was clear I had to make up for such a failed attempt at self-proclaiming myself a Broadway star. Maybe I should just focus my energy on producing for bit and curb the acting for a while. Yeah. That's a good idea. And in fact, that's how *Wonderland* came to be…

CHAPTER 14: WONDERLAND

Like I said, the play went to shit and drifted into a fuzzy memory quickly. It wasn't just Minnie either, I was trashed as fuck in between matinee and evening shows regularly, which possibly hurt my performance, though I always felt more relaxed when I wasn't sober. But so yeah, the bartender knew to pour me a martini in a margarita glass every lunch, so when I got back to the theatre for the evening performance I was pummeled—shit-face drunk. Then Minnie and I would have sex in the greenroom six minutes before the show while Lip and Louie grit their teeth. Maybe I need to improve my acting?

But anyway, I had started planning *Wonderland* around the same time I was planning *Manuscript*. *Wonderland* had actually been a long-time idea brewing in my treasure chest of get-rich-quick schemes. It started like a month after I found *Manuscript*... I was always starting something, then finding something better and starting that too, right away. I had no patience.

The idea for *Wonderland* came to me when Louie and I were holding auditions for this rinky-dink festival I came up with called *The Six Nights to Live Festival*, a six-day festival where one night was stand-up, another spoken word, another hip hop, another short plays, another night was called Friday Night Live—sketch comedy—I thought that was brilliant, even though I've since seen ten million other Friday Night Lives, so I guess it was a dull idea but we did it.

The thing I realized early on was the more people involved in a production, the more family and friends they invited, and the easier it was to sell tickets. So, the thinking behind it was all we had to do was produce a festival with millions of performers, and do it in a cheap venue, and really make people think tickets were limited so the performers would scramble to buy some for their friends and family. Then we wouldn't have to spend a dime on marketing.

It never worked though. We did *The Six Nights to Live Festival* like five or six times and lost a bit of money every time we did it, but point is, it was on one of those days when we were holding auditions that I stumbled upon the concept of what soon became *Wonderland*. Oh, right, and before I get to that, I gotta tell you about the auditions for *The Six Nights to Live Festival*. They were goddam pathetic. The spoken word artists from the hood would walk into this grimy audition room that smelled of mildew and mold and be like what the fuck is going on here?

"You gotta audition," we'd say.

"For spoken word? Fuck type of shit is that?"

"Yeah, nah, I mean, we just wanna make sure you don't suck, right?"

"Spoken word is poetry. Poetry ain't suck ever. Not if it from the soul, the heart."

"Yo this guy is hired. Get him a fahkin badge," Louie said.

We had made these badges. I don't know why. Anyway, all the auditions were like that. They especially got uncomfortable when someone would be like:

"So, this is paid, right?"

"Paid honey? You know how many shows I had to do to get me to where I am today sweetharht?"

I wonder where Louie thought he was? We're in a moldy theatre complex on Ninth Avenue, you know that right? But if I said that to him he'd freak out. But the actress looked at him, unsure if he was legit. He's not. I didn't say that of course, I just walked outa the room and to the bathroom until she left because he was so embarrassing. But look, none of this is the point of the story. The point is this:

One day I became friendly with the owner of the theatre complex, where we were holding auditions and the *Six Nights to Live Festivals*, and I was helpin out with some clerical work in the office for sweat equity—not that I needed the money, but why not get free shit? Anyhoo… While shuffling papers around, I hear him—the dude who runs the theatre, I hear him say sarcastically: "*The Strawberry One-Act Festival* is going to be here next week, *that should be fun.*"

I perked up. "What's that?" I asked.

"Some guy… This guy holds a festival with about thirty plays and puts them all up at once. He makes a *ton* of money doing it," the old theatre venue guy says.

"Yeah? How much he make?"

"Well let's see…" And he started doin the math. "Thirty plays times two hundred bucks—"

"—Wait, what's the two hundred bucks? He charges two hundred bucks for tickets?"

"No. Entrance fees. Scummy. Yeah, that's how he makes his money. The entrance fees. Tickets are probably all profit."

This was news to me. "Entrance fees? You can charge entrance fees? For what?"

But he didn't answer. "So yeah, two hundred times thirty plus all the ticket sales… Maybe around ten thousand dollars in a weekend."

That's when I realized that fortune and fame was closer than I thought. All I had to do was study this guy's business model and completely jack his idea and produce it ten times better than he does. Reverse engineer his process and rebuild. That was the plan.

I got home to my apartment and locked the door. Obviously. Who doesn't lock their door?

I took out my jug of weed, grabbed some whisky—scotch, of course, cracked some ice, put it in a dirty glass that I washed out with hot water real quick, and got to work. I'm drinking too much. I can't do this forever. I'll have to stop. One day I'll have to stop. But how? My body needs it. Whatever, I'll think about it when it's dire. Right now, it's fine. I think. But it did become dire, and it became a much bigger problem than I coulda ever imagined… more on that later.

Anyway, I was obsessed with keeping track of the money in my safe, but for some reason I only had two grand left and couldn't figure out where I'd spent all the rest of it. I thought long and hard. Where did it all go? I spent all that money already? Jeez, my investments need to *make me money,* not lose me money.

Could be all the restaurants I've been eating at. I went back to brainstorming...

The Strawberry One-Act Festival. Fuckin lame. Lame-ass name. I'll call mine... hmm... Like some magical place. Like a happy place. Somewhere happy. Disney World. That's happy. Like a carnival. Clowns. Circuses. Alice in Wonderland. *Wonderland.* Oh shit. Yes. I'll call it *Wonderland!* Not super creative, but at the time I thought I was like a fuckin genius. I hired a graphic designer for the logo and called The Dramatist Guild to reserve a full back page ad in their magazine. The Dramatist Guild is the playwright union for all you non-knowers of that shit.

"Hi there, I'd like to place an advertisement in your magazine. I want the entire back cover."

"Well, let's start with your name?"

"So sorry, I'm just excited. My name is Greg."

"IIi Greg," I could hear her writing things down. "So, this sounds big. Tell me what you'll be advertising?"

"We're producing the greatest play festival known to man. And woman."

"Oh, well that sounds grandiose. Tell me more."

"Well, we're gonna produce thirty plays—no, fifty plays. And uhh... We're gonna take submissions. Right? From uh—playwrights. And we're gonna then take fifty winners and produce them all. And we're gonna do it on 42nd Street."

"Oh wow. This sounds very exciting, Our members will be thrilled. Okay, well what month are you interested in advertising in?"

"Can I call you back with that information?"

I jazzed up the festival synopsis and said there was a fifteen-dollar application fee. I put that in small type on the ad but said nothing about the entrance fee. I didn't wanna scare anyone off. In the ad I said the festival would be on 42nd Street because *The Strawberry One-Act Festival* did his festival at that shit-ass theatre on *Ninth Avenue*. No. I had to go to Broadway with this. Well, Off-Broadway. Off-Off-Broadway. But yeah. I read his website—the Strawberry guy—and downloaded his application forms and all the other stuff he had available to download and copied everything with a bit changed so it wasn't like plagiarism or anything. Everything he said he was gonna do, I said we were gonna do ten times better, and double the amount. I wasn't sure how I planned on actually doing any of it, but all that can be worked out later. What's the worst that can happen?

I also said there'd be an awards show after the festival at the "hottest venue in NYC" (whatever the fuck that means) and that the best play would get a thousand-dollar grand prize. I had no idea who the judges would be. I *also* said the set design would be built by professional set-builders and that everyone would get *three* performances instead of the *two* that the shitty *Strawberry One-Act Festival* offered. I figured I'd wait to tell people about the entrance fee till they were all hyped. Like I said, I didn't wanna scare anyone off. It's not like I was being shady or anything. People do this kinda thing all the time. Then I started doing the math in my head:

If I could get fifty plays to sign up at $200 each—or $185 since the application fee would be deducted—and get like five hundred playwrights to apply, that'd be like seventeen grand! *Plus the ticket sales!* Then I could stop selling drugs and become a full-time producer like I was meant to be. This was all coming together so fast I was overly excited, and that's not a good place for me to be. That's when bad decisions come out, like my idea to sell cocaine.

I figured I could make *ten times* more money selling coke, which meant I could spend way more time producing theatre. So, I called this Puerto Rican Jew I knew from middle school, Trax.

"Trax! What's up my dude. Hey man, can I come over?"

He hated talking on the phone, and you could tell by his tone. "I won't be good till tonight."

"No no no," I told him. "Just wanna come over and see you. It's important."

So I went over and walked into his apartment and his bed was raised over a makeshift day-trading office he had set up. It looked nuts, like ten monitors with graphs and moving green lines. Not for me. After some basic chit-chat, I asked him:

"How much for an ounce?"

He eyed me up and down. "$1200."

"Wait, but it's $150 for an eight-ball. That won't leave me any profit."

"Ohhh, you trying to slang, huh? Aiight, aiight… $1,000."

"$800. Cash, right now."

"You got money now?"

"In my pocket."

"Aiight," come back in an hour.

I went to the bar next store then came back an hour later, got the coke, then called my buddy who I met at Brooklyn College—right, I had enrolled in the film department at Brooklyn College to get my screenplay up and running. Maybe I could build a crew there and use their equipment? Anyway, I called him, this fuck-up, just like me, some kid who'd been to jail like me from Hartford, and told him to come do a line with me. The ounce was three-quarters gone in three days. We snorted it all. I flushed the other quarter down the toilet. Bad idea altogether. Anyway, that was the end of my coke-selling days. But back to *Wonderland*…

All I had to do is encourage the actors in each of the fifty plays to bring just *one* friend and *one* family member to at least *one* of their three shows and I'll sell a fuckload of tickets. *And* I can sell popcorn and shit! LIKE A REAL FESTIVAL! I was so pumped. I even got these tee-shirts designed. All along I thought I'd be a famous actor, but no! *I'd be a famous-as-fuck theatre-festival producer!*

Best thing about it? I wasn't gonna spend a dime on any of this till I knew it would work for sure, which it will, but still, just to be safe. You learn that type of thing in business. So, I didn't reserve any venue space just yet, even as I was advertising the living shit out of the festival. I just said in vague language the festival was "coming soon." After I placed the ad in the magazine, I checked the mailbox that I rented at the UPS office every day to see if anyone had submitted their play. After all, I didn't want a buncha strangers knowing where I lived…

But I checked and checked and nothing.

Every day I checked and not a goddam play was submitted. For weeks, nothing.

This is around the time we began auditioning for *Manuscript*, when I met Lip, and when I hired Beth, then fired her so I could make out with Minnie, who was now my girlfriend. So, that's where we are right now. We're rehearsing for *Manuscript* while in pre-production for *Wonderland*. A lot going on, I know. Plus the failed coke business, Brooklyn College, and my weed clientele.

Anyway, one day after rehearsal, I went to the mailbox and there were *seven plays!* ALL WITH CHECKS! YES! I did it! KC will be so miserable once she sees how well I'm doing.

It was time to amp shit up and get this show on the road…

CHAPTER 15: BENIGN CROOK

But here's the thing… even with my newfound bourgeoning success, and even though Minnie was ten million times hotter, I was *still* jerkin off to KC all over my apartment and it consumed all of my spare thinking juices. And then there was Robyn, who I hadn't really talked to since Minnie—she also sucked up my thinking juices. I still texted her though. I had to. That's why Robyn never went too far, till she disappeared, but point is, every time I fucked Minnie, I thought about KC. I wonder if I'll ever move on?

"You won't."

"Huh? Who's that?"

"God."

"You're real?"

"And you're a fraud."

"Fuck you god."

"I see what you're thinking. Do it."

"I'm not thinking anything."

I walked over to the fire escape and screamed "YOU DON'T UNDERSTAND." You hear me? Are you deaf? "ARE YOU FUCKING DEAF!?"

"Do it."

"Oh look, you're there."

"Jump."

"See? You don't love me. You want me gone."

"What do I care?"

I lifted the window up and put my right foot outside and ducked my head under the bottom of the window and stood up on the fire escape and fuckin jumped. The entire apartment complex saw me. My head cracked on my downstairs' neighbor's fire escape on the way down and there was blood streaming down my cheek from the deep gash.

"Should I cut it?" a voice asked.

"Cut it?"

I looked over at the kitchen. It was Minnie. She was making a peanut butter and jelly sandwich. Holy shit. Minnie is here? She slept over last night? I took a Xanax before a full-blown panic attack crept in. I hated feeling crazy.

"GREG!"

"I'm sorry I was lost in my head…"

"What else is new… Do you want me to cut the sandwich in half or not?"

"Please, thank you so much. I love you."

But did I love her? I think so. What a bum I was. No way, a bum? You got a goddam model making you PB&J sandwiches, you're the fucking man. Just take the Xanax and chill the fuck out you goddam lunatic. Was I talkin to myself too much nowadays? Is it getting worse? Is this normal?

Another day passed. I went to the mailbox to check the fuckin thing and there *was twenty-two more submissions!* Yes! That was a total of... whatever! More than yesterday! The next day I got another *thirty!* Then I got more and more and more! Soon there were over a hundred submissions, each with a fifteen-dollar check in it—the application fee all the playwrights had to pay, not to be confused with the entry fee the winners would pay to participate. I still hadn't told anyone about that: the two-hundred-dollar entrance fee I planned on charging, but The Strawberry Festival did the same shit. I went to their website just to make sure. Oh shit. They *do* say they charge an entrance fee. Says it right on the homepage. Hmm... This is okay, right?

Then a new obstacle: how am I gonna read all these plays? I had like two-hundred and twenty-three plays by then. Manila envelopes were all over my already-cramped studio apartment and there was seriously nowhere to walk. Clients came in and had to sit in a mailroom. My Blackberry went off. It was Robyn. Jeez, what poor timing.

I answered in a light tone: "Hey, I can't talk right now."

"Hey yew sexy fuckin dick yew."

"Hey I can't really talk right now," I told her again.

"Yew think I give ah fuck if yew wanna talk? Sexy, ah jist wan tell yew I'm comin up to New York! To see yew! For chrismis! And to sit on yer face, an ah jus wanted t'tell yew that."

"Wait." I looked at Minnie. "No, you can't."

"Bullshit ah cayn't. Ahm comin, Okay, gotta go, jist wanted to tell yew thayt," and she hung up.

Oh man. That doesn't help. I had to figure this all out quick and make sure Robyn didn't dismantle my life, but I had till Christmas to figure that out. It was only April. Whatever, I have no time for this now. I told Louie and Vee to come over, and that it was seriously important. Vee was a busboy at Bolzano's, that's where we met. He had moved up here to New York from Florida to make it as a filmmaker. He was half black and then a mix of Chinese and Indian. But he looked regular black.

Louie was an asshole immediately upon entering: "See that Vee? The Godfather has summoned his brothers," he said as he and Vee came in together. I wanted to punch Louie in his balding Irish Native American face every time he said that shit, but he had a hard life, so I let it slide.

He and Vee both lived in Harlem, so they normally met up and came down to Murray Hill together even though they fought like mad; Louie was a hard guy to get along with.

Vee looked around and chuckled. "What the fuck—You in the post office business now dawg?"

I gave him a moment to soak in his decent joke, then I said: "It worked. The play festival, it's on."

"And let me guess Don Cayea and Miss Minnie need our help?"

Minnie paid him no attention. She hated him. For good reason. He kinda sucked.

Anyway, we decided to split up the profits three ways, but even Vee was skeptical about how I'd set this shindig up… "Yo, do these ma'fuckers know they gonna be payin *more* money if they get in?"

It made me a bit self-conscious actually. "Nah…" I said. "I didn't really tell them yet about the other fee. You think that's a big deal?"

"SNAKE! My brutha," and Louie came over to hug me. "You're a SNAKE! I LOVE IT!"

"You think I did something wrong? Should I've told em about that? Fuck. I should've."

"Yeah man, you should've," Vee said.

Minnie rolled her eyes. She didn't speak much, but when she did, she was generally right about whatever was finally making its way from her internal dialogue to audible speech.

"What? You think I'm a piece of shit?" I asked her.

"No. I don't think you're a *piece of shit*, but I do think you should tell them."

Vee was adamant about it: "Dawg, put tha shit up on the website dawg, fore it too late."

But I didn't really know how to code very well and change the website, but Vee did. So I asked him: "Can you do that?"

"Damn nigga how much you payin again?"

So finally, we put the entrance fee on the website. It read: *Playwrights lucky enough to be selected will contribute a $200 participation fee (minus the application fee already submitted) to help with publicity and production expenses.* I mean, I had no idea what else to write, and that sounded fairly close to what The Strawberry guy wrote on his site…

We stayed up on coffee and naps for three days reading all the shit-ass plays that people from around the world submitted. Some of them, man, they were *really* bad. But after reading like fifty, we just gave up and emailed every single playwright that they got in. Attached to the congratulations letter was an agreement and welcome package, which I completely stole from *The Strawberry One-Act Festival,* with the news of the extra hidden fee. I didn't even know I was snaking it in there. Really, I didn't, I just thought I was smart.

The first hundred and fifty playwrights or thereabouts wrote us back telling us we were crooks and to go fuck ourselves—some asking for their money back, but the other fifty-six were thrilled to be accepted, filled out our paperwork, and sent us a check for $185.

Now we had to scramble to put a festival together. Everything I had advertised had only been an idea; there was absolutely no infrastructure that had been built or venue that had been reserved—on 42nd street at that, as the ad said. In short, I had no idea how to pull this off, but if I didn't, there'd be a lot of people from all over the world that'd certainly try to have me arrested.

I had to move fast, so I bolted to a theatre complex on 42nd street and asked to speak to the general manager. After all, now I had enough money from the entry fees to reserve the space. And since *The Strawberry One-Act Festival* gave all their playwrights two performances, and I had to do everything better than they did, I told everyone that they'd have *three* performances. So, I had to sort that out too, somehow.

"Okay, so which days will you be holding performances?" the general manager asked me in her office at a complex called Theatre Row Studios.

"Uhh… Not sure. Can I just put a hold for the month of August?"

"The only month we have is May and then nothing for two years."

Oh shit. I never thought of theatre availability. I just figured there'd be *something* available in August. I mean, they had like seven different theatres, and *all of them* were taken? What a crock of shit. I tried to reason with her, "May? But that's *next month!*" I said with a jolt. "FUCK!"

"Excuse me?"

"Nothing. I'll take next month"

"How many shows are you planning to do for the month? We can do twenty—I think, let me see here who's working the box office on..."

"Wait, I need to do 168."

"Shows?"

"Is that too much? Oh wait, more actually, cause that's only the first round. We have four rounds. So maybe like 180."

"You're not serious, are you? We can't do more than seven shows during the week. We have to pay our staff to be on duty."

"But, well—so how do I do this? We need to have five shows every day."

"Unless you pay for the extra hours for our box office staff, I'm not sure we can accommodate that."

"Well how much is that?"

"Gosh, I don't know. Maybe an additional ten thousand?"

WHAT?! ARE YOU GODDAM KIDDING ME YOU DUMB CUNT? But I didn't say that. I just said, "Fine, just, we'll figure it out. But can we just lock it in?"

I went back to my apartment and told everyone that we had a month to produce fifty-six plays and had to make an additional ten grand to pay for the box office staff. Everything got pretty hectic. Especially when Vee threatened to quit.

"So how the hell we gonna make a profit now?"

"We'll sell DVDs of the performance. And tee shirts, and popcorn, and with ticket sales on top of all that, we'll be gold."

"You want us to work eighty hours a week to divvy up popcorn sales?"

"Snake. I told you Vee. Our boy's a snake. I love it. But also, fuck you Don Cayea."

So all that took some finessing—you know, to get them both on board again. And then I couldn't figure out how to give everyone one matinee, one mid-matinee, and one nighttime performance to keep it even. Like, I didn't wanna give someone a Monday show at 3PM and then a Tuesday show at 6PM and then a Wednesday show at 12PM, cause that'd suck for them and then people may not like me, and people liking me is very important. I had to be liked. No, I had to give everyone a weekend or at least a Friday night or something—FUCK! The scheduling was impossibly hard for me. I've never been good at that kinda thing—whatever type of thing that is. Organization possibly.

"Minnie? I need your help. I'm helpless. All these plays need to be scheduled."

She was on my bed, staring at the ceiling, probably wondering what the hell she'd got herself into.

"Color code all the plays on index cards maybe."

So Minnie ended up scheduling the entire festival. It overtook her life for about a week. I had no idea what a massive job all this would be. Then something seriously fucked up happened…

The Dramatists Guild of America, The Playwright Union, the people who ran my advertisement on the back cover of their magazine, they got some crazy calls from disgruntled potential contestants and delivered a statement in their email newsletter to their entire union saying they did NOT endorse our festival. They said I was a fucking crook and they apologized to their people for letting us advertise in their magazine. Apparently TONS of people were complaining. That newsletter *went out to every playwright in the world,* well, at least the ones part of the union, which was a dickload. It was signed by some guy named "Gary." I had to fix this. I had to find Gary.

And I did, but he turned out to be a real cowboy...

CHAPTER 16: GARY THE COWBOY

First we posted an apology online on some theatre forum where people were talkin shit about us. It wasn't hard to find people talkin shit about us, as I discovered. We were sending waves through the interwebs. Anyway, the apology explained how it was all a big misunderstanding, but that shit didn't go over well. Moments after the post, an explosion of insults erupted. Everyone made fun of us after Louie wrote he was "so proud of the festival he even wrote to his mom about it." He really shouldn'ta said that shit.

How sad. The crook is still looking for hugs from his mom, one fucker said.

Wanker can bask in his infamy in solitude, said some other asshole.

Hopefully, she's as appalled at his egregious actions as we all are. Shame. And the comments kept pouring in...

"You believe these fahkin people? Makin fahn uv my own mutha?"

"Okay. So... what do we do now?" I asked.

Vee shouted from my DJ Booth—now Wonderland office: "Yep. Another refund request...Damn ya'll, this ain't a good look."

Vee always laughed, especially when Louie pissed him off...

"Yeah, great job Vee. Big help," Louie bellowed. "Keep laughin and keep tellin us about every refund. Seriously Vee, tremendous job."

Trying not to lose his mind with laughter—or rage, Vee kept calm and said: "You the muthafucka who wrote about your mom, sayin sorry an shit. What was the purpose of that, huh? Gettin mad at me for tryin to help ya'll... Sittin here building fuckin websites and writin code—I don't even know code. Learnin this shit for ya'll. Ungrateful, man. I'm tellin you."

And right when Louie *shoulda* backed off, that's when he *always* brought it up a notch: "Yeah? Why don't ya stahp mumblin ova thehr in the corner and say it ta my face like a man, eh Vee?"

A goddam brawl was about to erupt in my living room. I had to stop this.

"Louie, Vee—guys. Please. Just—we gotta figure this out. Stop with this shit."

Vee went from zero to a million in less than three-hundredths of a second: "Tell your boy to stop talkin shit!" he said to me, like Louie wasn't there.

"Oh, now I ain't your boy no more? I'm Greg Corleone's boy, but not your boy? I'm not your brother Vee?" Then Louie got real close to Vee, like he was asking for a hug—a kiss even, but it was a threat. He got all touchy feely all the time in these weird moments. It was bizarre.

"Dawg, back up."

"Oh now you're hard? You're a tough guy now are ya? Eh Vee? You a gangster all of sudden?"

Louie was from a rough background, but he kept it a secret for the most part. The only time I truly saw how fucked up his childhood musta been was when his younger brother—who used to run jobs for the mob in Providence—showed up to the theatre a few weeks later. He had just gotten outa prison and looked it. Looked like a convict gone stale. And his older brother was murdered by a cop. Apparently one day he was out at the local market getting milk and shit for his family—all fucked up on heroin, but still, just getting milk, and he realized he didn't have any money. So, what do you do when you need milk but ain't got the money? You steal that shit. And that's what he did. He ganked the milk and got in his car and started to drive away. That's when the cop drew his pistol and pounded a bullet through his skull. His baby son was in a car seat in the back and saw it all go down. Not sure if he'll remember that shit when he's older, but man, talk about starting off on the wrong foot. But anyway, that's Louie's family. His dad was out of the picture and his mom was a poor Native American woman in Cranston. But still Louie looked Irish white, like it didn't get much more Irish than he looked, but he was half Native American.

Anyway, see this was normal. He and Vee… They'd always fight then make up, and sometimes the fights got really bad, like the time we were in the middle of the street by Bryant Park and Vee actually pushed Louie into the middle of the road in front of oncoming traffic and threw his backpack down on the sidewalk like he was ready to really make it happen this time. Somehow, the fight always stopped just shy of the first punch. Point is, all this bad publicity stirred up our melting pot, people started withdrawing their plays, and the heat was on. My whole life had been working to get to this point of notoriety and now this fucking goddam magazine—who I paid good money to—wants to tell the world I'm a thief?

But... Greg, you are.

Who said that?

Me.

FUCK YOU VOICE.

Do these people have *any* idea who the fuck I am? What I've been through? All the fucking hoops I've had to jump through to get here? I was goin nuts. Bullied, popular, scummy, drug-addict, rehab one, rehab two, boot camp three, wilderness four, runaway, homeless, hookers, needles, crack, acid, hitchhiking, Miami, Boulder, Queens, KC—FUCK! I couldn't take it.

"Eyo Cayea, relax. My brother. C'mere. Let me hold you. This is normal! You wanna be a big shot produca, well *this is what it's all about.* You want my boy Tony up on that wall? Well Tony's only go home with producas with BIG BALLS! And I know my boy. Big balls. Am I right? Huge fahkin balls."

But I was already halfway out the door.

"Bro, where you going? To whack someone?" Even Vee made the mafia jokes... This is what I mean. Now, *he's* on team Louie. Two seconds ago he wanted to murder him, now he's makin Godfather jokes. And why? Cause I figured out how to make money selling overpriced weed to successful New Yorkers, that's why. Jealousy. It's a sick disease. Well, I wasn't about to let ten years go by without me being as successful as my clients. No.

I was *not* a fucking drug dealer. I was a theatre producer, with big balls, and I had to straighten all this out.

"I'm goin to see Gary. At the Dramatists Guild. I'ma sort this out."

Louie threw up his hands as if he lost the fight. "Okay, see? That's what the fahk I'm talkin about. BIG BALLS. I'm comin, My boy ain't goin at this alone." Louie said in his deep, *I'll take care of it* voice.

"No, I got it."

"What's wrong, don't trust your brother?"

"Don't say anything stupid."

That made him real mad.

"Oh *sorry* lord Cayea, please let me know when I'm allowed to speak!"

"I'm just sayin that... You know, sometimes you get... Aggressive."

"You can say that again," Vee said with an eye-roll.

"Don't you worry about me, okay Don Cayea? You neither Gandhi. Let's go," and Louie grabbed his Kangal flat cap.

When Louie was determined, there was no changing his boisterous mind. He took the lead and walked in front of me, opened the door, and off we went to The Dramatist Guild, which was, of course, headquartered in Manhattan.

We walked in without an appointment, obviously.

The office was ordinary: receptionist, waiting area, and a few offices. Small bits of meticulous artwork placed specifically in odd places gave the joint a bit of quirk, but overall not a place I would ever take a job at. Not that they were hiring.

"We're from Wonderland. Here to see Gary," I tell the woman through the thin-paned glass.

"Do you have an appointment?"

"No, I need to speak to Gary—"

"We just got reamed out by your boss honey, I think he can spare a minute for us, eh!?"

God fucking dammit. This is why I didn't wanna bring him. The secretary looked at us like: You've *got* to be kidding me. At least that's how it looked to me. I was so mad at Louie. Why couldn't he just relax and be respectful for once in his life? He really made me look bad. Wait. Am I like that too? Am I a piece of hypocrite shit also? I'm a fraud—a phony. A fake. I'm a fuckin—

"Greg?" A massive gay cowboy stood in front of me. Holy shit. He was so big. "I'm Gary, why don't you come back to my office."

Louie and I stood up. Louie, for once in his miserable existence, kept his mouth shut. Gary was a tank, and there was no disputing that, no matter how many gay jokes Louie would make later. He could bombard his cock into us at any moment to flex his strength, so I just played it cool.

We entered his office. It was clean, organized, very feng shui. I think. Not that I read books on feng shui. Gary barely fit at his desk. It looked like a toy desk in front of him. Louie and I sat on two uncomfortable padded benches bordering the office. You could tell he bought the damn things so people wouldn't get too comfortable and sit for too long. You could tell they were expensive benches too. Uncomfortable though, like I said. I took a deep breath:

"Gary, we never meant to cause anyone any harm. I swear I just—we just really wanted to do this right and we fuck—messed up bad. I get it. But we're willing to do whatever it takes to make this better."

"We spent a good buncha thousands on this, ya know Gary?"

But that didn't help. Gary liked me, he hated Louie. That I could tell right off the bat. So I just tried to keep in control.

"It's not just about the money Gary; of course we want to make money. I was homeless a few years ago and I've never had a real education and I've made some mistakes but I LOVE theatre." And that wasn't a lie at all. I did in fact *love* theatre. And the rest was true too, sob story as it may be. But Gary sat motionless in his tiny chair behind his miniature desk flexing his big cock. He looked at me like shut up with your sad tale of life and get on with it. But after a moment of consideration, he says:

"I knew there must be *someone* behind this with a heart."

And he smiled. Then the smile disappeared.

"But I won't retract what I said in our newsletter." My stomach shot down into my gut and my breath fell short. "I saw the apology you wrote. It was… okay. Not bad. The stuff about the mother though… well, that was laying it on too thick. Our members see right through that sort of hogwash, as you can see, and I see that you have. You've taken quite a beating on that forum. So, you know how important public response to something like this can be. Well, look… I'll tell you what I'll do: I'll publish your apology letter on our website and send a link to it in our next newsletter. But edit it a bit. Take out the part about the mother. Was that you?"

"It was me, sir," Louie said, respectfully at last.

"I figured," Gary said.

Louie didn't react the way I thought he would. "I was only being honest, Gary."

All this was good enough for me. So we went home and fine-tuned the entire apology letter so that it was more polished than it was before. We deleted that dumbass comment Louie wrote about his mom. We sent the revised apology to Gary and waited. After he posted the apology to the Guild's website, our inbox exploded with more hate. The hater jokes rolled in faster than before.

Maybe we should scrap this shit? But we already found directors to cast and rehearse all the plays. I already locked the theatre down in full *and paid for their box office staff.* I also hired a publicist and spent all of the money on set design and the awards show was being planned. Not to mention all the damn posters and tee shirts we made with our logo on it. There was no way to even refund anyone at this point.

I had to be as honest as possible from here on out. And you know what? By the time opening day came around, we were completely broken even, fifty-six plays had been cast and rehearsed by a director, a revolving set had been built for each of the plays to share, and we had staffed up the ushers with chicks I used to date. It really was an efficient way to recruit workers.

Now all I had to do was convince all the actors to invite their family and friends to buy at least a couple tickets and we'd be rich. But I had to make it worth it to them, so I called our publicist and told him to get us written up in every damn paper in town. Once our contestants see how much we're spending on publicity,

I thought to myself, they'll see how well-spent their entrance fee was. And THEN—

There was a knock. Tech Zach looked stunned at Minnie when she opened the door. I don't blame him.

"Come in dude, forgot you were comin."

"Oh boy, what're you fellas cookin up in here? It's cramped, huh? You can barely move in here. I've got a book for you, all about feng shui. I think you'll like it."

"I was just thinking about feng shui," I told him.

He actually gave me that book a month or so later and it's still on my bookshelf. Never cracked it once, and I'm thirty-seven now. Anyway, I sold him what he needed and it was back to business as usual. Where were we again? Ah, right… Time to begin planning the awards show.

"What should we call it?" I asked Vee and Louie.

"The Wonders," Louie said immediately.

"I love it."

Then I picked up my Blackberry and called an old friend. He picked up with his brash, and crackily voice.

"Yo."

"Sahar!"

"Brah."

"We're doin a *massive* awards show for this theatre festival I'm producing and I need a venue. Hook it up."

"Def brah. How many people you bringin?"

"Tons."

"A hundred? Gotta be at least a hundred for me to get a spot."

"More. Like *three hundred.*"

"Girls? Or guys?"

"Both man, it's everything the club wants." Of course I didn't even know what club it would be, so there was no way for me to actually know what they wanted, but that's beside the point. The point being I was so confident in this idea I told him: "Hundreds of people from all over the world dude. Diversity man."

"Black people you mean?"

The only thing about Sahar was he was kinda racist. And by kinda, I mean very. But since he was Israeli, it was expected. Not that Israelis are racist, it's just the Israelis *he hung out with* were racist. Some of them weren't even Israeli. Look, I don't know. I don't have an excuse. But still he was my friend, I think. We even had a threesome together—no, no, not like that. Like we both fucked De'Ena at the same time. More on that later. It was Valentine's Day when that happened. It was pretty gross actually, especially when I looked up and his hairy Israeli balls were by my forehead. Sorry, I digress. Back to him being racist. It always made me feel so fucking shitty every time he talked about black people like that cause I never defended the race the way I should. He obviously hated them for some reason—no reason, really. And my second mom is black, my nanny, from when I was growing up, she raised me. So it more than offended me when he dropped those slurs, it drove me insane and made my blood run cold whenever he used those words. Such foul language. Who talks like that? But still, I needed a venue. So I said:

"I mean no, well yeah, some black people—of course, but that's not what I mean. That's not the fuckin point man. People from all walks of life. From all over the world! We have a play from Ireland coming!"

"A play?"

"It's a play festival, don't worry about it. Point is I need a venue. Can you help or not?"

"Right but it has to be a certain type of—Are they hot? The chicks?"

"Dude, they're actresses. They're *all hot.*" Again, not true, but it had to be said. I could see he wouldn't budge on that. So we locked in a deal, and I overcommitted myself once again to bringing *three hundred attractive girls* to some random club for the awards show now entitled: The Wonders. All the while, Minnie, usually lounging on my pitifully situated mattress, made me look like an accomplished human given her loyal companionship, but that didn't last for long. She was about to issue me the last sex, and frankly, I blame it on the panic attacks, which were growing more severe by the week...

CHAPTER 17: THE LAST SEX

One day I was in the lounge of the theatre on day five or so… Earlier in the morning I had been dry heaving, which happened often, roughly every time one of the shows only filled up with five people. I wasn't cut out for this kinda work whenever it went poorly, but good days were better—no dry-heaving at least, but still embarrassment for the crap we were producing. The plays were all dreadful. But anyway, on that particular day, I was dry heaving with anxiety so I hid out in the lounge and poured myself a drink from the still-closed-to-the-public bar and washed down a Xanax to calm my thoughts. I hadn't eaten all day, so I was more nauseous than usual as I lay on the couch, hiding in the darkness of the lounge, hoping nobody would walk in.

The lounge was on the third floor, and our theatre was on the fifth, so when Minnie came down to look for me and I was drunk on Xanax wondering what to do with my life on the shadowy couch, it made sense that the look on her face was of defeat.

"What's wrong *now*?"

"I'm just dizzy."

"You need to get back up there."

"I just need to relax. Can you please just keep everything under control up there for a bit?"

But that pissed her off for the last time. She was sick of being my bitch... Oh man, did I just say that? Did I just call her my bitch? *Was* she my bitch? Jeez, that sounds horrible. I'm a horrible man. I'm drunk. My mind was racy again. Then I felt sick as ever, so I turned over and faced the couch.

Later that night, Minnie looked at me while in bed with a look I'd never seen on her face before. She seemed like another person, like the same body with a different soul. She was usually soft—a beam of lust and a twinkle of kindness. Now, without warning, she was a devil in model's clothing, which turned me on immensely. I had to have her right away. So we fucked, which at this point was *all we did*. We had no emotional connection in the least. But on that night, I noticed the sex was *way* too good, and it was because of that I knew it'd be the last time we ever fucked. When I bit her lip and came inside her—she was on the pill—her look read: *Hope you enjoyed that.*

"What's wrong?" I asked as she got up and put her clothes on after I came.

"I need space. I'm going up to my apartment."

She lived in Washington Heights, which is the neighborhood above Harlem, like thirty minutes away.

"You're leaving? It's like midnight. You'll be at the theatre tomorrow, right?"

"No, I won't."

After a brief exchange of curt one-liners, I concluded the argument with a: "Fine, fucking go. You suck anyway."

And so she did. I chased her—well, I didn't actually chase her, I called her a million times and sent her a text that said: *on my way.*

I picked up some flowers from a bodega and hailed a cab and paid like a million bucks to hightail it up to Washington Heights and knock on her door, but she wouldn't let me in. So I paid another million bucks to get back down to Murray Hill to my apartment.

I had no idea what to do.

So I cried, for the first time in my life I think. I cried and poured a drink and wondered how the fuck I would ever replace her. She was perfect... looking. She was perfect looking. I just lost the most perfect looking girl ever. Wait—*looking? The most perfect looking girl?* What was I? Some sorta asshole? Yeah, I guess I was. I watched reruns of *Entourage* until I passed out. Ironically, Minnie was cast in the movie *Entourage* ten years later and was naked the whole movie. So, you've probably seen the girl I'm writing about right now, naked, if you've seen that movie. I told you I wouldn't even say which movie it was, but I did, so to keep some sort of my word, I won't tell you which girl she was. At least I can see Robyn now for Christmas. We celebrate Christmas even though most of my family is Jewish.

Anyway, I woke up a mess the next day and headed over to the theatre. I had to keep focused. I woefully took ticket stubs at 12PM and failed to mention to anyone that I was the producer of the festival. I never wanted people to know I was behind this atrocity. Then I got a Blackberry message from De'Ena, the southern cocktail waitress I first cheated on KC with.

Whatchya doin sexy?

At Wonderland. Wanna meet?

Why you think I'm text you... Be there in twenty.

So I told Vee I had to get some papers.

"Papers? Fuck kinda papers you need, I got like five thousand in the back," he told me.

"Nah, it's not that kinda paper, I needa go to Staples for some shit." I really had no excuse. I made no sense.

"Dawg, the festival is running. You the producer. You just gon up an leave like that?"

He really didn't understand. "Dude, I'll be back in like ten minutes, I'm not *leaving* leaving, just running a quick errand."

I ran downstairs, frantically hailed a cab, got to my apartment thirty minutes later, met De'Ena outside, brought her up, fucked her ASAP, left the apartment with her still in it, got in another cab, and made it back to the theatre. All in all it was about an hour-and-a-half I was gone. When I walked in, Vee took one look at me and was like:

"Where the 'papers'? Thought you had to get special papers from Staples. Thought you'd be back in ten minutes. Dawg you left two hours ago."

"I did—I had to run home, I didn't think I'd be so long, sorry man, I just, I don't know."

"Yeah, you don't." And he left all pissed, obviously. Maybe I have a sex addiction? I used to be terrified I'd die a virgin, now I can't make it through a matinee without a blowjob.

And look… without going through all the rest of the festival details, and what happened and who won and all that, cause who gives a shit, right? Without going through it all, let's just skip to the part where it ended—the awards show.

I told the playwrights we'd be giving out all these awards at the awards show and the thousand-dollar grand prize too, but they all had to show up to find out who won. So, that was how I got three hundred people to show up. Now, the problem was they weren't all that beautiful the way Sahar wanted them. I mean, most of them were like fifty-year-old dudes that sure as fuck weren't the hot actresses I told him I'd be bringing. And once everyone was inside, I was terrified to take the mic. I had some drinks to simmer my nerves but was waiting on Louie to get there cause everyone was waiting for the event to start and I was too much of a pussy to actually say anything. In fact, I hid so nobody saw me. It was utterly horrifying. Super humiliating. Where the *fuck* is Louie? Louie was good for talking. He could talk and talk and no matter how dumb I *thought* he would make himself look, he *always* killed it. I can't explain it. But what if he doesn't show up?

Fuck.

What if he's drunk somewhere at some pub across town? Then I'll have to do this alone. I took another drink. I had all these drink tickets that I was supposed to be giving out to the actors and directors and playwrights, but I kept half of the tickets for myself. Jeez I was so nervous. Where the *fuck* is Louie? People started looking at me like… uhh, dude. Are we doing this or what?

Oh fuck! I gotta write out the grand prize check! I don't even know how we picked the winner. I felt a little guilty. MY PARENTS ARE HERE! Oh my fucking—My parents showed up? WITH THEIR FRIENDS?! This was probably their time to prove to the world that their son wasn't a fuckup. And this was *my* chance to *finally* win their affection. I can do this. I just don't wanna have to pick up that damn mic. I ordered another martini with a drink ticket. That didn't look as bad as scotch—a dirty martini, so when I went up to my mom and was like:

"MOM! Howaya?!" I didn't look like such an alcoholic.

"A lot of people came!" she said excited. "The whole venue is full!"

To see my mom in a club was very odd. Then I started to wonder: why was she surprised? Did she think I wasn't capable of getting a lotta people to come? What the fuck was her problem? Finally, Louie walked into the club.

"Louie!" I shouted in a whisper. "What the—get the fuck on the mic dude!"

"My brother." He was crumby-ass drunk. He put his arm around me. "Look at all these people." He looked me in the eyes real close, like he was gonna kiss me. His Irish whiskey coffee breath could murder a llama. Did my breath smell like his? "Ya know who did this?"

"I know."

"*We did.*"

"Louie you gotta get up there man, they're all waitin on you!" I handed him a buncha papers. "Here, these are the awards."

I scribbled random names on a paper dictating which play had won, best actor, actress, all that nonsense, and shoved it in his hands. The judging process had been complete within one five-minute flurry of panic. He put his hand on my cheek and spoke eloquently—he always spoke eloquently when he was drunk—and said, "I got this my brutha. You just enjoy the show..."

He took to the stage and gave one hell of a performance. He was never scared of a crowd, that's why I loved working with him. Not like me. I was terrified to be me. Everyone look! Look at me! But when they looked, I ran to hide.

He announced the awards... "And best actor goes to..."

All that shit. The night was a blur. I handed someone a thousand-dollar check. I don't remember much. When all was said and done, the festival—to anyone on the outside—was a success. We pulled in many thousands of dollars, all of which were spent when I gave bonuses to the people who helped me make this work, but really I gave it to them to make sure they liked me. That was more important than money. I walked away with only $400 when all was done.

I woke up in my apartment with one of the actresses from Wonderland. I don't remember who she was or when she got there. I rolled over and sent Minnie a text. She hadn't responded once since my outlandish burst of text messages had begun. She was done with me. I had to do something to get my mind off her.

But unfortunately, I ended up in jail.

CHAPTER 18: GEORGIE BOY

I was twenty-three years old when I auditioned for the Atlantic Acting Conservatory. I got accepted. Then kicked out after one semester. But that's not the point. The point is the acting conservatory is where I met Georgie Boy, and Georgie Boy got me sent to jail.

It all started when I had a crush on this other student at the school named Lizzie. I later found out she was the youngest Olsen sister. I was determined to ask her out after our final scene day, which was the last day of the semester when all the students performed their... well, final scene. I did a scene from Edward

Albee's *Zoo Story,* but not cause I wanted to, cause they made me do it. Anyway, I went up to Lizzie—Olsen, that is, who I think did a scene from *Stop Kiss,* in the lobby of the theatre afterwards when all the scenes were complete. "Awesome fuckin scene," I told her.

"Oh, thanks, yeah, you too, nice job," she said back. Then some dude in her class pulled her away from me. "Oh, I'm—sorry, I'll be right back," she said. I was fuckin pissed about that.

That's when my friend Georgie Boy came up to me, dressed dapper in a suit after his scene from *Glengarry Glen Ross.* "You finally fucking talked to her. How's it feel?"

Now, Georgie Boy was an odd fellow. He looked like an Eastern European gangster, like he could crack your bones with a firm stare but spoke with a voice like he was cradling you to sleep; a soft and overly compassionate tone—even creepy at times. So, I was never sure if he'd break skulls or read his enemy a bedtime story if it actually came time for war, but so yeah—that's just how he was: Tough to read.

"I was just about to… and that damn kid pulled her away—we were, what the fuck, mid convo—"

"Let's go smoke this blunt," he said abruptly.

I couldn't believe he had wrapped up the good weed I sold him in tobacco. I had started selling Georgie Boy weed somewhere around the first week of classes when we both realized we were broken individuals, and so we could be friends. He became another frequent client—like The Perfume Man. They both came over every other day to buy an eighth or a quarter when they coulda easily just bought an ounce and come over once a week. And

Georgia Boy always rolled blunts. Who smokes blunts anymore? It didn't matter. I wasn't interested in smoking at the moment. I wasn't addicted like he was.

"No, not now. I'ma ask her out," I told him.

"But you look stupid just standing here, come on man. Brando never waited around for a girl."

He was *always talking about Marlon Brando.* Brando this, Brando that… And he always wanted me to watch these old Brando interviews on YouTube. The dude never shut up about him. But at that very moment, he was also right. I looked at my feet. I *did* look stupid. And Brando would never wait for a chick like this. Of course, he was famous, and dead, and I was just Greg.

So, I reconsidered: "Yeah I guess we could go for a sec," I said.

We walked outside and crossed the street. It was snowing and we were both in full costume: me in my preppy sweater, and he in his pinstriped suit. We lit the blunt on some icy park bench. "Who are *those* guys?" Georgie Boy asked, shivering after half the blunt was toast.

The guys he was referring to walked straight at us. They kinda looked like they might be—FUCK. One of em pulled out his badge. You're kidding me.

But no, they weren't kidding us. And as it turns out, the park we were smoking the blunt at was actually an elementary school playground. The kids were on recess. I swear it was impossible to know. One cop said, "You fucking kidding me? PUT THAT OUT!" as Georgie Boy took one last—"DON'T YOU FUCKING TAKE ONE MORE—PUT THAT SHIT OUT!" The cop yelled. Man, they were mad. Georgie Boy clipped the blunt and placed it on the snowy bench we were sitting on. I was shivering. Jeez, it was so cold. "STAND UP!" One of them told us. They pulled out two sets of handcuffs and walked us in front of the theatre and kept us there for a buncha minutes, handcuffed in front of *two* cop cruisers.

"PUT YOUR HEAD DOWN!" Georgie Boy yelled in a whisper. So I put my head down. People were leaving the theatre. Fuck! Lizzie is gonna be gone by the time I get back! We stood on 16th Street while all the students left the theatre before we were chauffeured to the Chelsea Precinct and escorted to our cell.

We sat in a small jail cell in full costume next to these three kids who musta been like thirteen. I asked the kids what they were in for, and one kid said to me:

"Aiight. You know Myspace?"

"Huh?" I asked.

"Myspace. It's like, you know, w-w-w-.-m-y—"

"Yeah I know what Myspace is, what's that gotta do with anything?"

Then he gave me this whole story about how some kid gave him a jacket, but the kid's mom found out on Myspace that it was him, and now he was sitting in jail with his friends for assault and battery. The story made no fucking sense. "What aboutchyou? What chya'll in fo?" another little kiddie gangster asked me.

"Uhh… We were smokin a blunt at an elementary school playground by accident." They all cracked up at that. Outside the cell were two girls—same age, young, handcuffed to the railing.

"Girl you lookin good all chained up like dat," one of the kids said.

"OH SHUT THE FUCK UP NIGGA!" she screamed and she got up as if she could rip the handcuffs off and walk through the cell bars and slap the kid in his face. Georgie Boy and I were just exchanging glances here and there, stoned as fuck. Some fat Puerto Rican cop came by to calm her down.

"Sit down! Don't play into his shit!" the fat and friendly and somewhat hood cop said, as if he was her eighth-grade teacher. There was also some vagrant black dude asleep in the cell with his head against the wall in the corner. It was a small cell but he felt far away. He was out cold, so nobody talked to him.

"Why you niggaz in suits an shit?" one of the kiddie gangsters asked us.

Georgie Boy replied with an elegance that he shouldn'ta necessarily had: "Oh we're *actors*," he proudly stated.

"OH SHIT! THEY ACTAZS!? WE IN HERE WITH SOME ACTAZS?!" Then they all started laughing again. After a while, like a couple hours or so, the fat cop came back.

"Eyo Shane!" Shane was the Myspace kid. "So you know I got your back right?" The cop said.

"Nigga I ain't need yo help! I'm from the BX!" Shane said all thug-like.

"Come on homie, don't be tryin to act all hard in fronta these people. Your *grandma* is from the Bronx. You're from the Chelsea projects. You can't even *rep* the Chelsea projects, aright?" Then the cop looked at all of us: "He's just tryin to impress ya'll."

"AAAAWWWWHHHHhhhhhh SSSShhhhiiiitt Shane that nigga PLAYIN you!!!" One of the girls chained to the pole said from outside the cell.

"Man he ain't playin me!"

"No but on the real though," the fat cop said. "You know I got your back right? But now we got a *real* nigga comin in, and it's gonna take me a bit to get the cell door open you know, so just keep quiet, aright?"

"Psst, I ain't scared!"

But then this dude appeared. He was in handcuffs. He was a short stocky black guy with bloodshot eyes and a red-hot complexion. He was about to fuckin pop. Nobody said shit. The gates opened and closed and the dude circled the small cell, but it was like five feet by ten feet maybe, so he was brushing up against all of us as he circled. I was petrified. The little gangsters sat on the bench of the cell and kept their eyes down. It was the loudest silence I'd heard in a while. At least Georgie Boy is here, he'll protect me if something happens. But with his personality, he might wanna talk about the goddam problem and try to work it out first, so I don't know if he'd even be much help. Suddenly, the guy turned around to us. I looked down. He's gonna hit me. He's gonna rip the hair off my head. He looked like he was waiting for someone to say something, but nobody said anything. He was ready to pounce on anyone. Then, out of nowhere, he *punched* the cement wall furiously and clung to the cell bars with all his might and screamed: **"FUCK!"**

I had no idea where this was going. I kept my eyes to the ground. Hours later, the guy came down from whatever methamphetamine he was on and told us a story about how he killed a man when he was nineteen years old, or maybe he killed a man that was nineteen years old? Or maybe he was in prison for nineteen years for killing a man? I don't know, but something with nineteen years in it, and something about killing a man. He said he broke his parole and was goin back to prison for life. And I thought *I* was having a bad day...

Another guy, some buff Hispanic dude, came into the cell in a sleeveless shirt and some funny mesh gym shorts and sneakers. "My name I tell you alreddy, okay? Javier Nasgales." Then the cop who let him into the cell walked away and Javier turned around and looked at us and said, "I not suppose be here." Then he turned to the bars of the cell and screamed, "I wanting my lawyer!" Then he turned back around and looked at us like *we were* the degenerates and turned the other way.

"See my man? That's what you gotta rememba, they ain't care bout chyo rights." Oh right. That was the cracked-out murderer was now giving me life advice. "See I know the system, know what I'm sayin? I'ma get my meds, I'ma get that government aid, see what I mean?" I had no idea what he meant, but I just said:

"Yeah I see exactly what you mean man."

Then the cop who brought the Hispanic dude in came back, "Javier?"

"Yes sir."

"Javier Nasgales?"

"Yes sir."

"That's not a real name."

Javier looked at the cop, very confused, then his expression changed, "I tol' you. My name in birth by my mom es Lucio Ramirez."

"So... Your name is *not* Javier Nasgales?"

"No sir."

"So why did you give me that name?"

"Because in home at my mom she calling me Javier."

"So if I go run this name, it's going to exist, right?"

"Yes sir."

The cop came back a minute later. "Okay, what's your *real* name? Because that name, also, does not exist."

"In the States, when I coming here, it make it Roberto."

"They changed your name to Roberto?"

"Si."

"And so your name is Roberto."

"Si—Yes."

"Okay Roberto, we'll give this one more try. What's your last name?"

"In the states, when I is coming, es Bulok."

"So Roberto Bulok."

"Yes."

The cop came back and said that name didn't exist either. I think the conclusion is: this guy was totally fucked. Anyway, I sat in jail in that goddam costume talking to a murderer for eight hours, got out, got a letter the next week telling me I was not invited back to the Atlantic Acting Conservatory for the next semester, and I never saw Lizzie again—not until I was watching the Golden Globes ten years later and saw she had won some award or whatever. Goddammit. I totally fucked that up.

I needed a break. That's why Chloe's brother, also a faithful client, invited me to Oahu: To help me get my mind off of things. So I did, and twelve hours later, we arrived in Honolulu. And that's where I met Agustina…

CHAPTER 19: HONOLULU

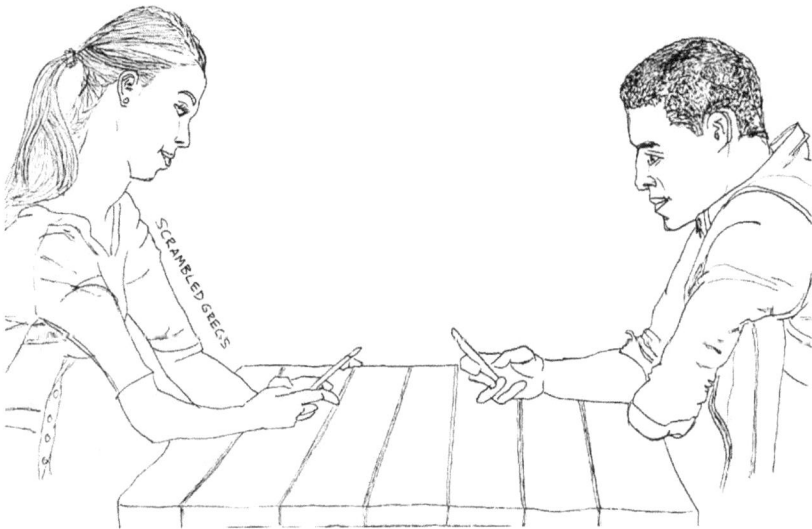

It all started at Señor Frogs. It was our first night in Hawaii. The club was overflowing with men in army fatigue. Chloe's brother was nowhere to be seen. I saw a girl with dark brown hair at the bar, darker skin than mine, she was about my age—twenty-five or so, and with a curly-haired white dude who was clearly drunk. I thought she seemed to be looking for something more substantial to do, so when for a brief moment she was alone, I took a swing…

"Are you two here together?" She didn't respond for some reason. So I asked again: "Is that your boyfriend?"

"I surry. I no speaking. No entiendo."

I did my best in Spanish, but it came out sorta like:

"He the man is boyfriend?"

But she understood me somehow and said: "Heem? No no no, es Pablo!" and then she said many more things, all of which was babble to my ears. I had no idea what she was saying, but I loved her already. We spend the night chatting in broken sentences and at some point, later on, she pulled me outside the club into the outdoor mall where it was located—on the second floor to be precise, and what she said to me was meaningful and direct, but I don't know what it was. But she spoke forcefully, as if the more serious she became the more likely I'd be to understand her, but that wasn't the case. What was she was getting at? "Holding on," she said at the finale, and so I held on, but she walked away and disappeared. I left the club once I realized maybe she meant to say goodbye and roamed around looking for her, but all I found was Chloe's brother.

"Duddde! Nice work! I saw you talking with her! Sweet!" His voice was squeaky, and anything he said sounded nerdy, though he was a prestigious businessman with a serious weed addiction.

"Man... She left. I don't know where she went. Did she pass here?"

"Nooooo duudddeee, she left?" He was a bit drunk.

"Yeah, did she pass?"

"I don't know man. I hope not."

It's almost like whatever I said went over his head and around the corner, like he wasn't paying attention, yet somehow responding with coherent replies. Just then, I saw a row of hookers across the street. In Honolulu, as I learned, they didn't crack down on prostitution because it's a big reason the Japanese tourists come to spend money at the hotels. In fact, the hookers were on display, almost as if in a retail storefront.

"Those girls. Jeez. They're really fuckin hot for hookers, right?" I said, totally defeated as we walked back to our hotel.

"Do you… wanna get one?" he asked me.

"I would love to but… I don't know."

"It's on me."

When I saw that he was serious, I froze. Hookers made me nervous. The last time I was with a hooker was with Sahar. He and I had just come back from a club.

"Brah. Let's get a skank."

"A hooker?"

"Yeh. A skank."

"Where?"

"Where you think brah? Craigslist." So we found a listing and called a number, but by the time she showed up, it was nearly 5AM and Sahar was like: "Brah. Tell eh we ain't want her no more."

"But she came all the way from Queens. I can't do that," I told him.

"Well I ain't payin for her brah."

Well look, I didn't wanna just send her away after she put in all that effort to get here. So I buzzed her up.

"Just pretend you're asleep, okay?" I told Sahar. He was laying on my couch right next to my mattress, which was still on the floor in the corner of the living room. I buzzed the hooker through the second glass door and heard her heels clanking up the stairwell. I bet she was thinking: four flights? Fuck this. "Close your eyes, okay? Don't move," I told him before opening the door.

Whoa.

She was *nothing* like what her picture looked like online. In fact, it was a totally different chick. She was gross. I can't bang this girl. How will I get hard? But still I felt bad, so I invited her in. She was a forty-year-old Vietnamese woman. She blew me on the mattress.

"Beeg kuk. Beeg kuk," she kept saying. The way she said it was nasty—and not because of her accent, that'd just be racist. But yuck, the whole experience was disgusting.

"Wait, can you maybe turn over?" I asked her.

I just had to somehow cum and get this whole thing over with, but then she handed me a flavored condom. The whole thing got worse by the moment. I put the strawberry rubber on, envisioned KC in my head, and finally came, but it took so much concentration I was pouring sweat from every pore in my soul and the sheets were drenched. I paid her three hundred dollars and she left. The second the door closed Sahar's laughter lasted into the early morning. Anyway, that was the last time I was with a hooker, and that experience left a terrible taste in my memory. I wasn't sure I could do it again.

"Yeessss! Dude!! Let's go! Pick any girl you want! It's on me!"

So I picked the trashiest blonde on the strip of building where they were all hanging out. But thing is, when I asked if she was working, it was awkward to say the least. She looked at me like *what a drag, I have to work?* And so as uncomfortable as it already was, now it was ten times worse. Within moments of her grabbing her shit off the ground, a car swung around the block and stopped in front of us, a minivan, and its sliding doors opened.

"Go, get in. Come on," she told me. She was really pushy... Then the minivan drove a few blocks then jerked to a stop in front of a convenient store. "Out, let's go," she told me. Jeez, this was tiring. We went into the store and she picked out a condom and some lube. Ew. Lube? Is she that dry? Then she put them on the counter by the cashier and waited for me to pull out my credit card. The whole process felt very rushed.

"Make shure ya say I'm yurh sista when ya check me in," she said in a trashed-out accent from nowhere in particular. So we walked to the concierge and I checked her in as my sister. Clearly, this woman was a prostitute, but the concierge had been through this gimmick before, so we went up to the room without a problem. "Get undressed," she told me immediately upon entering. I took my clothes off and I was soft as pie. "Get hard," she then yelled at me. Well fuck. I know what I'm supposed to do you cunt, why don't you blow me or something? Get me in the mood. But I didn't say that. I was too nervous. I just said:

"One sec," and I tried stroking my dick out of its coma into an attentive state. But by the time it was stiff enough for me to configure it inside of her, I came after two pumps. The hooker looked at me and laughed. *She actually laughed.* Then she pulled out a blunt roach from her purse while shaking her head, as if to say: what a loser. She lit the blunt roach and started smoking it in our room without even asking if it was cool while Chloe's brother finished up in the bathroom. She gave me a hit off the blunt as if to say: *cheer up kid.*

When Chloe's brother finished up and the girls left, he looked at me and said:

"Yooooo that was sick!!! Don't tell Chloe about this, okay? How was yours?!"

So that was that.

The good news is the next day I saw the chick from Señor Frogs on the beach. She was wearing a thong bikini lying next to Pablo.

"Yo! That's her!" I told Chloe's brother.

"Say something!" and he nudged me.

I pushed back, "No man stop, she's in a thong! With her boyfriend!"

"That's her boyfriend?"

"I don't know. She said something… I don't know."

"Duuuddee! Say something!"

But the moment passed and I pussied out and we walked along the beach back to our hotel, where I got in a chair and stared at the ocean while pondering if that was a sign or meaningless coincidence. I just walked by the girl I'm probably meant to marry, and I said nothing. I was beating myself up about it all day.

A few hours later, I opened my eyes and saw her again. She was on the payphone talking to someone. The payphone was right by the pool of our hotel. I couldn't believe she kept showing up in my life.

"If you don't go up to her, I will for you," Chloe's brother said.

Nobody wants something like that to happen, so I approached her. But she was in a heated conversation. I nearly turned around when it became obvious what an unpleasant call she was on, but it was too late, she had already made eye contact with me.

"It's me! From the club!" I softly said to her, aware of what despicable timing it was.

She pulled the phone away for a second. "Yes," she said. And waited.

I didn't know what that meant, so I just said: "Come to bar. When done. When done with call, come to bar, there," and I pointed to the beach bar. I said it in broken English as if she may understand that easier.

"Yes," she said then went back to her phone call.

I waited all afternoon for that call to end, and when it finally did, she vanished and never came into the bar.

Later that evening, in our room, Chloe's brother and I were smoking a joint of weed that I'd sold him on the balcony, looking at all the surfers in the ocean. It looked like god had sprinkled pepper on the water, not that I believe in god. Maybe I do.

"Holy shit dude! It's your girl! GO!" Chloe's brother said in a startling tone.

There she was again, walking along the beach. Fuck it, I thought. If this isn't a sign, I don't know what is. I rushed down to the lobby to try and catch her and nearly smashed into her right outside the elevator.

"Hey!"

"Sorry, sorry. I looking for you," she said. Pablo was standing next to her smoking a cigarette with a crazy sun burn. He didn't seem to care.

"I thought you didn't understand me," I said to her.

"No no, iz not thees. No. Ehm… tonight. Yes? Tonight is same place. Okay?"

She said all that in English.

"Right here?" I said in Spanish.

"Yez, here at them. Uh. At them elevun—eelayvan?"

"At eleven?" I said in shitty Spanish to her shitty English.

"Si, a las once."

"Okay! I'll see you here!"

"I, Agustina. He, Pablo."

"I'm Greg."

Then Pablo said: "Today here it's is."

"No es nada! You say nothing!" Agustina yelled at him, as if his English was so far inferior to hers that she was embarrassed.

That caused them to argue for a bit. Then Pablo said: "Here we see."

And that was how a new love entered my life. Agustina was here to stay, and without her, I may have never quit selling weed. In fact, I may be in prison had it not been for our burgeoning romance.

Later that night, I met her at 11PM by the elevator in the hotel lobby. The entire evening moved quickly and was full of intoxication. When morning came and our time together had expired, when the vacation was over and we were both scheduled to leave, Agustina looked at me and said:

"Next stopping for me iz New York. I calling to you when get." That was promising—so much better than moving to South America, as I had already played out in my head if this all worked out. I gave her my email and she told me: "Don worry, I getting to you when I arriving." And she left. I had no idea if I would ever see her again, and I hadn't even gotten her email. I didn't wanna seem insane.

Chloe's brother and I flew back to New York a few days later and I waited for Agustina, my soulmate, to email me. It took a week, but finally it came. All the email said was:

Soy Agus.

From that day forward I called her Agus. She told me where she was staying. It was at a Comfort Inn on Central Park West I think. I got to her room and it was only her.

"Where's Pablo?"

"Pablo had go back for work. Is in Buenos Aires."

I'm totally gonna fuck this girl, I thought. But I never did, well, not on that night. I fumbled around like an awkward toddler. I had no idea how to be romantic with someone I could barely communicate with. We used translator sites all night long and did nothing but sit in front of a computer for hours typing to each other, laughing hysterically at all the Internet translator's fuckups. I invited her back to my apartment the next day. She said her sister would be arriving that evening, so I invited everyone to stay at my tiny apartment.

Her sister was a blonde version of Agus. She was spunky and kissed me twice when I met her outside the Empire State building. Her suitcases were enormous and wrapped in saran wrap.

When she walked into my studio and saw that Agus and I were sharing a bed, she said nothing of it. I learned later that sex was far more casual in Argentina, not that we were having sex. Her sister let out a small smile and onto the next subject. They spoke in fast Spanish, and I stood on the sidelines waiting for a moment when I could understand what they were talking about, but it rarely came, and when it did, I said something a bit unrelated. That made me feel insignificant. If only she knew me in English, how special I was. I was certain I was special and worthy of her love.

Her sister refused my invitation to stay at my cramped living quarters and went to stay at a hotel.

"I having a friend in Bronx. For cocaine," Agus tells me. I was slowly starting to pick up enough words to have small talk with her, expanding on the little Spanish I remembered from Kitchen Kabaret during my days of being a pizza boy. "Thees guy is Colombiano. He having best cocaine. I knowing him from Argentina. He coming. But telling me he in here. So I call."

What in the fuck? I don't know, but an hour later a massive bald Colombian man showed up to my apartment with a thugged out sidekick. I had money and weed all over. I was certain this would all end in a tragedy. But it didn't. We blew coke all week and before she left, she held up my largest jar of weed and said:

"Thees you have stop."

"I'm stopping at eighty grand," I told her.

"Remembering movie with Johnny Depp? He saying always stopping but never."

"I swear, only a bit longer," I told her.

And that became a contention of our relationship, which lasted for a long time; we're still close to this day. I promised to visit her in Buenos Aires, and just like that, she left—back to South America. We never even had sex; we didn't even kiss, but we were in love, and I swore to myself I would marry her. But for now, I had to get her off my mind. So, I decided to make my biggest entrepreneurial endeavor yet and produce the greatest sketch comedy festival of all time, and this go-around, to ensure no Wonderland-esque mistakes were made. I was high on life with a new romantic future. Little did I know, this would be the start of a brand-new addiction: producing comedy festivals.

But what ended up happening was a giant setback and a humungous leap forward, all at the same time...

CHAPTER 20: SKIT SKAT LIVE

It was called Skit Skat, which I now realize sounds like porn.

I had to attract the greatest troupes in the city all at once. So, we had to have a grand prize that was enormous—but that's not why people should want to submit, they should *want to submit for the prestige of being a part of it*. But still, the grand prize had to match the prestige, so I decided to make it five grand—rather than one grand that I used for Wonderland—to get the biggest sketch troupes to apply and really sell the sizzle of the honor it would be to even be accepted into Skit Skat. And look, I did do one little thing that's not so kosher...

I worked out a deal with a waiter friend of mine named Matthew, who also had a sketch comedy troupe, to award him the grand prize—he would get the publicity from beating all the big troupes, and in exchange he'd return me the money.

"But what if we bomb?"

"Don't bomb," I told him. "Do the devil skit."

"You love that sketch."

"It's hysterical, you can't fuck that one up."

And what happened? They fucked that one up and still we had to award them the grand prize of five thousand dollars ahead of like ten other troupes who were ten times funnier. Anyway, I digress, point is I needed help executing all this but I was sick of Louie. Deep down, I knew that I couldn't keep him around anymore—he was too much of a liability. He certainly drank way too much… Couldn't have an alcoholic on the team. So that's why I decided I would have a go at this with Sahar. He was Israeli and good at business, so I figured he'd make the perfect partner. After all, he had all the venue connections for the awards show that I didn't have—and the awards show was almost a bigger deal than the actual festival. So, I pitched him the idea:

"I'll have two hundred girls there, smoking hot. All of them. My word," I told him.

"How?" Sahar asked me. "Last time they weren't so good."

"I got a plan, don't worry."

Then I got nervous that I couldn't do this alone, cause after Sahar agreed to work with me, he was nowhere to be found, so I caved and called Louie *one more time.*

"Ma brutha frum anutha mutha! Let's do this!"

So Louie was in. He *loved* my plan—Oh right, I didn't tell you what it was yet. But seriously, don't judge me for this, okay? I only did what I had to. The plan was to audition hundreds of actresses that wanted *on-camera hosting experience* and tell them we were going be filming a documentary, and that the awards show was a big part of the film. We told every girl during the audition that we wanted them to go around with our cameraman (Vee) and interview contestants.

"Only thing is," I would tell everyone, "we're not sure which host will work best for the documentary, so we're going to be doing a few trials with a few different hosts, but we want you to be one of them."

"Oh! And is this paid?"

"The trial isn't paid, I'm sorry, but it'll get a ton of publicity and you'll get free drinks and possibly be cast for the entire documentary, which is paid, but if you're not available for unpaid gigs, I understand, however—"

"That's fine, I was only asking..." most of them would inevitably say, because when you're an actor, you take anything— whatever will get you in front of a camera. I knew this cause I was one of those people.

So I auditioned a million actresses and cast them all on a "trial basis" to see how they did and they ALL showed up to the awards show cause that's where I told them the gig was... Which it was. Wait—Is this sleazier than I remember it being? Maybe. But don't worry, all this has a happy ending. And I wasn't trying to be sleazy, I was just trying to be creative and what not. It's only a marketing tactic.

Sahar was like "HOW'D YOU GET ALL THESE GIRLS TO SHOW UP!?!?"

"Don't worry about it," I told him.

The festival was okay, but the awards show morphed into a colossal event. We even had a billboard in the middle of Times Square that Sahar negotiated. He also negotiated that I'd get two bucks per girl that showed up, or some shit like that, not a lotta money, but a little pocket change to cover any gaps in the fifteen-grand bar guarantee I agreed to at the beginning of all this. Yeah, I gave a guarantee to the club—through Sahar, that if the bar didn't do at least fifteen thousand bucks, I'd cover the difference. Risky I know, but I had a plan for that as well…

To meet the bar guarantee, I was just gonna drag out the awards show as long as possible so that people would rack up their credit cards… But that's not what happened. It was like ten minutes into the night when this one girl—I mean, one of the "hosts" for our "documentary" we were filming, came up to me and was like:

"Umm I thought you said we'd be getting free drinks."

"You do," I said as I was checking in more girls for the "documentary."

"Well, he's trying to charge me."

"Who?"

"The bartender."

So I ran up to the bartender and saw the fiasco. Fifty actresses bombarding him about the drink special that he, apparently, knew nothing about.

"What happened to the free drinks?" I frantically screamed over the chaos of a million people running around amidst the anarchy.

"No one told me anything about free drinks."

WWHHHHAAAAAA?!

SAHAR!!!

WHERE THE FUCK IS SAHAR?!!?

All the girls were about to leave. The people were getting mad. I had to rectify this at once, but there was no time to look for Sahar—he could be anywhere. I had to do something. So, I took out my Amex and just gave it to the bartender:

"*Please* stop charging it at two grand."

I don't know why I said two grand, I just did. FUCK! TWO GRAND?! I better get this sorted out before they max my credit card out. Then girls kept coming over to me asking where they should start and who they should interview.

Interview?!

Oh right... You're here for the acting gig. Fuck, this was getting confusing. Hold on, I gotta make sure the bartender doesn't max my shit out. I'm bleeding money from the ass right now. But there were too many girls asking me questions, then they started asking each other questions, like:

"Wait, you're here for the job too?"

"No I'm just on a trial basis for tonight."

"ME TOO!"

Oh no.. They're starting to talk. FUCK! Breathe Greg, breathe. I had no idea where Sahar was or Louie and—

"SAHAR!"

"Great job man!" he said as he walked by.

"WAIT!!"

He stopped short, "What?"

"Free drinks till ten!"

"Huh?"

Holy shit I was gonna kill him. "FREE FUCKING DRINKS THE BARTENDER IS CHARGING MY CARD PLEASE GET THE GODDAM DRINKS!"

"Okay, okay. Relax man. I'll take care of it—"

"—Are you... Greg?"

"Um... Yeah?" I said, scared that at any moment all this would explode. It was one of the actresses. They were everywhere. "Where do I set up?" She had *all her gear!* Like a clipboard and all this shit. Oh man, I felt horrible. But wait—Why? This *is a gig Greg!* Don't feel bad, you're providing jobs for everyone! BUT NO ONE IS GETTING PAID BUT YOU! No, that's not true at all, the bartender is charging me thousands of dollars at the moment—

SHUT UP GREG!

Jeez my head was spinning. Then I see a redhead... Man I love redheads, so I see this redhead. Well actually, she was right in front of me. So, of course I saw her. I calmed down for a brief moment of flirtation.

"Are you here with your boyfriend?"

"I'm here with my girlfriend," she replied.

"Oh, so you're a lesbian."

"I'm bi."

"We should have a threesome," I suggest casually.

She looked me up and down. "I might be into that, but I'd have to ask my girlfriend."

"Well go ahead, ask, where is she? Is she here?"

"She's right there."

And there she was, a brunette… what a lovely couple.

"Well go ask her!"

So she goes up to her girlfriend and all I see is a pair of whispers. Then she comes back—the redhead.

"Yeah. She's into it. But we're not ready to leave yet," as she sips her wine, or whatever she was drinking that was now on my Amex.

"Leave? Nah, me neither! Shit I'm running the event!"

"I know, you auditioned me."

"Right! You're a host!"

"I thought I was, till I realized you just held the auditions to fill the club up with hot girls." Holy shit. She was on to me. Fuck. "It's okay, I like it. But yeah, we're not ready to leave yet."

"No I swear, you're going to get a chance to—"

"Really, I don't care. So, stop."

So I stopped. It was 11PM—Fuck. We were running an hour late! We had to give out awards! So I just said:

"Well come and get me when you're ready!"

Just then I heard Louie on the mic in the awards show room. It was a three-story club and we were on the third floor and there was a bar section and a club section that we converted to a theatre for the awards show, and Louie was now on stage, with the mic, completely drunk, damaging my legendary name. I had to stop him before he did something stupid. I know Louie, and when he's *this drunk,* there's no telling what'll happen.

My parents, I saw my parents. They showed up. Wow, they really love me. Then I saw Chloe. Chloe was here too. What a good friend. I never said anything to her about the hookers her brother and I got in Hawaii. Unless she reads this book, then she'll know. Then I thought about the lesbians. Was this really gonna happen? Don't think about it right now, GO DO THE FUCKING EVENT! Then more girls came up to me:

"I'M LEAVE YOU FUCKING ASSHOLE"

"SCUMBAG!"

Shit. Shit. Shit.

"LAAYYDDIEES N' GentSS…"

Man, Louie was FUCKED up… I just let the girls call me names and ran into the awards show room. He was falling all over the stage—well, not like literally falling over, but he looked terribly bad as the comedy troupes waited to hear whether or not they'd be crowned Skit Skat winner.

I got on stage, or at least I went to the part of the stage where he was standing and tried to get his attention, but he was in his own belligerent world.

"The Skit Skat Awards showww!!! Let's get a round of applause for my brotha! My brotha, the handsome lad that got us all here… my brotha…"

He kept saying, "my brotha…" Jeez.

"My brudder Grehory the Kay-yasss! Right before our eyes ladiezz and gentZ!"

You're kidding. Right? Are you fucking kidding? Get the fuck off stage you dumb drunken Irish prick fuck face dickwad dipshit!!!

But I didn't say any of that. I just said:

"Louie! YOU'RE FUCKING UP!" But that just made it worse, because then he looked at me and was like, "C'mere Cayea! Gih'uphere! C'mn folks—let's gihim up here!"

I stepped on stage and grabbed the mic from him before he did anything else dumb as fuck and looked around the room. It was silent. All the actresses were onto me. They detested me; I could see it in their stare. I was a fraud. But I wasn't trying to be, I was just trying to impress my parents. Wait, what? My parents? Where did *that* come from? Is that true? That I'm doing all this shit to impress my parents? Nah, that's probably just something that came out.

Anyway, I grabbed the mic and gave some stupid speech and handed out the awards, the grand prize going to my buddy Matthew, of course, who I rigged the festival for so I wouldn't have to pay any money out. But of course this story isn't 100% true, otherwise I'd be breaking the law. So, that's why I like to reinforce that this story is *mostly* true, you know, to keep safe and all... Anyway, I was up there on stage, fumbling through everything I had rehearsed in my head so clearly—wait, that's a lie. Why would I lie to you? I rehearsed nothing. Winged it. I winged life. Nothing was planned, though I always made agendas. So while up there, I cursed a million times cause I was nervous. I was wearing a cool suit by the way. I looked pretty awesome. Is that cocky? Am I an arrogant prick? Whatever, I just had to find those lesbians.

CUT TO 4AM:

Everyone was basically gone. My shirt was drenched in sweat and my temples were damp with anxiety, whatever the fuck that means. I grabbed the entire PA system that I had rented, a bunch of speakers and amps and other accessories to make sure Louie's presentation of the awards sounded professional, and found the redhead from earlier:

"Ready? Let's go!"

She was with her girlfriend when I said that, so they both heard me. I wasn't about to lose this opportunity. I needed it. She seemed a bit more hesitant than she had been a few hours ago, so I got nervous Louie had possibly ruined it all. Still, they both followed me down the couple flights of stairs and followed me as I rushed us out into the middle of the street to get us a cab. We all got in. I was thrilled.

"Hey! I'm Greg," I said to the redhead's girlfriend.

"I'm Emily."

"35th and third, PLEASE!!!" I yelled to the cabbie who was one foot away from me.

SUBTEXT: Hurry you motherfucker before they change their mind!

CUT TO MY FRONT DOOR:

I open the first set of glass doors with my key, smashing the PA system in my hands against the scratchy brick walls and nearly dropping everything on the crooked slabs of cement which made up my trashyard. Still, they followed. I couldn't believe my luck. Together we went through the second batch of doors and climbed the four flights of rickety stairs to my apartment door.

"Umm, what floor are you on?" Emily asked on floor two.

"Just one more up!" But that was a lie as you know; it was two more flights, but what was I supposed to do, tell her that? I had to keep the momentum going. But then they walked in, took a brief glance at my mattress on the floor in the corner of the room, looked at each other like... huh? I thought this guy was a big deal—then said:

"We have to go to the bathroom."

Fuck fuck fuck... "Sure! right there!"

And they both went into my tiny ass bathroom together. What the fuck were they doing in there? Shit. shit. shit. This was a horrible idea—no, a brilliant idea gone horrible. Then they came back out but with no toilet flushing, just walked out, and the redhead says:

"Emily isn't feeling good."

I was somewhat relieved to be honest, all the pressure was getting to me. "Well, we don't have to do this, but you also don't *have* to just run out. I mean, sit down, it was a long night. Relax, I'll get you a glass of water."

So I get a glass of water and Emily sits in this crescent-like chair I got next to my bed and the redhead stands and stares at me and waits.

"You should give your girl a massage," I tell the redhead, and motion for her to sit on my bed. She sat down. "This'll make you feel much better Emily." After a bit, I said, "I know we're not having sex or anything, but we should just lay down for a second." So I laid down on my bed. They were hesitant. I don't know what came over me, I just felt confident. "Come on, lay next to me at *least*." So the redhead lays next to me, and Emily lays next to her. I'm on the end. "If I told my friends that I had two beautiful lesbians in my bed and I wasn't even laying between them, I'd get made fun of forever. Lemme just at least get in the middle for a sec." So they give me the thumbs up, but with caution. "Kiss her," I say to the redhead after a moment. "It'll make her feel better." She looked at me like *you're an idiot if you think I'm falling for that.* "What?" I said innocently. "It's just a kiss!" So she leaned over and gave her a peck. Emily kissed her back. And then…

Anarchy.

They start frantically making out with each other. I interrupted them and kissed them both on the lips. Then they sat up, both of them, and in one single swoop, the redhead grabbed Emily's dress while Emily raised her arms to make it easier for the dress to slip right off, and just like that, she was in her underwear. This can't be happening, I thought.

Then the redhead raised *her* hands as if to say, *okay Emily, now undress me!*

Emily grabbed the redhead's dress from the bottom of her skirt and slid it up over her girlfriend's shoulders. They both kiss their way down to my dick and blow me for a bit before giving a: *Aaahhhh fuck it. To hell with 'not feeling well'… LET'S FUCK!*

They stopped blowing me and continued making out, laying stomach-to-stomach. They were right in front of me, but it all seemed like a porn video in another dimension. My dick was throbbing so hard that even putting the condom on wasn't a hindrance like it usually was. I hate those damn things. I'm always losing my erection. Does that make me not a man? Nah, that must happen to tons of guys. Does it? I took a second to just watch them make out and rub clits with each other while the condom was on before I slowly slid into Emily, then pulled out and slid into her girlfriend, then out and back to Emily, then the redhead. They kissed each other harder than ever—like hate-kissing—like how I shoulda kissed Minnie in *Manuscript*. Their shaky movements, twitch-like, indicated they were *actually* gonna cum. It was all very exciting. Emily pushed her clit up into the redhead's clit while I was inside her and bit the redhead's tongue and lips and the redhead grabbed my dick and took it out of Emily and puts it inside her. They were fighting for my cock and I could feel myself uncontrollably quivering as I tried to pummel my dick inside them as many more times as possible before I couldn't hold it in anymore. I leaned in and started kissing the redhead all over, missing her lips I was so in the moment. The more she moaned and whimpered the less time I had before... no...

AAAAAAAAHHHHHHHHHHHHAHAHAHAHAHA HAAHAHHHH

FFFFUUUUUCCCCKKKKKkkkkk....

Aaaahhhh...

Fuck.

I came. Before they did. I was so close. It was about 6AM by then. I threw my condom on the floor and went to the kitchen sink and put my mouth under the faucet and gulped down as much water as I could. I was sweating like crazy. Not sexy. I turned around and they were both still in bed, making out, fingering each other—it was remarkable.

They left my apartment and took a bus back to Jersey sometime around 7AM. I offered them money for a cab, but they said they liked the bus. I didn't see the redhead again until five years later on Hollywood Blvd in Los Angeles… But I'll get to that later, maybe.

Then it dawned on me that my credit card was still at the club—an open tab for the public to get drunk on my hard-earned dollars. I called Amex to see how much I had been charged. Everything. $15,000. My credit limit. And that was the biggest setback and leap forward I'd ever made in my life. And just when I thought I'd seen my share of crazy, I was introduced to a whole other level of insane.

And it all started on HotorNot.com…

CHAPTER 21: THE PSYCHO FROM SAN DIEGO

My sex addiction was rampant, so rampant that I created a premium account on HotorNot.com. The only girl I met from it came over and slept in my bed but wouldn't let me fuck her. She was eighteen from Floral Park, Long Island with lots of dark make-up and flat ironed hair. She was wearing these white leggings with a blue thong before it was fashionable and kept getting up to look at herself in my full-length mirror outside my bathroom door. She left shortly thereafter; no sex, no nothing. Couple kisses, and that was it. A year later she texted me to ask if she and her friend could come over.

"Can you buy us some vodka?" she asked when they both got up my four-flight stairwell.

"Ahh… so that's why you're here."

But truth be told, it turned me on. I liked it when girls used me. I can't explain why, but it turned me on. She told me her friend was from San Diego.

"So what brings you to New York?"

"I want to be a stripper." I looked her up and down. Not really cut out for the gig, but I didn't wanna spoil her enthusiasm. "They have some open calls tomorrow so I'm going," she told me. Then her friend says she's leaving. The wannabe stripper looks around my small studio apartment. "Can I sleep here tonight?"

I had no idea how to reply. "Sleep here? Ummm…. Absolutely."

FASTFORWARD TO:

JAM!

She shoves her finger in my ass while she's on top of me having sex.

"You like that?"

"Uhhh…. [still thinking]" She rides me harder, finger still in ass. "Uhhh… I don't know about—" She jams it in further. I hang on for dear life. "I'm gonna punch you in the face," she says.

"What?"

"Shhhhh." She puts her hand on my throat and squeezes. "You like that?" She clenches her fist.

"Don't punch me," I tell her.

BLAM!

Right in the fucking nose. I gush blood everywhere and throw her off me.

"Oh my god! Are you okay? I'm so sorry!"

"Yeah—" She rushes to get me a towel. "—it's all good."

"Are you mad? Can we still have sex?"

"Nah I'm done. I gotta do stuff anyway."

"Like what?"

"Work."

"But you don't work."

"I have an appointment tomorrow."

"An appointment with who?"

"A big photographer."

"You're getting photos taken?"

"I'm selling him pot. Let's just go to sleep."

"Is it cause I punched you?"

"It's 2:43AM. You're drunk. So am I. Let's just go to bed."

FAST-FORWARD TO THE MORNING:

"I need you to leave, he's almost here."

"I'll just wait."

"No, you can't be in here."

"Why not?"

"Cause he likes privacy."

"I'll hide in the bathroom."

"Are you serious? No."

"Why not?"

"What if he has to go to the bathroom?"

"Then I'll just sit quietly on your bed and not say anything."

"He won't come in if anyone is here." Of course, no one was actually coming over. Fuck. How do I get this psycho outa my apartment? "I'll tell you what... just go to that deli across the street, let me just take care of him then come back. Okay? Cool?"

"But why do I have to leave?"

"You're *not* leaving, you're just grabbing some bagels while I do business. Can you grab me a bagel?" I hand her a twenty.

"But I don't wanna leave."

I walk her to the door. "That's okay. You'll be right back... Let's go." We go down the stairs and I hold her hand to make sure she keeps moving. I can still feel her finger in my ass every step down I take. We go through my shitty cement trashyard then through the other set of doors then to the front door and out to the street. "This way..." And we turn right. I walk her to Third avenue and show her to the deli. Just wait here and buzz my apartment in fifteen minutes. K? See you in a sec..." I play it cool as I walk away, then my walk got faster. I cut the corner, waited till I was out of sight, then rushed to my brother's apartment around the block and waited till nightfall before I went back home. I'm in the clear. Phew. Until one day... Four months later, my Blackberry buzzes from an anonymous number.

I'm pregnant.
Who is this?
Fuck you faggot.
Who is this?
You'll never see him. It's a boy.
WHO IS THIS?

I call. No response, no voicemail. I call again. No response.

Fuck you I'm not picking up your fucking calls.

Okay. Did I do something wrong? Give me a clue.

I mean look, this could be anyone. My life was riddled with random sex with random girls from random nights from random places, all of which were too blurry in my hazy brown-out of a life to recall accurately.

Wait till I sue you for child support.

What?!?!?!?!?! WHO R U?!?!? Nothing. *You're not pregnant whoever the fuck this is.*

Okay...

No, you're not.

Yes I am. And you're NEVER seeing your child.

Right. Okay... bye.

Don't believe? Fine. Wait till I sue you for child support you fucking faggot.

I change my tactics cause actually this might be true. Could it be? I mean, I *never* used a condom for fear it would make my erection that much harder (no pun intended). So, all this might be true, I thought. No, I would—shit. I need to know who this is.

Okay, look, do you wanna talk on the phone?

Too late for that.

I call again anyway. She doesn't pick up.

Too late I said.

Whatever.

Every day for the next three months another text came through telling me how shitty of a father I would be. I began to get scared. Finally, it's clearly the crazy stripper from San Diego, so I start calling her out by name. She acts as if she doesn't know who the fuck the name I called her was. Months and months of constant texts, maybe another three months of this shit. I start to wonder, *is* she *really* pregnant? How in the fuck would she know it was me anyway? Did I cum in her? I can't remember. Did I? Well we stopped after she punched me…

Oh shit.

That was the *second* night she punched me. I immediately recall the first. It was right after the girl from HotorNot.com left. I had told my friend Johnny Red I would go to the bar his new girlfriend was bartending at. I knew them both from my dinky stint at Brooklyn College… right, and I told the San Diego stripper she could come with me.

Ok… Then what happened?

We took the train to Brooklyn… Brooklyn Heights. And we walked into the bar: some hipster pub. Johnny Red was at the other end of the narrow joint and I nodded to his girlfriend who was tending drinks.

"Who the *fuck* is that?" the stripper says.

"She's my friend's girlfriend. It's his birthday."

Oh right, that's why we were there. It was Johnny Red's birthday.

"You want to *fuck her* now?"

"What? Huh? Relax."

Oh jeez. She was starting to scare me. I tried to lose her in the crowded bar, but she came up to me after every person I talked to getting visibly angrier after every girl who even looked at me. She made a bit of a scene actually, I remember that.

"Can you calm your girlfriend down?" Johnny Red's girlfriend asked me aggressively, obviously pissed I even brought this trash to her place.

"Girlfriend? Oh no no no, that is *not* my girlfriend."

"Well, whoever she is. She's acting nuts."

I go up to her.

"Come on, let's leave."

"Oh now you want to FUCKING leave? HEY! HANDSOME!" and she screams to Johnny Red. Then she lifts up her shirt and shows him and the rest of the twenty people in the bar her tits. Her tits *were* really nice. Maybe she *could* be a stripper after all?

"GREG! GET THIS GIRL OUT!" Johnny Red's girlfriend screams.

So I drag the girl out. I was furious, but horny. The whole scene turned me on. I hailed a cab and we sped home to Manhattan and I fucked the shit out of her. I think I came *on her* but some of it coulda been *in her*. Fuck. Maybe *she is* pregnant?

The next night is when she shoved her finger in my ass and punched me in the nose. Immediately, I realize she might be telling the truth. What a horrible mom she would be. I text her back and say:

I'd like to work this out.

Nothing. I freak out.

LOOK YOU FUCKING WHORE.

I call her a million times. My head was going crazy. I had no idea what to do. Finally she says:

It's too late to talk. I'm back in San Diego preparing for the baby.

So it *is* her. Okay, at least now I know it's her and not the Muslim girl from Turkey—my filmmaking partner in one of the classes I nearly failed at Brooklyn College. What had I gotten myself into?

Then one day I go to a concert—Bad Fish, this fucking Sublime tribute band. I get to Terminal 5, the music venue they were playing at—I think that's where it was, and I'm on the top floor of the venue when...

HOLY. SHIT.

Guess who's NOT back in San Diego like she told me she was? Guess who is THIN AS FUCK? Guess who is DEFINITELY *not* pregnant? There she was. With some other dude. I take out my phone. A grin crowds my face. I smile with relief and a chilling vengeance pumps me up with adrenaline. The first text:

I see you.

Huh?

Sublime fan?

I see her looking around.

Who's that dude you're with?

Next text:

You're pretty skinny for seven months into your pregnancy... maybe you shouldn't be drinking at the bar of Terminal 5?

I don't know what the hell you're talking about.

YOU UGLY ASS SKANKED OUT WHOREBAG CUNTLICKING WHITE TRASHY PIECE OF GARBAGE SHIT!

I'm kidding, I didn't say that. No I'm not kidding. I totally said that. That's when I knew I needed someone stable, like Agus in Argentina, to help me get my career—and life—where it needed to be. Maybe I'll buy my ticket to see her after Robyn comes up for Christmas in a few weeks...

CHAPTER 22: ROBYN AT XMAS

It was like December 23rd and Robyn wanted to go out the second she arrived at my apartment from the airport.

It was like midnight when we got to The Groove, my favorite funk joint downtown by NYU. I got some cocaine for the night to keep her happy and keep me awake. It was dark and the tables were all sticky with overpriced cocktails. I ordered us two dirty martinis after the hostess sat us at a table with two Europeans. The tables touched each other and there was no privacy to have any meaningful conversation.

"Wut the fuck is this playce Grayg, where you go to feel hard an shit?" she asked.

"Fuck you mean?"

"We ain't but two've the only white people here!"

"So?"

"Oh shut. The fuck. Up. You're so funny, thayt's why I luv yew."

"Look, they're white," and I gave a slight nod of the head to indicate the Europeans.

"Why yew bein so shy, hi ya'll!" and she got their attention. They were handsome guys in their thirties maybe. Old. Nothing to worry about.

"Ehm, ello. Are yew tew from, ehh, how you say… locul?"

"Oh goLLLY! Listen t'thayt accent, where ya'll from?"

"We'hre both from France. Yew have been?"

"Nah, we met in Louisiana," I said.

"See thayt shit ya'll? Thayt's his way've sayin '*ahm* fuckin thayt shit ya'll!" And she cracked up. "Gimme a kiss yew, yew sexy New York fuck yew."

"Ah, yew tew are visitour tew?"

"No no, I'm from here. She's visiting."

"Look it yew tryina be all tough," and she leaned over to kiss me then turned her attention to the French guys.

"Maybe yew tew know where to get ehm, how you say…"

"Droges?" the other finished his sentence.

"Ehm, yes. Maybe some, white it is?"

"Blow?" I didn't wanna tell them I had a bag in my pocket cause I hated sharing. So I just said: "I can call a guy, he'll be here in like twenty probably."

"Oui, oui, yes, that would be very, ehm, purfect."

So I call the guy and he shows up an hour later, just as Linard takes the stage, the funk band I wanted to show off to Robyn to prove I was cultured, but instead I had to leave her alone in the club with those French fucks to get them coke. When I got back inside, after a few hours of blowing rails in the basement bathroom of the club, Robyn invited these guys back to my apartment. What a whore…

We got to my apartment and I showed them my weed and they were impressed, we smoked a bit, and then they left. I thought Robyn might try and fuck all of us, which put me in a bit of an uncomfortable mood for the entire time they were in the apartment, but at like 3AM, they left and I tried to slide my flaccid cock inside Robyn till I had mediocre success, then we miraculously fell asleep.

The next evening she wanted to go out *again*. I hated going out with her cause every guy wanted her. It was too much attention for me and too much work to defend myself as the winning suitor. But anyway, I had to text Sahar cause he was the only way I could get into a club. I took a photo of Robyn and sent it to his Blackberry with a message that said: *This is who I'm with. She wants to go out.*

Then I called him when he didn't reply. He picked up after ten rings.

"Brah. Holy shit."

Now, usually when I went to meet Sahar at a club, I had to tell the bouncer that I knew him and that I was on his list and all that bullshit but this time around he and his Israeli crew were hanging outside the club waiting for us. He flagged me down and pulled me to the side when Robyn walked in front of us and was like, "Brah. This is the hottest bitch I think I ever seen in person."

"She's good," I confirmed.

We walked in the club and again he pulled me close over to him. "Brah, you got like the hottest whore in this whole club."

"Yeah, she's fuckin hot," I replied to his insensitive comment, just to be cordial.

He really was a piece of shit, but I liked him. I don't know why. Maybe cause he thought I was cool, and that was enough to win me over. I'm really not that complex a being. But anyway, Christmas dinner at my parent's house arrived, which we celebrated even though we're Jewish cause my dad is Italian Catholic, so I invited Robyn to Long Island to meet the fam…

🕊 * * *

My parent's big grey house—formerly blue—stood attention as Robyn and I pulled up in a cab. I told her to tuck her tits in but the sweater was dying for air as her breasts stretched the cashmere to its last fiber of strength. Still her makeup made it clear she was perhaps a former stripper—which isn't true, mind you. She worked at Hooters, and when we went to Bourbon Street in New Orleans and went to the strip club and all the patrons and strippers begged her to get on stage, she didn't even take her top off when she grabbed the pole, so she was far from a stripper. Not like Renée, who you'll meet later. But still her dark past was painted on her face and my entire upper-class Jewish family raised an eyebrow when we walked in.

The dining room had gaudy trim around the ceiling, a wooden cabinet with glass doors showcasing fine china, and the "holiday table" had been elongated to fit the entire outer-nuclear family, along with a few family friends. The party consisted of my mom and dad and brother, my two grandparents—one Jew and one Italian—my three uncles—two Jews and one Italian, and their girlfriends, my two cousins, my nanny, my aunt, and four family friends of my parents. Everyone had went to high school and graduated college. Everyone except me. Everyone had a legal job and didn't launder money. Everyone except me.

"Haigh ya'll!"

Robyn wasted no time introducing herself to everyone. I couldn't believe how good with strangers she was. It's almost as if she wasn't aware of how odd the situation was. Later on in life, I would be reminded of that Christmas often. Apparently, though Robyn felt completely at home, the rest of the family chatted about her tits for the rest of their lives, and so far the rest of mine.

"I like your friend. She seems… she's *very* friendly." My mom said something of that nature.

"Hi Gregory," my dad probably said.

What else was there to say? Nobody knew anything about what was occurring forty miles away in Manhattan, and two inches away in my head. My entire life was a façade. Only my brother knew everything, and he seemed to be okay with it all, so as long as he thought my life was decently put-together, in my eyes I was just fine. Just living a life nobody would really understand. There was no fixing my past, only remedying my future, and if one day my parents and I chatted longer than a few minutes at a time, perhaps we could rebuild, if any bricks were still left standing. But for now, it was time to eat some Jewish Christmas dinner and get the fuck outa there. And after a few more nights of showing Robyn off to the world, she went back to Louisiana and I never saw her ever again. She went missing and I haven't been able to find her since.

It was around that time I drunkenly stumbled my way to Orbitz and bought a flight to Buenos Aires. It was time to profess my love to Agus. If love wasn't here in New York—or Louisiana, surely it was in Argentina.

CHAPTER 23: BUENOS AIRES

I grabbed about five thousand dollars in cash and headed to the airport. I was nervous about the trip. She was expecting me to fuck her, but what if I couldn't do it? What if I couldn't get hard? That kinda thing was happening all the time by now.

My neighbor came over the other day. She was a woman about thirty-seven years old from the Czech Republic. Her husband was paying to fuck her. They met on some sugar daddy website, but she was bored with him. One day after a photoshoot—she was an ex-model and still did these milfy photoshoots—she sent me a message on my Blackberry asking if she could swing by. Her text was something along the lines of:

I'm lonely. I have picture to show. New pictures. I need know if good or not.

She spoke with a dense accent, but generally I could understand her choppy, and aggressive English. She buzzed my door, walked up the four flights of stairs, brushed the unlocked door open, and chucked her CD in my laptop. Her photos popped up. She was on a boat.

"Oh, very nice. Where is that?"

"Look… more."

And I kept flipping through them. Suddenly her shirt disappeared and she was topless on the boat.

"Oh," I said. "Good tits—I mean, you have nice tits." What the fuck else was I supposed to say?

"Oh, thank you baby," and she kissed me on the cheek. She was always calling me baby. "Come, we go darrrink," she insisted after her last nude.

So we went. "I'm too drunk," I told her after the four martinis she ordered us at the bar across the street. The woman just kept ordering more. I couldn't keep up.

"No, no, pliss. I don't want darrrink alone. Please baby," and she kissed my cheek. Then kissed me again. Then on my lips. We ended up in my bed. She kissed me everywhere and got naked. She blew me and my heart was pounding. I couldn't get hard. I woke up the next morning in total shame. She slept next to me, naked, snoring, and remorseless. I couldn't believe I missed out on that up. I never got over it. All I wanted was a do-over, but when she woke up and put her clothes on, she gave me a kiss goodbye, and that was it.

"Sorry about last night," I said to her before she left. "I was… drunk. Sometimes that happens when I'm drunk."

"No no no, iz okay baby," but she didn't come over to kiss me like she usually did, she just left.

It happened another time with the Polish bartender from my old restaurant I used to wait tables at. Maybe it has something to do with Eastern Europeans? Anyway, I was at the bar after a shift—a shift I didn't need to even take cause I was selling weed to the city, as you clearly know, but I liked my manager. And the bartender. So after my shift one day, I sat at the bar flirting with her.

"You're trying too hard," she told me. "If you want to take me out, just tell me that."

Her accent was so faint it practically didn't exist. "Okay, I want to take you out," I told her.

"Maybe," she said.

"Tonight maybe? Or tomorrow maybe?"

Later that night the same thing happened. She came over after a few drinks at a bar and she took my clothes off, then her clothes came off. She had a birth mark all over her body, which also ran up to her face, but she covered it with makeup every day, which I didn't know about. Still it didn't hinder her beauty.

"Just relax," she told me when my floppy cock wouldn't stand up.

"Yeah, I know what to do… just, can you blow me for a bit longer?"

And she did, but to no avail. It was a lost cause and again I woke up with a feeling of failure in my scrotum and watched her perfect body walk out my door for the last time. I blew it again. So, yeah. I was goddam nervous as fuck by the time I got to Agustina's apartment in Palermo.

I was so nervous it was almost as if I wasn't present. I blamed it on my Spanish, and some of that was true, but really I was obsessing about the fact that in less than ten hours, I would be expected to perform miracles, especially after all the confidence I'd projected the entire time we'd been chatting on Skype since I met her in Hawaii a year ago.

She picked me up from the airport and her smile was bigger than I remembered. We walked to her car without understanding a damn thing each other had said. Usually, we had shitty Google Translate to help us out, but not in person. We got in the car and she said something. Who knows what she said? Not me. We drove through Buenos Aires and arrived at her apartment. Next to her apartment were train tracks. It's where kids from the barrios would come into Palermo to rob houses and shit, but when she told me that I had no clue what she was trying to get across.

"Es where the poor peoples coming to rob."

"The train tracks? Poor people come on the train… to rob?"

"Que?"

But it always ended in a "QUE?!"—most conversations, at least. How was I gonna make this work? Whatever, we got inside her apartment and her dog ran over to me. A shaggy mut. I can't remember his name. She had a mini-split AC unit by the ceiling.

It was a tasteless place with zero art hanging on the walls, which were coated in shitty primer white paint.

"Come, we going to Pablo," she said after we ran out of things to say.

So, we got in her car—it was fucking hot. January. Which is summer in Argentina. Anyway, we got to Pablo's apartment and his beer gut hung over his pants while he strummed one chord over and over on his guitar. His feet were planted on the sheets of his bed and his ass on the ledge where you may put a water before going to sleep. He drank a beer and continued teaching himself basic notes.

"Holaaaa Aguss!! Ey! From New... New Yerzy!"

"No, de uhh... de Nuevo York," I corrected him. New Jersey? No way.

"Ahhh! Si! New YORK! I remember!"

Agus and Pablo chatted in Spanish after my short-lived interaction with Pablo. I understood nothing. Then more friends came over his miniature apartment. I had no idea where to stand or sit. Nobody spoke a word of English. My face read uncomfortable, and I suppose Agus could see that cause after not too long, she said:

"Okay, we going, okay?" as if to make sure I was still hanging in there. What's she think? I can't fuckin take it? I can take it. I just look uncomfortable cause I got nothing to say. Nothing wrong with staying quiet till there's something to actually talk about, right? I didn't see the problem. But she shuffled me out and as night fell, she asked me: "You liking casino? Hay un casino on... ehm... Bota? Boat?"

"Yeah! Let's go to the casino!" Finally a sentence I understood.

So we went to the casino. She parked her car next to some big boat and a man shouted at her in Spanish when we exited her car. She took out some pesos and handed it to him. Then came back over to me and grabbed my hand and pulled me to the boat.

"You having to geev the money. They watching auto so no... bang bang. But if no give then he bang bang."

"Oh. Okay." I think I understood, but who knows?

So we entered this casino and I played the maximum bet on every slot machine. Our horrible communication went for many hours till we left to come back to her car, only to find it in shambles. All the windows were smashed, and everything was gone. She flipped her lid in Spanish and we drove back to her apartment. Fuck. Now I gotta initiate sex after all this? Oh man. I was seriously nervous. Maybe I should go home? And when what I had hoped not to happen *did* in fact happen, I didn't just leave, though the conversation the next morning was severely awkward:

"Las nigh, I like. Is fun. But frens. Is okay?"

"Yeah, that's okay."

Cause truth be told, I wasn't really into her, especially not after I learned about her politics and crazy viewpoints on life. But still to this day, fifteen years later, we chat all the time. Whatever, point of this story is I ended up staying for three weeks before I finally told Agus I had to leave, which I don't think she was too upset about. I had spent a good chunk of change and had to do another trip to Colorado. At this rate, the eighty grand will never be raised.

"The… the… geeft. You need stop. Remember. In the movie. He always say he stopping."

She was talkin about *Blow,* you know, the movie with Johnny Depp? She *hated* how much weed I sold and was sure I would one day get caught. I assured her that would never happen, and actually, I was right, but that doesn't mean I was in the clear.

In fact, it was time to ratchet up the ante and go all in…

CHAPTER 24: THE WOLF GUARDED THE POT

I took a Xanax in the cab so I could weather the anxiety and not set off security with my nervous system. Beads of sweat soaked the interior of my soul as I stared at my ticket to make sure it hadn't been lightly stamped with: *SSSS*.

A ticket marked *SSSS* meant I was a security risk, or something of the sort, and it meant I would be taken to a corner and searched thoroughly. Sometimes when you buy a one-way ticket on short notice or your roundtrip only lasts for a day or so, they stick you with an *SSSS*. They probably stick it to you for other reasons too, but those other reasons weren't of my concern. I figured that out—the *SSSS* thing—cause one time I had it on my ticket, and I had no idea what it meant, and by the time I asked somebody what the deal was I was taken off and questioned and searched... Which was okay cause I only had nine grand on me, the legal amount you can have in cash.

"Sir what is this?"

"My money."

"What is it for?"

"Art."

"Art?"

"I'm buying art... The guy needs cash."

"And do you always keep your money on your... person like that? In that... area?"

"When it's that much cash, sure. Always."

"Always?"

"Is there a problem? Am I not allowed to buy pricey art with cash I'm careful with?"

So that was my line... I was buying art. I was a goddam art dealer, okay? Fuck off. My last-minute roundtrip ticket that would land me back in NYC the day after tomorrow had *nothing* to do with drugs you imbecile, it's a GODDAM ART TRANSACTION! I just couldn't *stand* authority. So I lashed out and actually reached for his gun—which was a bad move maybe, but he stopped me and threw me to the ground and so I headbutt him in the nose and I heard it crack and blood spilled on my face and I couldn't breathe cause the blood was getting in my nostrils and mouth and—

"Huh?"

"That line please."

"Line of what?"

"The security line sir, please step to the security line right there."

Sorry, I got lost in my head there for a bit, but yeah, that was a few weeks ago and that's how I learned about the *SSSS*. I got lucky cause it was only 9k, but today was a bigger order. Twenty pounds. My biggest order yet. I had to stop selling weed as fast as possible, and the only way to do that was to sell more, quicker, so I could stop.

The money was rolled up in two fat, clunky rolls, wedged inside my boxer briefs, one to each side of my dick to act as overgrown balls. Every step jarred them a bit loose. There was a lot of prison time dangling from the transaction I was about to make, and I knew it. I searched the ticket fiercely in the cab, and found nothing. There was no *SSSS*. I was safe. I was now at the security checkpoint. Game time. But the money was irritating my crouch and I had to itch it without fumbling the money down my pants leg. I couldn't keep that itch; it had to be scratched.

So I scratched lightly, carefully, and—

Fuck.

The money shifted outa place a bit. I could feel it. Oh no. If it fell down one of my jean legs I'd go to prison for ten years… Would

I? FUCK. I'm fucked. Ten years? I think that's right. The Xanax was taken hold. I was numb. I could do this. I wasn't sweating. My heartbeat was smooth. I was gonna do this. This was gonna work. My backpack went through the x-ray. Step one, done.

"Sir, please step down."

Oh god. Oh god. Oh god.

The money is comin loose. Am I walkin weird? ARE THEY ONTO ME?! And then...

I MADE IT!

YYYYYYEEEEESSSSSSSS.

I rushed to the bathroom to take the cash from out my balls and put it into my backpack and ran to my gate. My flight was taking off literally ten minutes ago. But when I got to the gate, my name was being paged over the loudspeaker. Oh no. They know. They're onto me. I'm fucked. So I go to the gate attendant and he says:

"You've been bumped up to first class."

Lol, WHAT?!

I just unstuck seventy grand from my balls and they wanna move me to first class?! This is weird. This never happens—not the money on my balls, that always happens—the first class thing. *That* never happens. I've never been lucky in my life. Well wait, I just made it past security. I guess that's lucky. But I never won prizes at county fairs. I'm actually really unlucky. What if the package gets lost, or the FBI finds it? FBI? Do I mean DEA? Whatever, what if they find it, whoever they are? Just enjoy the goddam first-class ticket to Denver.

So I was sitting in first class next to this first-class type of woman, and she was telling me about her oh so silly problems as she drank red wine and I drank scotch. I told her all sortsa bullshit.

"So what do you do?" she asked all drunk and flirty and forty-something. I just sipped my scotch and said:

"I produce theatre. I'm a theatre producer."

Which is true. Right? I wasn't lying. Was I? No, of course not.

Whatever, this woman isn't important. So we land in Denver. I transfer to another plane to take me to a small town that only a small plane can get me to on the border of New Mexico and Colorado—I'll keep the town secret, after all... this is illegal. But there's no way for anyone to prove this is true. It isn't. Is it? Of course it is. Maybe...

I greet my grower outside the one-gate airport. He was in his truck with his wolf in the backseat. That was the first time I met her. He tells me through the window before I get into his truck:

"She might growl a bit."

"All good, I love dogs."

"She's a wolf."

"No problem."

But it was a HUGE problem. I opened the front door and:

CHOMP!

My face almost came off.

"BAD GIRL!" he shouted at her, like that worked. This was no domesticated animal. This was a fuckin wolf. I nearly pissed myself. The whole bottom half of my body was unable to clench and keep anything in. I felt paralyzed. My breath was erratic and my heart was thumping. It slowed down by the time we got to the edge of town. There was snow on the tops of all the mountains, but the weather was sunny and breezy.

We didn't talk business at all. In fact, we went to his garden and picked some mushrooms and chives and other vegetables to begin a three-hour cook session. The fireplace was lit and crackling with sound of comfort while the best pot in the country sat on the living room table in front of the TV, which played weird cooking shows. I was bored as fuck watching that shit, but we watched it all night long. We ate a three-course meal, fed the fireplace more wood, and inhaled the finest marijuana on planet Earth while slowly dozing off.

I woke up the next morning alone on the couch with Bianca right next to me. Bianca, the wolf. She examined my face but didn't remember who I was. I looked at her. She looked at me. I slowly took a Xanax outa my bag and put it in my mouth and had to pee for like two hours but thought even the slightest of movements may set her off. So, I held still and held my pee till my grower woke up. Then my grower came out of his room in full snowboard gear.

"Let's hit the slopes!"

"Man, I barely remember how to ski."

We got to the ski mountain and took seven million chairlifts up then took some shuttle that only *real* snowboarders contemplate, and were towed even higher, to the part of the mountain that's covered with signs that say:

DANGER, NO HELP IF YOU GET FUCKED.

We were no longer in *ski territory*. We were completely off the grid. I was horrified.

"I'll see ya down there," he tells me, and leaps off into the wooded mountain area, swerving in and out of trees like an Olympic athlete. I went two feet and nearly crashed into a pine tree. Then my ski fell off six feet up the mountain. I tried to get it back on, but my foot sank into the snow up to my waist. I stayed stuck for many minutes before I was finally able to climb myself out.

No one was around. I stared at the way down. I couldn't even remember which way the bottom of the mountain was. I mean, every way was the bottom, but if I ended up where the chairlift wasn't, if I ended up where my grower couldn't find me, where no one could find me, I'd be dead. There was no service on my phone and it was fucking freezing.

A couple other lunatic snowboarders skated past me and I shouted for dear life:

"WHICH WAY IS THE BOTTOM!?"

"Are you lost?"

"WHAT?!"

I couldn't hear them. Then they were gone. So I slid my way down the mountain on my ass, two feet at time, nearly bombarding into a pine tree on every slide. It took me like two hours. I ended up, miraculously, in the right place and my grower was waiting for me like he'd already done ten trillion runs. I told him I was done for the day and we headed back to his house.

Again, Bianca didn't remember me. She growled like I was a total stranger. She growled louder.

"BAD GIRL!" my grower said. "Not sure why she's acting like that."

Ummm cause she's a fucking wolf dude, but I didn't say that. Then came the one and only hour we discussed business.

"Want to take a look at what I've been working on?"

It was like I was scared to ask about weed, even though I had just taken two planes to get there for that exact purpose. I was always so scared about people not liking me. I wasn't sure if I should bring it up or wait for him to steer that boat. But do I want to see what you've been working on? Fuck yeah I do. Why the hell you think I'm here?

So, he led me down the stairs to a room fully dressed in plastic with a billion-dollar ventilation system and complex lighting arrangements and all sorts of hydroponic shit that I knew nothing about. I stared at about hundreds of artisanal plants illuminated in some basement that felt like it was on the edge of the world.

"Northern Lights over here, Silver Haze over there, and Sweet Island over there."

"Right on."

We put on gloves, grabbed some cardboard boxes, the vacuum sealer, and began precisely and methodically packaging up twenty pounds. Each pound was so fluffy it was the size of three pillowcases, so it took five enormous boxes to get it all together.

He drove me a few towns over to the local shipping center and waited in the truck. The shipping center was a mom-and-pop joint; small and probably profitless. The front counter was two feet from the front door. It was a tight space. Very uncomfortable. The woman behind the counter looked at me curiously, like *why in the fuck are you here?* I couldn't explain my presence in a town of ten, or why I had five large boxes which took three trips to get inside, or why I had to overnight everything from a somewhat undisclosed location in the Rocky Mountains in a tiny offshoot of a town which I'd never even visited before. So, I just acted like I was in a rush.

"Delivery?" she asked me.

"Yes please. Overnight if possible. To this address. Thanks." I handed her a paper with my address on it.

"New York?"

"Yes ma'am."

"Contents?"

This was the hard part…

"Art."

"All the boxes?"

"Yes."

"Value of content?"

"Like how much does it cost?" I always played dumb.

"Yes sir, don't want to buy the wrong insurance. Better safe!"

"Right. Well, I mean, art is priceless, ya know? So I don't know, a trillion dollars."

She laughed. I gulped. There's no scent at all. I'm in the clear.

"We'll just put a hundred dollars. Okay, do you want noon, 10AM, or an 8AM delivery?"

The less time it's in the air, the less time they have to catch me, right?

"8AM please." I land at 7AM New York time, so I should be back by 8AM. But what if I'm not? "Wait. 9AM," I say at the last moment.

"There is no 9AM sir. 8AM, 10AM, and noon."

"Oh, right. Okay, 8AM is fine."

"Okay, you're all set. Should be there by tomorrow at 8AM."

"Great." Fuck I hope the flight isn't delayed.

Then we headed straight to the airport. I left him the seventy grand—all my money—and boarded a small plane to get to the bigger plane in Denver to get back to New York at 7AM the next day, precisely one hour before the packages were scheduled to arrive at my front door.

As soon as I landed at JFK I sent a mass text out to my list that said:

New Line, Full Of Exotic Arrangements. 8AM to 10PM. With love.

It went out to many people, some of whom you've met. Lawyers, celebrities, real estate moguls, talent agency execs, artists, and high-profile photographers. Within fifteen minutes I received appointment requests. 8:30AM in the East Village, 4PM in the Lower East Side, 5PM Upperwest Side, 6:30PM Harlem, 9PM Jersey City, 10PM Williamsburg... and so on. All of it sold—well, most of it. I had a few wholesalers by now I could offload most of it to, but I still had to get home and sign for the packages. But what if the packages never get there? What if the DEA comes with the delivery? I took some more Xanax then jumped in a cab and scurried back to my apartment. I arrived at like 7:55AM.

Before I even had time to take a shit: DING DONG. I trembled to my buzzer. Through my speaker I say, "Yeah?"

"Delivery," the voice on the other end says.

I'm shaky as hell. This is the last package, I thought to myself. The last one. Then I'm done.

"One sec," I told him.

I headed down like James Bond to make sure it was just a delivery man and no feds.

Phew. I'm in the clear.

I signed for the packages and hauled two at a time upstairs. There was about one inch of space on each side of the boxes to the hallway wall as I fumbled up the stairs. I couldn't see in front of me so I felt for each step carefully with my foot. Don't wanna fall down the stairs and die on my last package, I thought. I put the boxes in the apartment and scrambled back down to get the others.

I had to be real quick about unsealing and re-packaging the pot in their respective jars and bags. Even twenty seconds of exposure would make the entire building reek. I moved like a fox, and then... it was go time.

It was a fast run, and I had to up my clientele to rid the inventory, so I asked my list for referrals, and it was around that time that I met Mike Z... the man that changed my life.

CHAPTER 25: SIX MONTHS OF MIKE Z

BzZz

I woke up and reached for my phone, which was dead smack in the center of my hardwood floor. It was just far enough out of reach from where I'd fallen asleep in a drunken slumber and not moved a muscle since so that grabbing it was nearly an impossible task. I stared at the screen, which read 9AM, and at the caller ID: *Tech Zach (Survivor) (Train)*

I cleared my throat to make sure he knew I was up, hard at work already.

"Tech Zach," I shouted into the phone to keep my voice clear and distinct.

"Yo. What's up... *man!?*"

I could tell he already forgot my name.

"What brings you to my Blackberry?" I asked.

"You sound tired, I wake you up?"

I spoke louder to clear out any crackle. "Me? No man. I'm always up. Whattaya got?"

"Sounds like you're screaming! Pull that receiver back! Just kiddin ya. Gonna give your info to Mike Z. The guy is a character, but a good guy. He's got tons of stories like you. I bet you'll get along. He'll order a lot."

I hated when people said the word "order" or any words in the slightest bit similar to that on the phone. Why use words that could incriminate me? Just say some shit like "he's always hungry and eats big meals" or whatever. But it was Tech Zach, so I tried to be patient. Besides, the government isn't paying attention to me.

Are they?

Anyway, the guy sent me a message, I sent him my address, and prepared my apartment to make it look like I was more than a drug-dealer. You know, a couple dense books about producing theatre on the dresser, screenplay on desk, coffee and a bagel to my right, bed made, all that shit.

bZZzzzz.

I buzzed door number one and waited for the twelve seconds it generally took people to get to door number two and—

Zzzz…

Shit. This guy is a fast walker, I thought. I buzzed the second door and quickly positioned myself as if I didn't even remember he was coming over, at my desk, fake writing. The sound of his footsteps in the hallway walking up the four-flight staircase sounded like he was wearing metal boots. His knock was as clunky as his footsteps—loud for no reason.

I got up slowly, brushed my valor sweat suit to smooth the wrinkles out, and opened the door.

In came a bald man in his early forties with a leather jacket and a motorcycle helmet.

"Just sold EVERY SINGLE BRITNEY SPEARS TICKET. EVERY FUCKING ONE. DO YOU KNOW WHAT THE FUCK THAT MEANS? 700 GRAND. OFF ONE FUCKING DEAL."

The guy talked a mile a minute. I wasn't ready for it. "That's a ton of money," I said. I wasn't sure if he was lying or some big shot. Coulda been either or. I took out my weed, all three jars, and prepped my station. "So you produced a Britney Spears show?"

"Dude. Listen to this. I was meeting with Randy Phillips— you know Randy Phillips? CEO of AEG?— anyway, big fucking deal, dude's huge… runs Madison Square Garden and every other major venue you know, anyway—holy shit. Stuff stinks. STINKS. Whatever you give me, package it good. MUCH better than it is now. What was I saying?"

"Uhh… Britney Spears."

"Right. Every fucking ticket." He put his motorcycle helmet down.

"Always wanted a bike," I told him.

"Yeah? Give you a ride right now, want one?"

This guy wants me to get on the back of his bike? No way. "Nah man, thanks though. I'm good."

"You sure?"

"I'm good."

"Any time, just let me know. Gotta experience the world we live in. Who knows how long we got, right?"

"Right. No, yeah, you're right."

Then he looked around my apartment as I waited for him to signal to me he was ready to discuss the different strains I had.

"So, how you doing my man? Zach tells me big things about you. BIG things."

"Yeah Zach's a good guy. I met him about—"

"Whattaya doin? Writing a book or something?"

I was so glad he asked. "Better, screenplay. Writing a screenplay about this girl I used to date, a chick I knew from rehab who said she witnessed a murder and—"

But he cut me off again and said: "What's *that?*" and looked at the ginormous posterboard I had on display that read: *The Wonderland One-Act Play Festival.* It was like eight feet tall, another thing crowding my miniscule living space.

"That? It's a play festival I produced."

"Oh yeah? Wonder World huh?"

"Wonderland."

"And it's what? A play thing?"

"Yeah, we produced fifty-five—well, actually fifty-six—"

"When is it? I'll bring my partner Alan. HUGE in the industry. HUGE."

"It's done, over, it was fuckin awesome."

"Yeah? Make any money on it?"

He had a sly grin. So, I lied.

"A shit ton. We made 40K in profit in three weeks."

"Wow, not bad."

"Want in? Got some other ideas brewing."

I was just trying to be a good businessman, know what I mean? Can't show your whole deck, right? I think that's right. Besides, if he knew the whole story he wouldn't be interested. So I lied about the entire enterprise.

"Ever heard of William Morris?" he asked me.

"Of course. I was repped by them when I was an act—"

"Fuck repped. I got the head honcho as my partner."

Ever since I had been kicked outa acting school, I'd become resentful at acting, resentful at the entire acting industry too, including fucking William Morris. But maybe that chapter of life wasn't over yet...

"The owner of the company?" I asked.

"Fuck the owner. I got the head of legal."

Head of *legal*? I was thinking that sounded a bit... well, not like the head honcho. "So he's a lawyer?"

"Maybe I'll bring this wonder world thing up with him. Huge name. Head honcho of William Morris for two fucking decades, MORE even, he did the legal, all of it. Hired like fifty fucking guys."

"No, it's not wonder world. That sounds like some Disney World rip-off. It's Wonderland. But it's over. I got this *other idea though...*"

"Either way, you should meet him. Big fucking deal. Major."

"Totally, bring him over." Then there was silence. Better just sell the lunatic some weed and get him out. "So whattaya want?" I asked, not willing to inject any more personal relations into the visit.

"Oh just an eighth of some good shit, whatever, I don't care."

An eighth? Are you fucking kidding? I didn't say that obviously, but still… this guy is a big shot? A guy buying an eighth like we're in middle school?

"I can do an eighth today but usually if you can get at least a half-ounce that'd be preferable."

"How much is it?"

"An eighth? Depends. This one is sixty, this one is—"

"Sixty? Expensive! I'm in the wrong business! Sure, give me that, what's it called?"

"This is Sweet Island Skunk and this one—"

"Fucking names. You believe this shit? Unbelievable. Who comes up with these names? Give me the skank."

"The skunk?"

"Whatever. But pack it up good, real tight. Don't wanna stink up my next meeting. Know who I'm about to meet with?"

NO AND I DON'T GIVE A GODDAM MOTHERFUCKING SHIT YOU NAME-DROPPING DIPSHIT!

"No, who are you meeting?" I asked patiently.

"David…." And he said some famous person's name. But I didn't really care. I just wanted his money and to get back to writing this movie. I was now on my third draft of the Robyn Smith story that I was determined to solve. But the point of all this is to say that a few weeks later, I was eating sushi alone, on my second large sake, when I got a text from that douchebag:

U avail for biz call in 10?

YES!

I waited by my phone for two hours. Finally, my Blackberry buzzed.

"Hello?"

"I want you to come up with a name for a company and meet me at 7AM in Brooklyn tomorrow to meet your first client. I talked to my partner about it. Talked you up big time, BIG time… You owe me. But congratulations man, you can stop slangin weed like a freshman in college. Well, I'll still need some, but you can do it part time now, cause my man, you're officially the CEO of your own music booking agency.

"Music booking agency? Whattaya talkin about? I don't know how to do that shit."

"You'll learn. I've got faith. Don't let me down. Talked you up REAL big to Alan. Head of fucking William Morris. I'll text you the address right now. 7AM, don't be late. And don't wear that ugly valor suit, no offense. It's disgusting. DISGUSTING. This group is big, BIG. Rockstars almost. See ya then."

I was horrified. Music? I been listening to the same Eminem song for ten years. I don't know dick about music. But that's how Black Apple came to be, and that was my ticket to freedom. And in a strange way, it finally got me there…

CHAPTER 26: THE BERGERWITZ'S

Are you fucking kidding me? These guys are rockstars? Living in the projects? The fuck is going on? I walked to the address I scribbled down, all the while wondering why in the hell my first client lived in such a wretched neighborhood.

I got to their apartment and looked both ways to make sure I didn't get shot. I climbed up their rackety stairs and got to a splintery door full of poverty. I gave a knock, careful not to scrape up my knuckles, and was greeted by the dorkiest version of a man I'd ever seen. He looked like a nerdier version of the guy from *Honey I Shrunk the Kids*. His eyeglasses were thick-rimmed and looked like two magnifying glasses glued together—eyeballs zoomed-in by like 500%. His dorky nose kept scrunched so his hundred-pound glasses didn't crater to the ground and cause an earthquake on impact. To top it off, the guy said everything four times and was perpetually in a state of severe neurosis.

"Oh my my my my, this is exciting, please come in! Come come come, please, here, here take a look," and I walked into their kitchen from outside, listening to this blabbering madman ramble adverbs and conjunctions four times in row. "Here's what we're thinking...okay, okay, okay, okay... so, um, okay..." and he rolls out a map on the kitchen table without introducing himself.

"Here's where we'd like to start. Berlin loves us, and and and and, and Hamburg, they too, such a great city, they too, really, and oh!—"

"And Munich," a small girl off to the side says. She was about twelve and holding a ukulele.

"Right right right right, Munich, *all* of Germany really. And we can't skip the UK, so I was thinking we fly into Dublin and and and and, and we work our way through The Netherlands."

"We're *not* playing Moscow," his angry wife, a woman with red hair in a ten-inch bun declared from the stove. She was cooking terrible smelling something. I hope I don't have to eat that trash. I could see tofu and other vegan bullshit I didn't want anything to do with.

"Well, right, if we can avoid—well, Russia in general, that'd be—but Poland is good and... Oh! There was that one venue in Romania, honey where were we? In Romania—"

"It was in Vienna."

"Ah right, Austria. That's what I meant. There's a venue in Austria, in Vienna, and it's—well, wait. Was it Budapest?"

"It was Vienna," the small girl with the ukulele says.

"Well, there's a venue, I'll find out the name, and we must go there. Mike Z insists."

"Where is Mike Z?" I ask, wondering where the fuck who demanded I be on time was...

"He's late. He's always late," the wife says.

"So... is he your manager?" I inquire.

"Just recently, we're giving him a test run," she angrily says—the wife.

Test run? I was thinking these people are lucky to afford breakfast, and they're picky about their manager? Is this a joke? Where the fuck am I?

"Please, sit, sit, sit down, sit. Here," and he swipes a non-matching chair from the corner and chucks it up to the kitchen table, where all the other non-matching chairs are, so I can get a better look at his insane map with lines all over dictating where he'd like to go on tour. I didn't want to seem like I hadn't done my research, but I hadn't cause I had no idea who I was to meet, though I wasn't sure if I should say that. So, I tried to ask unoffensive queries:

"So, you all play together?"

A look of silence.

"We're the Bergerwitz's!"

I nearly cracked up. Who? What? Who the fuck are you? Just then, Mike Z walked in.

"Sorry got caught up talking with the Beastie Boy's ex-agent. Huge in the biz, HUGE. What's for breakfast, vegan enchiladas?"

"Tamales and bacon with fresh gluten-free pancakes and syrup," the wife says.

"Mmm! Yum mom!" their daughter remarked.

"Bacon! NICE!" Mike Z says, without even looking at me.

"Vegan bacon," the dad says, "we're not *that* different than we were ten years ago."

"What I'd tell you guys, whole new look. Totally new. New everything. Conan won't recognize you."

"Did he tell you that that that that we were kicked off Conan O'Brien?"

"Ahhh, no, I didn't know that. For what?" I ask.

"Long story," he says to me, cracking up, as if it's some inside joke that's not funny even from the inside.

"Aright, c'mon guys, what're we doin here? We makin moves or are we chattin about Conan O'fuckin, whoever he is," Mike Z jolts in.

"Right right right right, okay, but—"

"What's this," Mike Z interrupted. "Who did this, you? Greg, my man! Already at work, nice going. See that guys? What'd I tell you? I said I'd get you the best agent in New York, and here he is. Fuck union agents. We got the hustler of all hustlers. Tell them."

I tried to play along. "Yeah, I mean, I *am* a hustler, I suppose."

"Suppose? You're THE hustler. So what's cookin, what's this map?"

"Right right right right, well, it's it's it's…"

"It's what we think is best for the group," the wife says.

Mike Z looks at the map with lines scribbled all over Europe. "Great, looks like a great tour." Then he looks at me. "You good with this?"

Good with what? I was thinkin. With this? This tour? Can I set this tour up? I'm a goddam drug-dealer theatre producer, I have no idea how to do this shit. I didn't say any of that though, I just said: "100%. I'll get started on it first thing tomorrow."

"Great, let's eat. Oh no, guys, you're gonna hate me, HATE. I have to go. Big meetings today, BIG, good for all of us, trust me. Hey, great meeting guys," and he left me eating that shitty vegan breakfast alone with the Bergerwitz's.

"So so so so, yeah, umm, so you can put this together? We'd like to start touring next month cause well, well, well... The bills have to get paid HAHA!" and he let out this weird little laugh that sounded like a cat trapped in hell.

"No problem. I'll take care of it. Can I keep this?" referring to the map.

"Yeah yeah yeah yeah, we've got we've got we've got more. Another we've got."

So I rolled up the map and finished the gross breakfast, which wasn't that awful actually, and walked off towards the subway not knowing how in the *fuck* this would all get done. All I knew was this: If I *could* do this, my entire life would change. So, I woke up at 5AM the next morning ready to tackle the shit out've it.

The first thing I did was Google: *how to put a band on tour.*

Within three weeks, after navigating through German and Dutch and French websites, I learned what the "contact us" page looked like in a million different languages of a million different venues and sent everyone an email telling them the good news:

THE BERGERWITZ'S WANT TO PLAY YOUR CLUB!

And you know what? *Everyone* knew who they were. Within a few weeks, I had a hundred-thousand-dollar international tour booked for this crazy band of bizarre family members. I guess they were more famous than I thought... But the only thing was I didn't know what the fuck I was doing, so I had them in Berlin one day and then said yes to London the next day and then said cool to Prague the day after that and the itinerary became physically impossible. Then I had to go back to all the damn venue bookers and try to rearrange the dates the best I could to make it feasible.

But point is, it got done. They told all their "anti-folk" (that's the name of their genre) friends about the tour I booked for them and within a month, I had a roster of twenty bands all asking for my help. So, that's how the Black Apple music agency was built.

That when shit *really* got hectic…

CHAPTER 27: SPINNIN TOO MANY PLATES

SCRAMBLED GREGS

Mike Z's tenure as my boss was short-lived, the fuckin prick, but without him Black Apple never woulda existed and I'd still be stuck in a wave pool of shitty theatre production. But the guy was an outdated douchebag, and now that I had so many people who needed me, I didn't need that old fuck anymore. Still I gave him *one more chance*, even after he called me that one time and berated me about the Bergerwitz's tour—which they never even paid me for—while Gay Jason was over.

"One sec Jason, I just gotta get this real quick." I answered the call. "Hey man, can I call you back in just—"

"Greg. Dude. Quick question. How the FUCK are they supposed to play Ireland on the 18th, Rome on the 19th, and Oslo on the 20th? How are they supposed to get all their gear in a van and drive that far? Didn't think of that?"

"Drive? I thought they'd be flying?"

"Flying?! Haven't you done your research? Don't you know how many musical fucking instruments they play? GET IT RIGHT!" And he hung up. Like I said, he really had a problem. But I truly saw him for the total dipshit he was on the night he called me and said: "Meet me at Pianos."

Pianos was this music venue and bar. I went downtown and he Blackberry-messaged me that he was upstairs. I went upstairs and saw him in his leather jacket. I couldn't help to notice how old he was. He was for sure older than everyone else there. He was so old. Probably in his late forties even. I don't want to be like him when I'm forty, I thought.

"You like her?" he said to me without saying anything else, or even looking at me.

I looked at the singer-songwriter who was strumming her sad music on stage as he handed me a bag of coke, which was horrible, terrible coke.

"I mean, yeah," I tell him. "She's pretty good, right?" I had no idea what good sounded like. I had no ear for music. I was hoping he thought she was good cause I wasn't sure of the answer he was looking for, and I had to make sure he thought I knew my business, which was music… I think.

"She's a lesbian," he tells me.

"Well, that's always good, right?" Not sure what I meant by that.

"You think she's good?"

I really wasn't sure. "Yeah, she's good," I said with uncertainty.

"Go and sign her."

"What do you mean?"

"What're you retarded? Tell her you want to represent her."

He always used the word retarded. I wasn't sure about that word. It's not a good word, but enough people say it casually so that I don't wanna push back on it. Not like the *n* word, which Sahar *always* used. I really hated when he used that word. I rarely said anything when he used it cause he was always with these other middle eastern dudes who also used it. Then one day he asked me:

"Does that nigger still work for your parents?"

He was talking about my nanny. My black mom. The woman who raised me. I lost it. I wanted to set his curly Jew hair on fire and run him over with a semi. What a piece of dog shit. Without even realizing what I was doing, I tightened my fist and felt my heart burning hot. I slammed my knuckles into his Israeli nose and heard a crunch as he teetered backwards. Pussy. We were in his friend's apartment and he lived on the forty-fifth floor. It was a tall building. So when he backed his way onto the porch and looked like he may fall off the ledge, it made me happy. A person like this must die. All it took was a little push and..

I snapped out of it.

"Don't fucking call her that man, that shit pisses me off. You know her name. Why you always saying that word anyway? It's fucking embarrassing. It pisses me the fuck off."

"Yeh, I forgot her name. She still work for your parents?" he asked as if he missed my entire point. Then he started talking about other shit like the fuck that he was, though I think that was the last time he used that word in front of me, but definitely not the last time he used it. What a piece of garbage.

Anyway, I looked at the lesbian on stage. That's not bad to say, right? Lesbian? That's an okay word. Not like retarded. I hate all these words. I used so many of those words back in rehab, but that was when I was like fifteen. These people are *still* using them. What losers.

Point is, I walked up to the girl on stage, who had a Justin Bieber haircut and a pretty face—very country-looking, androgenous, pretty but boyish. I was attracted to her for some reason. Her eyes were blue and her freckles looked painted peach. Her skin appeared photoshopped and her outfit was a flannel shirt and jeans. Her smile was so inviting that it was easy to approach her in between songs:

"Hey, good shit. Question. Do you have an agent?"

Her eyes LIT UP as she looked over at Mike Z.

"No, why is that an agent?"

What the fuck? "Nah, me. I'm the agent." Then I got a bit aggravated. Does she not think I can do the fucking job? I CAN DO THE JOB YOU CUNT! Whoa. Calm down Greg, nobody even said anything. But then I felt the need to flex, as I always did.

I had to make sure everyone who ever talked to me knew about every accomplishment I ever accomplished.

"I can get you shows all over. I just booked a 100K tour all over Europe for my other client."

If only KC knew what a big deal I was already becoming—and Maggie, my old agent, she'll see I'm becoming a bigger agent than she could *ever* be. I was determined to out-agent her. I don't know why I'm so competitive.

Anyhow, Mike Z left and took his shitty bag of coke while I stayed at the bar all night long talking to the lesbian songwriter. That's when I made my biggest offer yet:

"How about I become your manager and we start a movement of lesbian fangirls that all wanna lick your face…"

"I love it. I'm in. You're my manager."

And that's how I signed my first management client, one more revenue stream to add to my already crowded arsenal of entrepreneurial activities, all of which were basically losing me money, except for the weed business. Good thing I had to let one go…

That's why I decided to bury the booking agency; too much of a hassle. Everybody went on the tours I booked for them, but nobody could afford to pay me my commission when they got back cause they had spent all their money. The Bergerwitz's never paid me a dime…

So I went to their house in Brooklyn and smashed their front door in and grabbed a pan with vegan bacon that was frying on their stove and threw it at the cunty mom. I didn't mean to hit her in the throat or smash her nose so it bent in a way where she couldn't breathe, but since I wasn't about to go to jail for these imbeciles, I just jumped off their fire escape and stole her wedding ring—

"Same thing?"

"What?"

It was the bartender. I was at some bar. I don't know which one.

"Dewers?"

"Oh right, yeah, please."

On stage was a guy strumming a cello. I remembered I was there cause Mike Z told me to check him out too. It was the last night I ever talked to that prick. He'd tell me to meet him somewhere downtown, then he'd message me saying he got held up and couldn't make it but I should sign whoever I was scouting if they were good. I just started leaving him outa the equation. He was trying to make me like his assistant even though I was doing all the work. Well, that shit just won't fly man. No, I am *not* your assistant you piece of shit.

So I sent him that message—drunk, as usual, which was more frequent every month that passed, and that was that. He never even hit me up to buy weed again. Fucking loser. But anyway, I still went out and tried to find great bands who could draw a crowd because it became clear the only way to make money in this business was to find local musicians who already had an audience, and then pair them up nicely with other local musicians who had an audience and go to the venue to collect the fucking money myself. So I had to go out every night and scout around town in search of quality talent. I had to make a name for myself without being Mike Z's little bitch. What a fucking tool that dickwad is…

making me do all the work then bragging about Britney Spears or whatever. Bet that shit didn't even happen. 750k in one night? Yeah right. Where's that money now when you ask me to cover the bar tab you cheap fuck?

Point is, all I had to do was figure out how much a band was worth, which would determine how much I could afford to profitably pay them. If they *said* they could draw 300 people, it was always half that. I learned that after a few shows. So, if they said *300*, I had to figure out how much I could afford to pay an act that could draw *150*—well, how much *we* could afford to spend, cause eventually I hired help. So, we came up with a way to assign a score to every act we stumbled upon. We created an algorithm that would measure, based on their MySpace, Twitter, Facebook, Soundcloud, all that shit—Bandcamp even, all those sites, we made an algorithm that would assign each act a score between one and a hundred to let us know how much money they were actually worth, and how much we could make with them on say... a fifteen-dollar ticket in a 500-person venue. What I'm tryin to say to you here is shit got mad sophisticated and eventually, we got it.

In fact, what follows became the best money laundering scheme I ever came up with. First thing I did was convert the music agency into a music promotions company. Now, instead of *me* reaching out to the promoter to book a show, *I* would be the promoter that the agents would be reaching out to. If a big band was about to go on tour, I wanted to be the New York promoter all the agents wanted to link up with. I wanted people calling *me*.

There were a few BIG competitors I had to take down. I just needed to build a bigger name than them ASAP. So how do I do that? Well, with a great idea, of course. And with money. So I had to make more money to fund this strategy of becoming the most famous music promoter in NYC.

I just had to dip into my savings account—which was at eighty grand, give or take by then, and I had to make *big offers* to *real agents* and let these other promoters in town know that I had the hookup. That's how I met Jerrod. He was a big music agent in Los Angeles, and eventually, he became the reason I got sober, because he was part of the reason my life deteriorated so fast after I moved to LA. I'll tell ya about all that later. Point is, he and I started negotiations for a buncha shows that would put me on the map. But then what? Once the shows were on the books I needed more. I had to do something unique. Big bands, famous sketch troupes, that's all fine and dandy, but that shit is regular; basic. I need some way to brand myself as different, as the creative genius I was certain I was. My idea was to combine five genres into one and build a melting pot of live entertainment *only Black Apple* could conceive.

That's when I came up with the idea for *JACKPOT!*

CHAPTER 28: JACKPOT!

It was August of 2009. I was twenty-four years old. It was time to do this goddam right. Seriously, no more fuckin around. But I couldn't shake the doubt that perhaps I'm not as good at this as I thought I was from scurrying around in the back of my thoughts.

Truth is, I'd lost money on everything I'd done since Wonderland—and even at that I only made $400 after spending like forty grand. In my head I thought I was building an empire... Am I a phony? Should I stick to acting? No, not after what Sahar said to me that one day in my apartment...

"Personally, I think you're more of a producer than an acta..." and he said it like *dude, stop trying to convince the world you're an actor. You're maybe a good businessman, maybe... but that's it.*

I don't know, I just needed something to work. I was great at selling weed. Why is that all I can be successful at? Maybe I *should* listen to my mom.

"Have ya ever thought about... going back to high school?"

Again, she had this suggestion one day on the phone... it was seriously absurd. "High school? Mom. I'm goddam twenty-four. I missed the boat on that. You want me to be ten years older than the whole school?"

"It's never too late."

See, that's where you're wrong mom. You're right about a lot of things, but seriously wrong about others. Of course, I never said any of this. But I thought it. High school? What is this, goddam Billy Madison? Shoulda thought about your desire to have me finish high school when I was stuck at Hidden Lake. See, now that woulda been the opportune time. Then. When I was a fuckin kid. Now I gotta make money as an adult and look how disabled you've left me. Now I gotta do everything on my own, and it ain't goddam easy mom. Shit is hard.

Anyway, I had to make something work. I learned one thing: numbers work. Play the numbers game. And if I never give up, it's impossible to fail. I'm just one festival away from utter success; from my life altering in a way that only materialized in movies. If I just reach out to enough people, I'll get what I need. I just gotta play the numbers game. It's all about numbers. Just like girls are all about customer service. That's how to get laid. You provide great customer service.

"Bitches are all about customer service," I told Sahar on that same day he told me I was a better producer than actor. See, he started asking me how I got hot chicks—how I got laid so often. And though I was starting out with a bit of a handicap... My twitches and all, I still was able to capture the most rambunctious sex life imaginable. But I never told anyone about my twitches. See, I was diagnosed with Tourette's Syndrome when I was a kid, but I never told anyone that. My tics had gotten better since they started. Drinking helped, so did Xanax, which is why maybe I did them both so much. Not like it's a muscle thing, it's a brain thing, but still it helped calm the nerves—the booze, and when I was calm, the twitches weren't as bad. The drinking also helped me hide the tics from people if they *did* get bad, cause it gave me the courage to make up weird excuses that I could confidently get behind:

"Brah. Why you always shaking like that?"

"Wha? Whattaya mean—oh, I got a tag in a weird spot on this shirt."

Whatever, point is I never told anyone about that shit cause where would that get me? Nowhere. Made fun of. Called a crazy person. You know how many stand-up comics include Tourette's in their comedy routine? No way I'm tellin people about that shit. Nope. But point is, even with that I was able to fuck mad bitches. And I don't say "bitches" anymore, but back then I did. So that's how I'll say it here. But yeah, I told him:

"Bitches are all about customer service, you gotta provide great dinner, offer compliments, pay for everything, all that shit. Customer service. And business is all about numbers."

I could see the look on his face whenever I talked about business, like what do *you* know? You can't even produce a comedy festival… goddam failure. That's probably what he was thinking. That's why this time, with JACKPOT!, I was *determined* to take everything that had worked before, combine them into one idea, and take out all the shit that didn't work. The most important thing was to be honest with everyone, cause if not, you end up all over the news as a crook. That I hated. I didn't like that shit. So I sent out a message to every single comedy troupe I met during Skit Skat, and every single actor I knew from Wonderland, and all the comedians I knew from The Six Nights to Live Festival, and just…

everyone. Everyone I knew. I sent them this exact message, and I sent it to em on Facebook. Everything was done on Facebook. What a great website.

I just want you to know that I definitely want you involved with JACKPOT- if you have not already checked out the site, it is www.JACKPOTcomedy.com. If you want to get on our roster all you have to do is fill out the submission form. There are no fees or obligations at all. It's a free event for performers and for audience. You can read more about it on our website. We signed on to do JACKPOT once a month every month for a year at Crash Mansion and the winning troupe wins the $3-$5 suggested JACKPOT donation the audience makes at the door. The event is free to attend so if 500 people show up the Jackpot will be around $1,500- $2,500. If 750 people show up the jackpot may get up to $3,000- $5,000. Basically the bigger the audience the bigger the donations and the bigger the jackpot. Comedy Central is interested in making JACKPOT a TV show so they will be there on our launch on the 29th checking us all out. If you are free sometime this week I can explain everything a bit more in detail. I hope all is well, let me know your thoughts and feel free to give me a ring if you have any questions.

And so that's how it all started. With a venue, an idea, and a website. It was a wild idea with bursts of manic passion. Then one day Facebook shut down my account, saying that I couldn't use personal accounts to promote business. Luckily, this one dude I knew was one of the founding members of Facebook. He was the president of my high school when I was a freshman before I was kicked out of my parent's house and toured America's finest juvenile institutions. And when I left on that tour, this guy—the president of my ex-high school, fucked my ex-girlfriend at prom. You believe that? All the times I asked my ex for a blow job, nothing. Then after one date she fucks some goddam senior at prom? What a whore.

But I reached out to him anyway—the guy who fucked my ex—when Facebook implemented a new policy that made it so you couldn't promote a business on a personal profile anymore; exactly what I had been doing to promote shows. I hit him up and said:

Dude, you fucked my ex and that basically makes us family, and now I come to you for help...

And you know what? That piece of shit helped me out. I guess he wasn't so bad after all. He moved all my "friends" on my personal Skit Skat Facebook profile, which I was using to promote everything, even non-comedy-related stuff, but since I couldn't change the name I just left it as Skit Skat for all business communications—and he moved all my friends on that profile to a Facebook "Like" Page and made them all into "likes." It was confusing, but it worked, and that's how JACKPOT! got off the ground. It became a drunken shitshow because my drinking was *really* getting out of hand by then.

Well, it *really* got bad after Jessica, but I wouldn't meet her for a few more months...

One night at Jackpot I called an agency that represented dwarfs and hired a little guy to dress up in a leprechaun costume and run around throwing Lucky Charms cereal at the audience. I hired the carpenter who built the set for *Manuscript* to build a spinning wheel, like Wheel of Fortune, but this JACKPOT! wheel said how much you had to drink wherever it landed, or if you won money or not. It was this big game show, but only for sketch troupes. There was a stand-up comic hosting it too, so it was like a comedian sketch troupe game show, but also we had a rock band perform who I knew from my music promotions business, so it was like a rock game show for sketch comedy troupes with a stand-up comedian, who was also a magician... So, it was a magic show too. Literally I was going insane with ideas. My mind was cracking up. But I had to grow bigger and faster.

I hired two more employees and set up a row of desks in my apartment. That's when I moved my mattress into the DJ booth/ former Wonderland office. Now it was the only thing in that miniature room. That's where Jessica and I fucked while my team put together weekly game shows and booked bands at music venues across Manhattan and Brooklyn—but like I said, she didn't come into the picture just yet. Just wanted you to know something fucked up is about to happen.

My mind was obsessed with success, but there was no one to really talk to about it. It really was just me and my mind, which isn't a great neighborhood to be trapped in without a friend. I had to get this damn show on the road. I had to become the biggest show promoter in the world. I had to take over. I needed to be known. I wanted more. I had to be special. I just *had* to make this movie. Something needed to work. Then the friends will come. They'll see I'm worth it. They'll need my help. I was really going crazy. So I came up with another idea when JACKPOT! didn't become the raging success I thought it might be. The new idea was called Jukeboxx. It was Skit Skat but for music. Still I'd be working on JACKPOT!, but I needed something with music. Comedy didn't sell as well as rock bands did, and I just learned that. I shoulda thought of that earlier. FUCK! Why did I put all this effort into JACKPOT!? I shoulda done Jukeboxx to begin with—whatever. Fuck it. Just do it now. Stop being pissed off that you *didn't* do it and just do it. That's Nike. Fuck Nike. Now nobody can say *just do it* without promoting their shitty brand. But back to Jukeboxx:

The idea was to find a massive venue and make every room a different genre of music: like a Jukeboxx! I added the extra "x" to make it not as bland, but really I think the lack of creativity for the name made it even more basic with such a mindless addition like an extra "x". So, now I had JACKPOT! going on, I had a handful of bands I was booking, I started managing FUCT, a comedy troupe I loved. The Fordham Underground Comedy Troupe: FUCT. I just thought they were brilliant. I was also managing the lesbian singer-songwriter, and now with Jukeboxx in the works, it became clear I needed help. So, I contacted a PR firm in Tarrytown to help me publicize the living shit out of it. They cost me eight grand, which was a decent chunk that again ate into my magical number of eighty that I required to exit the weed business, which even with the large quantities I was now selling, the profit evaporated quickly, dried out like white out from all the shit I was producing... Anyhow, the PR firm sent me two junior account executives. Really, they were hot interns. And I'll warn you... life is about to get very real, very dark, and very bad. This was the beginning of the end.

And it all started with Jukeboxx because that's where I met Jessica...

CHAPTER 29: JUKEBOXX JESSICA

Why waste your time? Look, Jukeboxx never happened. It was supposed to be my most ambitious project yet, as you know, but between taking trips to Colorado every few weeks, flying back to sign for the packages, selling the weed, paying bands cash to perform and telling them not to declare the money, then asking the music venues to cut the check to me so it'd look like I'd just made fifteen grand, even though I was losing money, between all that and JACKPOT! and the movie—which still needed to happen, all of this was really stretching myself thin.

My mind was on repeat: Why can't I get one of these shows to work? I just need to do one more. I'll sell more weed. What if I get caught one day? Don't think about it. Just get Jukeboxx right and you can stop right away. But like I said, Jukeboxx never happened. It never even got close. I think about that first day—before all the horror, before the most terrible day of my life, how many different directions I coulda taken... but by then, it was too late.

It all started with that PR firm. I told the chick in Tarrytown, the owner, that I needed help picking out the venue. So, instead of coming herself—fuckin skank—she sent these two interns. One of them was an off-duty fashion model. Her name was Jessica. I loved her immediately. She was six feet tall. I straightened my back as tall as possible to match her height, but it never worked, especially when she wore heels. I had to ask her to stop doing that (except during sex), because it just looked too goddam silly. What's she wanna do, make me look like a fool? Anyway, when I met her on that day, I knew I had to be with her—to be with her forever. She was the most beautiful chick I'd ever seen—except for Robyn, and Minnie.

As we toured the potential Jukeboxx venue, I told Jessica and the other intern, a smaller girl who took her job seriously, which musta made it hard to do her job when I was clearly flirting with her coworker, I told them both all about my absurd idea for how I envisioned Jukeboxx.

"So that'll be the hip hop room. And that'll be like, EDM or whatever. We can do singer songwriters in there, and maybe add a wall there for like, hmm… rock bands maybe. But everyone can congregate out here, in the main space. And we can make like tunnels to get everywhere."

The venue owner looked at me. "I'm not sure that'll be possible."

The PR chick who took her job seriously kinda giggled, but I couldn't really concentrate on her with Jessica there, all tall and whatnot. I had to take her to dinner. What time is it? Hmm, it's too early. Fuck it…

"Okay well thanks for your time," I told the venue owner, or operator, or whoever she was. "We'll chat about it and I'll get back to you ASAP."

Then we left. Outside the venue I looked at the girls outside, but really my focus was on Jessica, and I asked: "Should we get some food?"

"We should probably get back," the smaller one said.

"I could eat," Jessica says.

"Great! So nice to meet you!" I said to the smaller one. "Ready?" I asked Jessica. And I hustled them apart from each other. What a dick I was acting like, but it was just so important I see if there was any sorta connection between Jessica and me. I *really* needed a girlfriend.

When we sat down, I told her to forget about Jukeboxx. I wanted to explore our relationship outside of work. Sounds bad, I know. But what am I gonna do, lie? But crazy thing is, she agreed. She came home with me, we slept together—no sex problems at all, which was meaningful, and two days later she moved into my apartment with her ferocious dog that attacked nearly anyone who tried to pet him.

I noticed she walked with her head down whenever we were outside walkin anywhere. Wherever we were going, even though she was far more attractive than the rest of the city, she hid her eyes and stared at the pavement. The only time I ever saw her feel comfortable in her skin was on the runway during Fashion Week, but after that her eyes fell sunken to depression as soon as she was back in the dressing room. I had to invite her into my life forever, because I knew that feeling she was feeling. We were the same. But things got confusing right away when I made a commitment. I mean, for starters, I had made so many dates with other girls in the upcoming few weeks prior to meeting Jessica that I totally forgot about Gina. And I'm not a mean dude, I just… Literally could keep track of all the things I told people I'd do. I did most of them, but Gina I forgot about, which really sucked cause she was incredibly important.

I met her in Connecticut. I was working with the creator of Felix the Cat, like he owned all the intellectual property, and I was helping him manage this musician he thought was promising. She sucked, but he thought she had talent, and he had heard from someone that I was a music agent and might be able to help. Anyway, Gina was his secretary and she and I became close. We became so close that we started fucking. Well, to say we were fucking is giving myself a bit too much credit.

I tried to have flaccid-dick sex with her a week before and it didn't work out too well. Again, another night I blamed on the "whiskey," but really she just made me so nervous. I was always nervous I wouldn't perform well; that I wouldn't match my outspoken confidence that when it came down to getting naked, I prayed to god I'd live up to my cocky sentiments and that my heart would slow down. The faster it beat, the less likely I would get hard. But still I told every girl I was remarkable in bed and then when it was my time to prove it, I froze. I was a phony. That's why I always had to start every date with whiskey, just so I could blame it on the scotch if my dick didn't work by the time we got into bed. It's a miracle I was able to put a condom on with those lesbians. Oh my god, how lucky I got. Best night of my life, but lonely thereafter.

Anyway, so I told Gina to be my date for a show I had booked when she got back from France to make it up to her—the flaccid dick—and to hopefully have hard-dick sex later in the evening. She thought it was her fault, that she didn't turn me on, but she did, and I assured her that. She was so hot. Wait, but maybe she can be hot and not turn me on? Was it the whiskey? Was I was trying to have sex with girls I didn't actually wanna have sex with? Was I only trying to have sex with them to prove to myself I was good enough to get laid? Was my entire confidence built on the premise that I could fuck hot chicks? Is that okay? I don't know, but all this escaped my mind and I accidently showed up with Jessica on the night I was supposed to meet Gina. Needless to say, when Gina showed up ten minutes into the show after the lights were already down and I was sitting up front with Jessica, she took one look at me and ran out.

I felt horrible. I really liked Gina.

"I'll be right back," I told Jessica.

This was totally going to get back to her boss and fuck up business—but what business? Not like he was paying me... It's just, I don't know, I never *wanted* to be a sleazeball, and it just kept happening over and over. Seriously, it was purely a mistake, and I just wanted to explain that to her, but she didn't want to hear it and slapped me in the face and threw water all over me on her way out of the venue. She was dressed up very fancy. I felt truly horrible. I went back inside Joe's Pub—the fancy music venue I had booked, drenched in water—maybe it was vodka, and sat back down next to Jessica.

"What happened, is everything okay? Who was that?"

"Oh, a work friend," I told her. Oh man, this was too much. I kept drinking. I was drinking too heavily, I thought. At some point, I'll need to stop. But then how will I control the tics?

But nothing stopped. Everything was heightened.

I redirected the other PR intern to focus on JACKPOT!, which I was certain was a wonderful idea. But month after month, the game show cost me more and more money, but I was in so far, I couldn't stop now. I had to keep going. I had the hundred pound wheel and everything. At some point, things will turn around. I asked the PR intern to join Black Apple as a full-time employee because I felt bad about all that had happened with Jukeboxx not coming to life. I don't know why I always felt bad about things; always felt the need to make it right with people, even though they probably didn't care. I thought everyone cared about every single thing I did, and I would pay whatever it took to make sure they still liked me and didn't badmouth me to... well, I don't know, whoever.

Meanwhile, the HQ—my apartment—was riddled with chaos, illegal activity, crazy ideas, concert promotion, set pieces, computers, flyers, pounds of weed, thousands of dollars in cash in my safe, and now Jessica and her killer dog...

CHAPTER 30: THE HQ

My apartment had become a nightmare.

I hired three more employees to work in the living room while Jessica and I fucked in the closet—meaning our bedroom—out loud, next to her killer dog, while everyone else worked on the other side of our hollow door on some outrageous idea I had come up with that morning while smoking weed.

I had to climb on top of the full-size mattress to get out of the room since it took up the entire width of the doorway. Jessica's vicious dog had to stay in there all day while everyone was working because he attacked the nicest of people. Like this one time when The Gak came over. He was a real pussy about it too...

See, I was still buying wholesale deals from him whenever I couldn't make it to Colorado—cause c'mon, I can't go out to Colorado *every time* I needed to re-up, that'd just be irresponsible. The Gak always wanted me to stop going out there cause I stole all his customers whenever I *did* go out there. But on one of the occasions when I was buying a few pounds from him, he came in and tried to pet her—or him, I can't remember the sex of the dog, and the damn dog bit him on the hand. Just a nip. But The Gak was a pussy about it, like I said, and bitched for a month that he might have rabies. He went and got all sorts of shots and tests for all sorts of bullshit that he thought he had. I found him to be overdramatic. But anyhow, all that is beside the point. The point is my apartment was a madhouse. Plus, I was selling larger and larger amounts of weed at once because I was short on time, so I upped my minimum purchase, which didn't look great to my employees since I was selling weed during business hours—not to mention drinking from 3PM on. So, bad decisions became more frequent, though now everyone who worked for me at least understood why I kept doing shows even when we lost money: to clean the money up. The music promotions business was important because we had to launder all the money so that eventually, I could exit the weed business, which I assumed they found to be no big deal. I mean, it was only weed. Plus, how else was I supposed to pay them their salaries?

"Wait, we're losing money?" One intern asked bashfully.

"No, we're making money. We're just losing some on the shows we promote. But we're making money overall. The concerts clean the cash, which we need for the festivals and the game shows, and that's where the real money is. Especially when we start making movies with the screenplays I'm writing." I sounded crazy, but it all made total sense in my head. So, I kept explaining it to whoever asked: "Look. We pay all the bands in cash, then tell them not to report it. We find *big* bands that can draw a *big* local audience, pay them more money than *any other* promoter in the city, make sure they don't report the income, then tell them to promote the show to all of their fans. It's like... look, we're payin you *more* than any other promoter and we're payin cash, so promote that shit. Right? But don't be asking for... whatever, a w-9 or some shit.

No reporting nada. Right? Then when the venue cuts us a check for 60% of the door—cause at The Music Hall of Williamsburg, they give us 60%, and it looks like we made real money! Plus every band wants to play that venue anyway... So yeah, we give them mad cash to be on the bill *and* let them put that shit on their resume. They can tell all their relatives they played a massive venue. It makes them look good, and gives us a clean check... see what I mean? Then I take that shit to the bank and deposit it. Looks like we made legit money. I even pay my taxes and all that shit. See? It actually looks like we're making tons of money from the music promotions business, but in reality, we're breaking even or even losin money on some shows cause we pay like seven grand to get all the bands on board, and comedy troupes—whoever, you know? The fuckin talent. So we lose a bit in the process, swap the cash for a check—like pay 8K cash for a 7K check basically, and then put that shit in the bank and keep the rest of the weed money in the safe till I get to eighty—don't tell your friends about this shit. Cool? Anyway, cause that's when I'm out. At eighty. But the real money is in JACKPOT! and all the other festivals cause that's where the longevity lives: in the brand. We gotta build big brands. You know what I mean?"

Everyone looked at me lost.

"So you're basically a drug dealer who has a music business?"

I was elated someone understood: "Yes! Kinda! But it's so much bigger than that. You see where this is all goin? You gotta think chess here. Long-term."

But I would listen to myself tell them that shit and hear how crazy it all sounded. So I came up with a new plan: Make a profit *while* laundering the money, *then* everyone would stop asking so many questions. And I *had* made a profit once… but only because Bowery Presents, the company that owned all the music venues I was working with, put our show on their email list and promoted it on one of their newsletters. But the only way to get on their newsletter was to book a huge band—one they'd wanna promote—and the only way to get a huge band, or artist, was to talk to an agent and negotiate a price. So that's what I had to do… And while all this shit was happening inside the HQ—and my head, a lot of it just happened in my head—Jessica listened in awe, like I was a superstar. Actually, most of the speeches I gave to the employees during the day were more to impress her than to maintain company morale. But my idea to make money during the money-laundering process actually made sense. That's how I met Jerrod the Agent—who I'll tell ya about in a moment, he was one of the big agents that repped big artists that I needed to book in order to get on the Bowery Presents newsletter! The important thing was to get organized. JACKPOT! was the big game show that would bring in the big money—eventually. I was sure it would get me—and Black Apple—on TV, where I would make my movie contacts to produce my script and solidify my reputation as the most powerful live entertainment producer in the world. Cause in essence, that's who I was: a live entertainment producer. Make sense?

And just as everything was coming together, we had to abort everything…

CHAPTER 31: ABORT!

One night, while Jessica and I were making love… That's right, I said making love… I came deep inside her. I knew I had cum inside her, but said nothing… Just a simple "I think I came a bit too early" throwaway line after we were done.

But that was a lie. It was a lot of cum inside her. I was as sick as I had ever been. I just wanted some assurance we would be together forever. But I had no idea what it would feel like on that one day, two months later, when I sat her down to break up with her. Our relationship had turned into a bloody mess, and by bloody mess, I mean we couldn't stop arguing and threatening to kill each other and the codependency was stronger than I'd ever experienced. I had no idea what it would feel like on that day when I sat her down on my couch in the living room, with a full office of desks crammed behind the couch where I stored my employees. I had no idea the pain that would thrust through my heart that day when I told her, ready to break things off for good:

"I need to say something to you."

"Me too. I'm so glad you said that. I have something to say to you too," she told me.

Perfect. She's going to break up with me so I won't have to break up with her, I thought.

"Who first? You. You go first." I said.

And so she handed me a box. I opened the box. It was a small hippie outfit. She knew I loved hippie outfits, but this one was for a baby. Then she handed me two books on how to be a father and told me:

"I'm pregnant."

A smile lit her face up for the first time. For the first time in her existence she was happy. I had no idea what to say. I couldn't think. I was absolutely paralyzed. All I knew was that I was a drug dealing fucked up piece of garbage and this poor girl was finally happy with the one thing she knew she was put on this Earth to do: Care for a child.

I had given her the greatest gift she could possibly ask for. I was so fucking scared. I couldn't be a father. I had no idea how to make my face look. I was shocked and in terror and couldn't hide my confusion.

"Are you not happy?"

"I…"

But I couldn't speak. She welled up with tears and stood up and her mouth opened and the veins in her throat clenched but her words were silent. My vision was blurry and my heart was fast. My thoughts were feelings and my feelings were darts blowing in the wind. Nothing made sense. I think she was screaming.

I grabbed a bottle of whiskey. I don't know how it got into my hands. I thought it was sitting on top of the fridge. But it was in my hands. I fell backwards. She was in front of me. Where was I? I opened the bottle and sipped. The bottle crashed to the floor but didn't break. What just happened? I looked at her eyes and she was yelling into me but I heard nothing. I picked the bottle up and opened the door, but I'm not sure how my hand got to the knob. I was blocked in by some force. I think it was her. She was six feet and bigger than I was. I reached for the knob again, whiskey back in hand. How did that get back there?

I was floating now. Was I high?

Should we break up then? NO! Okay should we get married? Do I spend the rest of my life with this chick, or should we break up and never see each other ever again? I had fallen in love with her dangerous dog, which didn't make it any easier. Plus, I loved when people saw us together, but I always felt short. I can't do this. I'm a drug-dealer who launders his money by producing one-act plays and comedy festivals. I don't have a very promising future, not yet. The night was a disaster.

I woke up to a strange Asian guy in my living room.

What the fuck?

Oh right, I hired him. Musta been drunk. I told him work was canceled. Jessica was awake, staring at me. Oh no, this all happened. I begged her to get an abortion even though I clearly remember cumming inside her and knowing what I was doing. Maybe I wanted an insurance policy to never be lonely ever again. But as soon as it actually happened, I realized what I'd done. She wanted to get married and I wanted an abortion.

I was twenty-four years old at the time.

Later that night I touched the knob and my eardrum almost popped. But why? Everything was silent. It was then I realized everything was loud. A fight had erupted. It was nighttime. She was blocking the doorway again. I got scared. I grabbed her with my hands. STOP THAT! But I didn't listen to myself. I moved her. I opened the door. I ran. I found a yellow car. I think it was a cab. I had my whiskey. My eyes got heavy. My sight fell blind. I went to sleep. She texted me forty times. I kept drinking. I kept hidden for three days then went back to the apartment. She blocked me in and asked me questions I was too scared to answer. I started screaming. She screamed back. I called my employees again and told them work was canceled.

More shouting.

A knife was pulled. I was the one who pulled it. A kitchen knife. I held it to my body telling her to kill me. This was bad. The moment died and we had sex. I'll figure this out tomorrow. Tomorrow came and I canceled work again. I agreed to get married but told her I wouldn't stop drinking. She told me I drank too much, so I ran out with my whisky again to drink some more, but she blocked me at the door again. I pivoted around her and went to my brothers to snort coke and drink in peace.

I asked my brother what to do, but he didn't fuckin know... I was supposed to be the older brother, but instead I was drowning in life. I couldn't breathe. My whole family was horrified by the situation. I told them she was pregnant and what was going on, but I left out the domestic violence part. I'll keep that to myself. I couldn't control my emotions and was scared the knife scene would happen again. I have to leave. I can't leave, she's pregnant. But we need to break up, right? I don't know.

I went back home again and told her I was sorry. Of course I was, I'm a total piece of garbage. I'm threatening my pregnant girlfriend. But she threatened me too. That's no excuse. Whose fault is this? Mine. Is it though? All mine? I don't know. Fuckin shit, I don't know. I need a drink. Actually...

"Should we break up?" I asked her.

"BREAK UP?!"

"Okay okay, let's get married then. But like, I'm a drug dealer."

"It's okay, we have a trust fund. You can produce anything you want."

Her parents were wealthy. A fashion model wants to marry me and let me in on her trust fund, what am I upset about? I can't be a dad. I'm a fuckup. I'll be in prison next year. No way I'll make it past thirty. Serves me right.

"But we barely get along," I said to her finally when it was clear a break up had to happen soon or else. She didn't take that well. We fought and again we said things that shouldn'ta been said. Today I know this was my fault. Well, I think it was. Back then I thought I was totally right about everything. Eventually she screamed that I would make a terrible father and she refused to have the baby.

I rushed us to an abortion clinic. The doctor told me to leave the room. They spoke for some time. She came out and was given pills. The doctor looked at me like I was a criminal. The next buncha days were horrid and I won't write about them. I went on a mini vacation with my parents cause they thought I was losing my mind. I came back to an empty apartment. She left me. We sexted each other for another year.

Five years later something crazy happened.

"Greg?" I heard someone say.

Oh my god.

I was in LA, my new home, and I sat down for a client meeting. I was signing my first PR client. I was a year-and-a-half sober. I looked to my right and it was her best friend, Jessica's best friend, the one that sent me death threats telling me all the terrible things I did. She was right. I had to apologize. I left my potential client and pulled her away from her date. We were at a bar, a trendy bar, and the world was watching, especially her date who she left at their table alone.

"I'm so sorry can I just talk to her a moment?" I said to both her and her date while they were sitting together. She got up and followed me. "I'm sober."

"I know, I can tell."

"Please I need to speak with her."

"That will never happen."

"What can I do?"

I was on the verge of crying forever.

"I'll tell her I saw you and you look better. Take care of yourself."

That was the last time I ever had any connection with her. Some things are just left unfixed. Nothing will ever make that right. There are so many apologies I want to make, but I wouldn't even know where to start. Sometimes the best apologies I think are to simply let that person live without ever hearing from you again. At least that's what I think. I don't even know how to finish this up…

I still remembered the first night I left after she told me she was pregnant. I stared at my phone buzzing and buzzing and lighting up and dying down then lighting back up to let me know the unanswered fifty-five text messages were not going to slow. I was at my brother's apartment. I don't know how I got there on that night. I envisioned my child growing up in a dysfunctional alcoholic drug-addicted mess that was my life—wait, alcoholic? Am I an alcoholic? Why would I say that if I wasn't? Was it just one of those things that rehab left buried in my mind? Was it true? These were the thoughts on that night.

I saw my child. All I heard were cries and screams. I have no idea if it was a boy or girl. I saw Jessica coming after me with a knife—Wait. That was me. I had the knife. Thoughts of suicide entered all over again, reliving this nightmare. I let them go. But I couldn't, I had traveled back in time.

Where is the knife?

I saw it. It was in my hand. I was in my apartment again. How'd I get here?

"YOU DON'T JUST WALK OUT ON YOUR PREGNANT FUCKING GIRLFRIEND!"

Jessica? Where am I?

She came at me. I wasn't sure if this was really happening. I had to protect myself. I grabbed a knife from the kitchen—Oh right. That's where the knife came from. Where's my brother? I was out of whiskey. I needed more whiskey, but there was a knife in my hand.

"FUCKING KILL ME!" I shouted and handed her the knife. It was a big chef's knife with a ten-inch blade. I was ready to die, but I couldn't feel my emotions. I couldn't feel my hand. I was numb.

"I JUST NEED TO TALK TO YOU ABOUT THIS!" She yelled. "I'M HAVING THE FUCKING BABY GREG! IT'S NOT YOUR DECISION!"

"I NEVER SAID NOT TO! I HAVE NOTHING TO OFFER YOU JESSICA! WE HATE EACH OTHER!"

She refused to grip the knife, it was still in my hands. I tilted it towards me, the blade aimed at my solar plexus. I walked into the blade and put her hands on the handle. But she wouldn't take it.

"TAKE THE FUCKING KNIFE BITCH! KILL ME!"

Why was I saying this? Was I self-sabotaging myself? Was I an abusive man? Was this a pattern? Is she really pregnant?

"YOU'RE ACTING CRAZY!"

She started to cry. The knife dropped to the ground. I ran to her to hold her but she squirmed to get away from me. I held her in place. Was that not allowed? I just had to get a grip on this situation. I was too sober. Was I? I couldn't think right. I grabbed her and all at once she grabbed back onto me and sunk her head into my shoulders and cried and tears wept down my neck from her eyes.

"I'm a drug dealer. I produce theatre. I'm a nobody. I have nothing Jessica. I'm not a father. I can't raise a child." She cried. "I have no money," I said. But I had plenty of money. But I'd have nothing once I stopped selling drugs, and I'd have to do that as a father, right? How would I afford this? What would my parents say? I've fucked up bigger than I've ever fucked up before. "I can't do it Jessica." The words just came out. She slapped me. I threw her into the couch.

What have I done?

"YOU'RE GOING TO BEAT YOUR PRENANT GIRLFRIEND!?"

WHY DOES SHE KEEP SAYING THAT?! I'M TRYING TO BE HONEST AND TALK ABOUT MY FEELINGS YOU STUPID CUNT WHORE WE NEED TO TAKE THIS FUCKING GODDAM SERIOUSLY YOU **FUCKING PIECE OF—**

But I wasn't thinking that. I had said it out loud. My hand was in a fist raised above my head. Was I threatening her? I was. I deserve to die. I had to leave this life and never come back. I could never repent for this sin. I was done. Life was over. I looked at Jessica covering herself as if I were going to kill her. But I was. Was I? WHERE AM I?! I backed up slowly. Nothing I said or did or anything could ever make peace with what had just happened. Nothing mattered.

"I'M NOT HAVING YOUR BABY!" She yelled.

Oh right. I kept remembering her saying that. I remember how fast I picked up the phone and called a doctor and hustled us into a cab to get to the doctor. I don't remember much. Oh wait I do. The doctor said, before she asked me to leave the room, she said:

"It's just very unusual that someone would ask for an abortion at this part of the pregnancy. Did something happen?"

We looked at each other, well, she looked down, I looked at her, then the doctor. We were at the most expensive doctor I could find. How did I find this place? When did this all happen? Is this an abortion clinic? What is going on?

There was a silence that was a different silence than I'd heard before. It was a silence so loud my ears were ringing. Time stopped.

"Greg, would you mind leaving the room for a bit? So I can speak with Jessica alone?"

I left her office—the doctor—and went to the waiting room.

The look on the doctor's face plagued my blinks. Every time I blinked my eyes I saw that face. She knew me. She knew what I had done. I'll never forget that office. I'll never forget that night— the night she agreed to induce a miscarriage. The sound of the screams. Her hands squeezed tightly over mine every streak of pain that came into her body after she took those two pills.

Those pills.

They went into her body because I made her do it. Did I? No, she asked for this. But she asked for it because of me. I was the reason. I was nothing. This was murder. Was it murder? Am I going to hell? WHAT DOES THIS MEAN?! Do other people go through this? How am I supposed to handle this situation? Is this a situation? I'm going crazy.

Then it happened.

The baby was gone. Nothing could fix this. I drank heavily for many days, that's why my parents came to get me and take me to Aruba. They would do anything to help me, which wasn't always the case. While in Aruba I texted her, begged for her forgiveness, we sexted each other still, we were unable to depart even though she was back upstate with her family.

What did her family think of me? I barely knew who they were and already I killed their grandchild. Am I being hard on myself? I checked my Facebook and there was a long letter from her best friend declaring what a distinctive piece of gutter shit I truly was. I agreed. That was the girl I bumped into in LA.

I got back from Aruba and the apartment was clear of all her belongings. I called my employees and told them to come in. What do I tell them? I couldn't be alone. I talked to them about it during work the next few days, but they typed away as I drank in my bedroom. I had nothing left to offer life. I had to do something. Maybe I should leave this country and never come back? I packed up my shit and moved to Brooklyn not long after that. I couldn't bear to see the sight of this apartment anymore. Everything was a mess. I was losing my mind, spiraling out of control, and I just had to leave. I woke up in Park Slope a month later, unable to think. I had to fix myself. I missed Jessica's dog. I needed a dog. She had a Doberman, so I got myself a Doberman. I named her Ooli—but I didn't get Ooli till a bit later. But when I did, it made me feel like she was still in my life. I loved her. I needed her back. WHAT HAD I DONE? How will I ever laugh ever again?

I had to keep busy, but little did I know I was nearing the end of my time in New York...

CHAPTER 32: RAPID EXPANSION

It all started when I began making insane business plans, like my idea to expand JACKPOT!, which wasn't even working in New York, to Los Angeles.

In my head, I thought sure, maybe JACKPOT! wasn't making money in New York, but perhaps it'll make tons in LA. I could even try it out in Kansas City too, and Seattle, and maybe even Austin. I should go big. But first I was determined to at least double my presence by setting up a show in Los Angeles. So I did what I did best: sent a blanket email to every email address I could find in search of LA venues to host the event. I pitched my big idea to anyone who replied. "I want to offer you the opportunity to host the very first JACKPOT! LA, which would soon erupt into JACKPOTS! all over the country," I told everyone.

This was it.

It started making total sense. I had to do one in every city. Every comedy troupe had to know my name. That was so important. I was so obsessed with being known. I tried as an actor and failed. I tried producing theatre and failed. I tried booking bands and failed. JACKPOT! was my only hope to free myself from the anxiety of smuggling weed across the country and to help me overcome my past. Finally, a venue replied: The Viper

Room—you know, Johnny Depp's old club? So I booked a night there. If this doesn't work, then I have nothing. Just selling weed, and eventually I'll get caught.

I thought about all the Xanax and scotch I was consuming. I'll probably have withdrawals if I stop. I'll have to explain to the prison warden that I need medically prescribed Xanax. But what if that doesn't work? Still, even if I get the Xanax, I'll have to detox off whiskey. I'll start shaking and break out into seizures. All the prisoners will look at me. I'll fight back if they fuck with me but I won't be able to see straight. All my fibers will be at attention, poking into the inside of my skin from my bones. I'll sweat everywhere and panic. The walls will close in on my face and crush my skull. I had to have my Xanax to keep that from happening. I had to keep myself calm. And the twitches would be seen and would get worse. Then I'd have no way to make them subside. I'll be living in hell on Earth. Holy shit. JACKPOT! LA has to goddam work. The repercussions were immense. It's either this works, or I suffer in inferno for the rest of my life. That's why I sent Autumn a message on Facebook: I needed a date; that'll help my odds.

Autumn was a hippie from Hidden Lake, the juvie place I went to as a kid. I jerked off to her Facebook pics every once in a while. I had always thought she was hot, and in my drunken stupor of panic one night, she seemed like the perfect person to help me calm down...

1/18/10, 11:36 PM: Autumn! Hiiii!

1/19/10, 12:41 AM: Hey there, doll!

1/19/10, 9:11 AM: well hello sugarplum, how are you?!?!? r u still in tennessee? whats going on w u??!

1/19/10, 10:29 AM: I'm exceptionally well, thanks! Tis correct, back in ol' chattanooga, TN.... sigh. Hmmm...(my goodness. it's absolutely wretched to give only the cliff's notes!)... I'm working as a social worker at a homeless shelter, caring for the unloved. It's truly god's work. Still combatting whether to remain post-grad or aspire onto certification for dream analysis and hypnotherapy... OR to splice ahead to where I become a cloistered promising novelist. Time will tell... Still moving around... Another move to another house with another group of people (precisely what was needed!)... Oh. Contemplating a bigger move either to Vancouver or perhaps Vermont. But still UNDENIABLY trying to move back to Africa in less time than too much, but too far to arrange mentally as of yet. How are YOU?!? I'm without the foggiest clue when last we conversed. Has it been since Hidden Lake?!... Impossible. Has it been a decade...(has it?!) Tell me of yourself! I await wondrous news of all sorts of wondrous affairs! All the best, love!

1/19/10, 10:48 AM: Seems like you are just where you should be. I would love to see you, it's been so long. I work in showbusiness now, mostly producing- comedy, festivals, theater, and so on... also concert/ tour promotion for hip hop/ soul/ funk/ dance music/ brooklyn band type shit basically. Are you planning any NYC trip any time soon? There is a small chance I may be in the chattanooga area soon, but not sure yet. Well, I totally wanna hear about Africa and the homeless shelter (I coulda used that when I was 16!) much love, Greg

1/22/10, 6:10 AM: Greg, it would be an absolute delight to see you!!! I have a couple friends in NYC who keep demanding I visit... Can you believe that I've actually never been there?! Isn't that... unfathomable?!! No sincere agenda to make the trip... but I'm sincerely not opposed (I'm just broke-er than hell). It sounds like YOU are just where you should be!! I regularly regret not keeping at acting. Envious! I'll await the fractional chance that you actually make it down here. Should it not materialize, we'll have to negotiate the terms of me catching the chinatown bus up there (after a lonesome hitchhike to Atlanta first, of course). KEEP IN TOUCH! ~Autumn

1/22/10, 6:25 PM: Proposition... Hitch your way to ATL... Catch the bus up here on Monday (on me). Come be my date or companion (or whatever you'd prefer) to our Los Angeles 2010 premiere of the live rock sketch comedy game show I produce, JACKPOT. It's the first show in LA. You can stay with me or your friends or whatever. Those are my terms, do you accept?

1/22/10, 6:42 PM: Holy mother of fuck!!! I hadn't expected true negotiations!!! I am utterly out of my element here! Hmm... I never took the bus on an overnight trip... On that account, I'd be unbelievably tense. But unless I'm forgetting something crucial, I say fuck it. I have exactly 2 personal philosophies: 1) the only thing better than a good adventure is a terrible adventure. 2) if you're gonna get wet, go skinny dipping all the way. So we've arrived at my impetuous decision to accept your terms, sir! And I follow through with my impulsions. So.. I guess I'm coming to see you! Of COURSE I'll be your date to your premiere! I'd be thrilled! I'll wholly feel like a complete ingenue in New York, but what the hell... I'm in.

Her language was as flowery as her name. Autumn had delicate features, not a scratch anywhere on her soft, cushy skin. Not a blemish or bug bite. Not a freckle or mole. Her entire persona was smooth and fragile. Her hair was dirty blonde with just the right amount of oil to give it a stylish bohemian look. Her makeup was scarce, except for her cat-eyes mascara—that was very dark and thick. She looked like she coulda been fifteen, but we were both twenty-five. Our relationship at Hidden Lake was never anything more than a playful stare from across the Lodge every now and then. We were practically strangers with a united past, but a past that made it feel like she was the only family I had left. To see her in New York was like to see a fairy out of an illustration, lost in 3D. Her smile billowed with organic sparkles and her vocabulary never shrank. It was as if she'd been studying the dictionary her entire life. But for some reason, she felt temporary. I was tired of temporary. Perhaps this would be its end. And so my adventure to California with Autumn began after a couple days of romanticizing about the ten years since Hidden Lake in my apartment and many war stories from the happiest decade of our lives. Though in shambles, it was freedom. We never kissed once, though we shared my bed till we left.

We were greeted at the airport by the comedian magician host of JACKPOT! and my employees holding the million-pound JACKPOT! wheel. It was built with solid oak by the same carpenter Louie and I met at the pub a few years back. The wheel folded up into half a circle, still massive in size—too big for any sort of carry-on, and so we had to wrap it up with thousands of layers of bubble wrap and put it under the plane.

What would happen if it got ruined? All the sketch troupes, the audience, my team, everyone would laugh at my inadequacy. That couldn't happen. I was a nervous wreck the entire flight there, but alas we landed and the damn wheel was still in one piece.

My employees and the host rented cars and went their separate ways, insisting they knew where to sleep and how to get to The Viper Room in a few days to prepare for the show. It almost seemed like they wanted to take a break from me. Autumn and I had no reservation anywhere, and so we rented a car and simply drove.

"Where to Mister Cayea?"

"Let's just drive till we see something amazing."

But amazing never came and the neighborhoods got progressively dicier until finally we pulled into a motel in Echo Park with distressed palm trees crowding the parking lot. We parked and grabbed our belongings and locked the door to the rental-Mustang a million times—my OCD's fault. We walked under the overhang to where the motel office was located. On the other side of the tunnel-like overhang was a pathetic tropical landscape around a cement pool with muck and such floating in the water. The pool sat center of the motel with all the rooms bordering around it. It looked like a scene from any prostitute movie ever made.

Since the motel was garbage and since we had gotten there a few days early, I thought going to Vegas would hide the fact that my premiere arrangements were less than satisfactory. I did my best to up my vocab as well, to show Autumn I wasn't just some dropout. She had never been to Vegas so the trip made total sense. We drove the four or so hours through the desert to get there, only to check into another crumby hotel, gamble a small amount of money, and pass a row of strip clubs on our way back to Los Angeles. Still we hadn't slept together, or even kissed. I was nervous she wasn't interested in me. How could she not want me to kiss her? Why would she want to "be my date" otherwise? Was she having second thoughts, or was this a plutonic date in her eyes? I was pondering in my mind whether or not she'd make a wonderful lifetime partner, and she apparently was only excited about comedy.

Not to think is always a better option than thinking sad, and so on the drive back, I had the mindless idea to stop off at this mini-golf course in Victorville that we passed on our way there. It looked fun, but in an axe-murderer type of way. Nothing but desert surrounded the mini-golf course. There was a human sling-shot ride next to it, which we did, and an arcade infested with hooligans looking to steal other people's raffle tickets from skee-ball machines so they could trade them in for a bouncy ball or some shit. I saw a teen couple in the corner pulling all the tickets out of a basketball hoop machine using some kind of contraption they had built. Anyway, that was the vibe, and after the human sling-shot ride came the mini-golf course.

Right behind us was some other couple, kinda like us, but a shittier version, and they were right on our ass the whole time so we had to rush through the course.

Trashy mini-golf in a trashy mini-town in the middle of the California desert with only future debaucheries passing us by on I-15 on their way to fuck their way through Vegas or go broke trying to, and us: on the side of the road, at some shithole mini-golf joint nobody in their right mind would ever actually stop at. But I had to provide an adventure—or even better, a *terrible adventure* for Autumn. Luckily, it happened…

Right before her putt, she placed her damn purse on the putting green for a goddam second and within moments, the dude and chick behind us on the hole prior were nowhere to be seen, and neither was her purse. All this was shitty, especially because she was now without an ID...

So, when we showed up to my own JACKPOT! LA premiere, *my own fucking show,* the bouncer wouldn't let her in (she didn't have ID). You believe that shit? And since she didn't know how to drive, and I didn't have time to drop her off at our seedy motel—a place nobody would wanna stay at alone, especially not this chick who expected literary adventure on every turn. I couldn't leave her outside the venue all night either. So I goddam left my own premiere and told my employees, who basically worked for free—salaries are expensive, you know?—to run the show. I have no idea what happened that night.

We got back to the shitty motel in Echo Park and drank some scotch—at least I did. I was so upset. I had a video camera. I was planning to film the whole thing. Instead I filmed Autumn. She was beautiful, and drunk, and under the covers. The only solution was to kiss her. I got on top of her but she moved her lips away from me many times. Was I harassing her? Or was she playfully saying "oh no, we *really* shouldn't..." but actually wanting to? I wasn't sure, but I loved her for a moment and pressed my lips against hers and for the first time she didn't move me but kept me firmly there. We made love. I mean, we fucked. I think. There's no way to know. I woke up the next morning and remembered very little.

The romance was over the second we awoke—awoke? I'm starting to talk like her. Anyway, I had to help my employees with the fifty-billion-pound spinning wheel we used for the show and somehow wrap it up again then lug it onto the plane. After we landed back in NYC, Autumn took the bus back to Tennessee as soon as she realized I was hopelessly in love with chaos. I got an email from The Viper Room telling me I didn't meet the minimum requirement for a payout, or some shit.

Are you serious? I bring you the greatest show in NYC and you gank my cash?

She wrote back an infuriating email: *Greatest show with only 19 people? Maybe it's not so great...*

She never paid me, and the show out there was ruined, maybe, it coulda been great. Who knows? But nineteen people? Are you fucking kidding me? Okay. I had to switch gears. I had to focus on music again. Comedy was out. I'm canceling all the JACKPOTS! from here on out. Time was ticking. Something treacherous was abound. Save me god. God? Do I believe in God? Should I capitalize it now? Or keep it with a little g? I need everything I can get, so God, if you're listening... GIVE ME ONE GOOD SHOW!

Goddam motherfucker...

CHAPTER 33: NYPD

I fired all my employees.

I just had to get rid of everything that reminded me of Jessica. And at my new Brooklyn apartment, I was completely alone, putting together shows by myself, doing everything on my own. The apartment was a studio. If ever I thought my old apartment was tiny, this one was half its size. It was probably three-hundred square feet. I couldn't even fit a bed inside it, so I had to sleep on my fold-out sofa. I'd pull out the bed every night then fold it back up into a couch every morning so I could actually walk around. Soon that stopped and the bed just stayed out all day. The walls were brick. There was a porch, and that's what sold me on the joint; it was about as big as the actual apartment.

There were many changes in my life. One of them being that none of my weed clients came to my new apartment, no one but one person...

There was a knock at the door.

It was Matthew from the Sketch Comedy Troupe who won Skit Skat. The waiter who taught me everything I knew on my first day. I still remember going up to him that first day on the job, after I was fired from Bolzano's. He was folding napkins. I was clueless and the lunch rush was about to come in...

"Dude, I'm Greg."

"Hey man. I'm—"

"I told Fabrizia that I had waited tables before, but I've never done it. I have no idea what to do. How do I use the computer system?"

He rolled his eyes big time. "Oh man. Seriously? Okay look, I'll show you but you gotta learn fast, okay? I have a huge party coming in today."

"That's fine... just... umm... what do I need to know?"

"Okay see this button? It says "course-break" and you push that between appetizers and entrees. So you put in the appetizer— and when you're taking orders, do it like this." And he drew a Y and X axis on his waiter pad and showed me a way to jot down orders quickly. "And remember, seat one is always at 2 o'clock. Got it?"

"I think."

"When the appetizers are done, you "fire" the next meal, like this. See?"

And just like that, in the course of an hour, I became a waiter. All thanks to Matthew. I was just happy I could repay the favor by rigging my sketch comedy festival to make it look like he won. Anyway, I totally forgot he was coming over. I opened the door to my new Park Slope studio and he took one look at me and jumped.

"Whoa. Guy. You look..."

He was talking about my hair. In a fluster of drunken cokeness, I buzzed my head down to a one, basically to the skin. I looked psycho.

"Yeah, I buzzed it."

"You sure did. It's uh… clean?"

"Agustina loved it."

"The girl with the dog?"

"No, she left. The girl from Argentina."

"Ooohh right! I remember when she was here. She was cute. Did you ever figure out how to say hi to her?"

"Yeah, of course, I mean, we could speak a bit."

"Yeah, a bit. Not much more than that though, right?"

"Not really. Well, with the translator we could."

"So what, you guys just sat by your laptop all day translating sentences?"

"Actually that's precisely what we did, and it was awesome."

"You're a weird dude, Greg. So, got weed?"

He never even mentioned the new apartment, like he didn't wanna get started on a whole new topic. But the new apartment posed very serious challenges. For one, Park Slope—the neighborhood in Brooklyn I moved to, the studio wasn't very well ventilated. The entire building reeked after *one* joint. It was very inconvenient.

Then to make matters worse, two lesbians moved to the basement floor apartment. It's not that they were lesbians, it's the *kind of* lesbians they were that mattered. One of them was a teacher, and the other one was with the NYPD. That scared the shit outa me, and it should have. It became a massive problem…

I found this out at the worst possible time. It was while she and her lover were outside in the backyard, right below me on the porch. I was smoking a joint and barbecuing illegally (the porch was wood and at any moment a hot coal coulda fallen through the crevasse of the planks and set the building on fire), when a conversation erupted:

"You must smoke a lot. It *really* smells up the building," the short-haired woman said.

"Does it?" I made it clear I smoked weed—a lot of it, you know, so she wouldn't get the idea I was selling it.

"Sure does. Maybe invest in some ventilation?"

"Yeah, that's a good idea. I work from home so I always smoke while I work."

"Yeah, whattaya you do?" What a nosey woman…

"I run a live entertainment production company." I sounded so official, and fancy. The way it should be. "What about you?"

The two looked at each other bashfully. The bigger of the lesbians said, "I teach eighth grade."

The shorter lesbian—the one with a crew cut of black hair; strong, butch, young—she says: "I'm a cop. NYPD. Don't worry, I'm off-duty."

She said that as a joke, but there's a tinge of honesty in every joke. That freaked me the fuck out. I had to *really* throw her off my tracks. Was she spying on me? "Well, I buy an ounce and smoke on it throughout the month. So, sorry about the smell. You don't care, do you?"

"You'll know if I come a'knocking with handcuffs…"

"What? You arrest people for that?"

"I'm just kidding. But seriously, tone the smell down."

I had to make her my friend. I thought of Scotty Guns' friend Sarge. The cop from Jersey. I had to get in good with her; then I'd know a cop. This might actually be beneficial. So this odd relationship began between me and my lesbian NYPD neighbor, but it got pretty sticky within a few months. And it all started with my idea to make a short film…

The film was supposed to be about a dude who walks his dog across the country.

That brings us to Ooli. I had just gotten Ooli. She was a twelve-week-old Doberman. I got her from a breeder in south Jersey—right by Delaware. The breeder asked me a few questions about the size of my apartment, which I lied about, and a few more questions. I presented myself as a human with a life who could easily take care of a puppy. And as a puppy, I was an okay dog-dad—I think, I was pretty drunk most of the day—well, from 3PM on, at least. But yeah, when Ooli became a dog, I was not okay. I was very bad. I was in a very bad place. I wasn't able to be a good dad—another thing I wasn't cut out for: caring for anything or anyone who actually needs my help. But I had to jumpstart my movie career much quicker now that there was a cop living below me.

Should I move?

No, that'll raise even more red flags. I'll just get started right away on my movie. I almost had enough money to exit the game. I was back up to like fifty thousand dollars in my tiny, unbolted safe, which anyone coulda fit in their backpack. Point is, I called up my friend Dusty and asked him if he knew how to use a camera.

"A Camera? Sure. I guess. Why?"

"Okay… We're taking a month-long trip to walk Ooli across the country. It'll be fucking hilarious. You in?"

I could hear myself; I sounded absolutely crazy. I was losing my mind. But any lack of motion could break me in half, so I had to keep my mind completely cluttered with bullshit, so I had to go fast, wherever I was going. And I couldn't be alone.

"Dude. I'm broke," he told me.

"No no, I'll pay. All expenses covered. Let's leave today."

"In whose car?"

"Hmmm… I'll go get one. Meet me at Prospect Park in like two hours and be ready to go."

So I went to an Enterprise booth at some Jersey City mall cause that's where I found the cheapest sedan for rent. I was fuckin losing it, you hear me? I jutted into a barrage of questions while walking towards the guy at the booth still about ten feet away like an incoming missile:

"So… Unlimited miles, right?"

"Yeah… Unlimited miles."

"So no matter how much I drive it's the same cost?"

"Well… I mean you gon hafta put in the gas an stuff."

Does this guy think I'm a fuckin idiot? "Right. Right. Okay. I'll take it."

So the rental car dude slowly starts typing the info into his computer at the speed of growing grass. "Impala…" he entered. Can this asshole take *any longer* to type? "How long a rental you want?" he asked.

So I think to myself hmmm… how long is this shit gonna take? How long before my soul heals? "Like… uhhh two weeks maybe?"

"Two weeks," he says to me in a solidifying tone as he puts it into his computer, tragically sluggish. Then I cut him off as he was typing—

"Actually I don't know."

He looked confused. "You don't know?"

"Maybe three weeks. Wait—if I wanna change the rental length can I? From the road?"

Jeez now I even sound crazy to the Enterprise guy.

"Where you goin? Africa?" He laughed. I didn't. "Just call us up. You can extend over the phone."

Gold.

I drove the Impala to Brooklyn and grabbed Ooli from the apartment, then picked up Dusty at the park and off we drove. I felt like a crazy man as we crossed the George Washington Bridge. No clue where the fuck I was going.

"You alright man? Where's Jessica?"

My heart jumped a beat and the car swerved a bit as small bits of screams and flashes of a knife passed behind my eyes.

"We broke up."

"Oh shit. I'm sorry. What happened?"

"She got pregnant."

Wait... Did I just say that?

"She got pregnant?!"

I guess I did say that.

"It's a long story. Let's go to where the Amish people are and make sure the audience knows that we're actually doing this. That *I'm literally* walking a puppy across America."

"Well, you're not literally walking the dog across the country, we're driving."

"You know what the fuck I mean."

I was irritable. This trip was gonna be a mess. Actually, it ends up in a jail on the border of Mexico... But we'll get there.

So, in Lancaster, I walk Ooli in front of a horse and buggy. In St Louis, Ooli and I walk by the Arch. In Kansas, we walk through a windy field of long dry grass. In Boulder... Oh man, I'm back in Boulder.

I thought of KC.

How could I not? Everywhere I went were splashes of memory in vivid image form—short films even. I had to get the fuck outa there immediately. Why'd I even come here? Was she alive? WHERE IS SHE? Maybe I should call her. No, she hates me. She's in Georgia. What if she moved back here without me? We quickly walked through Chautauqua State Park then got the fuck back on the road. Walked through the pine trees of Park City Utah. We really needed somewhere to sleep, so I called Jana—you remember her, right? The girl I took to the Ritz Carlton with me years ago to see that rich couple on a "World Tour Bender"? Yeah, she and I still hung out. Often, actually. In between every girlfriend I ever had was Jana. She would come to my apartment and drop to her knees and ask to blow me. She liked to be dominated, or be submissive, or whatever that shit is. She liked that type of thing, and so she was really hard to turn down, or ignore. I always found myself calling her after every tragedy. Anyway, her parents had a house in Park City. So I called her...

"Hey babe."

In a raspier voice than she used to have, "How's Ooli? Across the country yet? Miss me yet?"

She kept up with everything I did in life... "I always miss you," I told her. "We're actually in Park City."

"My parents have a house there."

"I remember."

"Oh, so *that* you remember? Let me guess… you need a place to stay?"

"No, not at all."

"Well, you can, if you want."

"Nah, I mean, we have Ooli and all…"

"Well, I know you have Ooli. I know you have a dog, Greg. You can stay, it's fine. The key is hidden. I'll tell you where it is."

"I love you. Kinda."

"You know you don't love me. You just love me right now."

"I deeply care about you."

"Whatever. I'll text you."

So she did. But then we had to go find some scotch, or any place to drink, and we weren't sure what to do with Ooli, so we put her in the bathroom. When we got back the entire bathroom was destroyed—scratch marks everywhere. The wood base molding, the door, everything. Ooli was pissed, and so was Jana.

But *everything* changed in The Biggest Little City in the World…

CHAPTER 34: RENÉE

A lonely sign in Nevada welcomed us to *The Biggest Little City in the World* when we got to Reno.

"What should we do?" I asked Dusty.

"Casino?"

"Should we find a motel first?"

"Will they let Ooli stay in the room you think?"

"Uhhh… We can just do it anyway, right?"

So we left Ooli in some shitty hotel room attached to some down-and-out casino, but like… since we had a dog, the building we stayed in was detached from the actual casino, like some add-on motel. Does that make me a bad dog dad? I mean, a dog doesn't know the difference between a shitty casino motel and a presidential suite, right? Whatever, we checked out the casino at our hotel, but it was full of old people and as silent as an elevator stuffed with strangers. So we left and drove around town. We went to another casino. More old people. "I thought this was supposed to be a cool town, no?" I asked Dusty. He shrugged. We left on foot and walked another block.

Suddenly we see a buncha cars piled up around some building. Upon closer investigation, we see that it's called, "The Men's Club." Hmm… Okay. So we enter the strip club and BOOM! The bustling city erupts. "SEE?! I KNEW THIS WAS THE SPOT!" I yelled at Dusty over the stripper music and wafts of cheap-scented perfume. Then I see this little redhead walking around, some stripper, a good one. She looked at me from across the room, I looked back. Then she left. Then from outa nowhere, a light touch of human perfection rested upon my lap and I looked up and it was her.

"Hi," she says.

"Hey there."

"I'm Brooklyn, who are you?"

"What's your real name?" I ask her.

"Renée."

I break the bad news to her….

"I'm Greg. I'm probably not gonna get a dance. So, you know, I feel bad taking up your time. But you are the best one here. The best stripper."

"I'm a dancer."

"Right, that's what I meant. Stripper just came out cause, well, we're in a strip club."

"Gentlemen's club."

She kept correcting me. Bitch. Some dude approached her and said: "Hey uhh.. my buddy really likes you…" and he shoves some money her way. "Can you come over?" and he pulls her towards his friend.

"I'll be right back," she says to me as she proceeds to give some dipshit a lap dance right next to me. Dusty is drinking a PBR and choking down cigarettes. I order vodka—the most expensive vodka of my life. Scotch here is trash, I'm sure. Trashy scotch is no good, so I drank trashy vodka instead. Meanwhile, Renée is staring at me the whole time… Wait, *is* she staring at me? Nah… she's a stripper—I mean dancer. That's what they do.

But the song ends and she's back on my lap, talking as if the conversation never left. I learn that she's named after the town she's from—not Renée, that's not really her name either, but for the story I can't tell you everything, know what I mean? Point is her real name was actually after a small desert town in New Mexico, which we can keep a secret for the sake of, well, not sharing *everything*. We're gonna call her Renée. Then another goddam dude approaches. He says… Well, yada yada yada… you get the picture. He wants a dance. How does this fucker know whether or not *I'm* getting a fuckin dance? Does it not look like I can afford a dance?! I can afford a fucking dance you piece of shit—I chucked my fake glass cup at his forehead—cause it was a cheap joint—the gentlemen's club—and it didn't break but he started swelling up right away, so Renée grabbed me and we ran out to the car and drove off to Lake Tahoe and got married. We fucked in every truck-stop bathroom along the way. The news reported on the radio that some guy was dead. I had killed him. Good, you fuckin piece of goddam dog shit—

"I'll be right back… Sorry!"

I came back to life. "All good, it's your job!"

What the fuck is going on? Why does she keep coming back? Does she like me? Aren't I not good enough? Wait—I'm the fucking man. What in the WORLD am I saying? LOOK AT ME! I fucking put on all these shows, I got a music agency and promotions company and I sell the best weed in the country to celebrities and lawyers and—But then I thought of Jessica. Oh man. I'm going to hell. She's miserable and I'm in a strip club. I should dump my head in sand and punish myself. No, that's dumb. That's a dumb idea Greg. Just move on with your life. Was that kid really a kid? Was the baby real? Does abortion exist? It does, cause she had one. And you're responsible for it. You ruined her lifelong dream of being a mom. You're a piece of garbage and you think you're the shit.

Wait—I'm a producer. No, a *live entertainment* producer. Shit, I'm making a movie. That makes me a *filmmaker*. But I sell weed… So I guess I'm a drug-dealer. Dammit, WHO AM I?

I see Renée behind a cloud of smoke. She's staring at me from across the room as she bounces her petite ass in front of some dickhead, not that I know he's even a mean guy, or even disrespectful at that, but he's in a strip club... Of COURSE he's a dickhead. But I'm in a strip club. Am I a dickhead? Definitely. The song ends and she's right back on my lap.

"I think I'ma go," I tell her. Dusty had been talkin to some other stripper—dancer, the whole time. "You ready man?" I ask him. He nods. I swig the rest of my drink. I've had about four vodkas by then cause like I said, they didn't have any good scotch and bad scotch is like... *really* bad. So I was drinkin vodka. Vodka cranberry at strip clubs, and dirty martinis at bars—if the mood strikes. Anyway, I tell her I gotta go.

"Wait... don't you want my number?" she asks me.

"Your number?"

"Yeah!"

"Ummm... Yeah. What's your number?"

So we exchange numbers. Then she says to me, "Do you wanna hang out after work?"

FUCK YEAH I DO! YOU HOT LITTLE STRIPPER! I WANNA BANG YOUR FUCKING HEAD OFF!!

"Ummm... yeah, sure, why not?"

"I get off at like 4, will you be awake?"

"I'll stay awake."

"Where are you staying?"

"At the shitty casino by the uhh... what's the name Dusty?"

Dusty said the name. Then we got up to leave, completely clusterfucked by this whole situation.

"WAIT!!" she screamed behind me. "Don't you wanna see me dance? I go on stage next."

"You want me to watch you go on stage?"

"Uh huh!"

Usher's *OMG* came on and she took the stage. Her moves were spectacular. She wore two thongs and climbed to the top of the pole, swung upside down, and peeled off one thong with her high heels, the other thong still intact. Super talented girl.

RING RING RING RING.

Huh?

I wake up. It's 5am.

NNNNOOOOOOOOOOOOOOO!!!!! **FUCKKKKKKKKKK!!!**

I check my phone; there're six missed calls. I look at Dusty passed out on the bed. The room only had one bed. I look at Ooli, sleeping next to Dusty. I was basically falling off the mattress. I look at my phone and frantically call the number back.

"Gosh. I thought you forgot about me... do you still want to hang out?"

"Yeah of course!"

I'm flustered as fuck trying to figure out how this was all gonna work. Where will we go? I didn't even tell her I have a dog. Should I fuck her next to Dusty? How do I even know she wants to fuck? It's 5AM, *of course* she wants to fuck, she's a stripper! No she's *not* Greg! She's a goddam dancer!!

"Good I'm almost at your casino. Meet me out front?" she says.

Did I tell her the casino I was at? I don't remember that. Get outa your head and figure this shit out. So I jet down to the concierge.

"I need a room."

"Great, check in is at—"

"—No, I need one now."

"Oooohhhhhh," and he winks at me.

"No no, it's not like that. She's a stripper."

"Right."

"She is."

"Right."

I get a room close to the other room and make it look like I've been staying there. She calls my phone, "I'm here!" I was in love already. I jet downstairs, but not before cleaning myself up, and there she is, in hippie clothing with bright pink heels and a sparkly dress sticking out of her small, Rastafarian-colored woven purse. Her face was tiny like a figurine. Seriously, this must be why I'm here. The trip wasn't about the film, it was the universe bringing me to my soulmate in Reno, Nevada.

I woke up the next morning, Renée in my arms. It was the greatest sex of my life. And by that I meant it went off with no complications. I was sure it was the best sex of her life too. I mean, I've *never* woken up with a girl still in my arms. This must be what true love is.

"Come to San Francisco with me," I tell her.

"Are you serious?"

"Yes."

"Why you going to San Francisco?"

"We're making a movie."

"About what?"

"A guy that walks his dog across the country."

"You have a dog with you?"

"Next door, I'll introduce you."

"Really?"

"Come with me."

"Are you serious?"

"Very."

"How will I get back?"

"I'll pay for your train. It'll be fun. Road trip."

"Well… okay!"

I go to the other room and wake Dusty up. "Where the fuck have you been?" he asks me.

"Renée came over!"

"Who?"

"She's coming to Sanfran with us!"

"What?" He says as he gets up and puts his clothes on, trying to put two and two together.

"Yeah! I really like her!"

"The stripper?" He's really confused.

"Her name's Renée. She's amazing."

"Uhh… Okay dude. Look, I gotta run to the roulette table real quick and make a hundred bucks." I didn't even question that statement. "Yeah man, I'm totally broke. I spent two hundred dollars last night. I'll be back." And he left the room.

Renée and I drove through the desert. She directed me to a college dorm room on some shitty college campus. "I'll be right back, okay? Gotta get my stuff. Stay here. Don't get out."

"Everything okay?" I ask.

"Yeah just wait. I'll be back."

I was so excited about this. She came back out with a small backpack and some poi—you know those balls on strings that hippies wave in the air at music festivals and raves and shit? Yeah, well, that's all she had.

"That's all your stuff?"

"Yup!"

FASTFORWARD to San Francisco.

"Come to LA with me."

FASTFORWARD to Los Angeles.

"Come back to New York with me"

FASTFORWARD to El Paso

Lights. Bright lights.

Shit… Border Patrol. We were at a checkpoint on Interstate 10. Renée was driving. I was asleep in the backseat with Ooli. Dusty was in the passenger seat. We had Jersey plates. By the way, we hadn't shot a minute of footage since Reno. So we had a half-done film, which was supposed to be the entire point of the trip… till I met Renée. Anyway, cops everywhere. The car doors open. They start rummaging through our shit.

"Any drugs on you?" one agent says to me. Dusty stares at me. Renée stares at Dusty. I stare at the cop. The cop stares at Ooli. "That a Doberman? Why didn't you clip the ears?" I left her ears floppy cause I didn't want her to scare any more people than she already did. It wasn't her fault she was scary looking.

"Cause I didn't want to," I tell the prick. I totally forgot about that weed I bought on Venice Beach. I had one gram—*one fucking gram*—from one of those medical weed joints that're scattered all over California. I didn't wanna lie and fuck myself over for one gram of weed, so I figured best to just let him know about it. I mean, at the rate they were going, they'd find it in a bit anyway.

"Uhhh…" I began, "I have like a gram of pot," I told the cop. He handcuffs me. "Wait, is that a problem?"

"Yessir, you've got drugs. You're under arrest. That's the problem."

He didn't have an accent at all. He was Mexican with no accent. I guess that makes him American. I tried to reason with him…

"But I have a doctor's card for it and all."

"This is Texas. Zero tolerance."

Renée and Dusty were handcuffed alongside me. They walked us all to jail. Fuck. Renée might break up with me over this.

We were each thrown in a different cell. I *really* had to piss. My cellmate was a pudgy black dude in his twenties with cornrows and was lying down on the metal bench in the cell when I got in. I rushed right by him and started peeing in the metal toilet.

"Whatchu in for?"

"They found a gram of pot in my car and they threw my dog in a big cage outside and now I'm here. You?" I say all that to him while I was pissing.

He let it rip… "Man they tryin'a tell me I got like… a ounce'a shrooms or some shit in ma bag?" I wasn't sure if that was a question. "But that shit ain't mine. I was on the Greyhound and they just pulled me off an said I had like… Yeah. What I said. I dunno man. Now they be sayin I got like a warrant out for my arrest?"

"Nah man you'll be all good. You're good." This dude is fucked, I thought. Shit. Renée is all alone, or is she? I start yelling for one of the guards through the bars of my cell. "EYO!"

"WHAT?!" one guard says.

"That redhead, she's my girlfriend. I just met her three days ago in Reno, and seriously she didn't do anything. She doesn't even really smoke. I'll take the charge or whatever, but can you just please let her out??"

The guard looked at me like I was a fuckin idiot.

Silence.

He's still looking. Finally:

"Shut the heck up," and he walked away.

Four hours later the door to my cell opened and I was taken to the front of the jail place. Renée and Dusty were waiting for me on a wooden bench. Renée looked fucking *pissed*. Goddammit, I knew this shit would be a bad look. So, I paid them $750 and they let us go. I went to get Ooli from the big cage they stuck her in way off the side of the road. Different Mexican Border Patrol dudes start asking me *again* why I didn't cut her ears and make them point up. She had these beautiful floppy ears and these imbeciles want me to chop em off? Go fuck yourself. "Cause I didn't fuckin want to."

The car was a *mess* when they gave it back to us. The weed was gone—obviously. Our luggage and things were everywhere. We drove to a small town like seventy miles away and rented a room at a rundown motel. Dusty went to sleep immediately. Renée ran outside and called me a dick. I poured myself some of the scotch we had bought after the debacle on our way to the motel into one of those single-serving plastic cups that the motel left by the ice bucket in our room, then went after Renée. I apologized profusely. Finally, she forgave me, kinda.

We had sex in the bathroom while Dusty was sleeping and eventually, we made it back to Brooklyn. She moved in with me and never left. Both of us tried to water our relationship in my three-hundred square-foot studio in Park Slope. Me, Renée, and Ooli in a closet. I assured her I'd take care of our lives, like I was some sorta millionaire. But I was just some medium pot dealer, which I failed to mention to her till she was moved in.

There were pounds of weed all over the studio apartment, a growing Doberman that kept eating her thongs and puking them up—which made her *seriously* mad, and a cop living below me. There were stacks of cash all over as we slept on the pull-out couch together—us and Ooli. It was tight. I failed to mention I didn't have a bed either. I left out a buncha shit. I thought well… all these things might put her off, but if I can just get her to Brooklyn, she'll see I'm worth it. And then there was the scotch. Bottles of scotch everywhere. Not sure if she knew just how much I drank, but there was no questioning it now.

Let's just say the relationship moved quite fast…

CHAPTER 35: WRONG STOP

It had been four months since I brought Renée back to my studio apartment with nothing but a pull-out bed, an alcohol problem, a growing Doberman, and about seventy thousand bucks shoved in my safe in stacks of hundreds, fifties, and twenties, though I had stopped accepting twenties. You know how much space they take up? Not like I had a gigantic safe or anything—that'd just raise suspicion should any unwanted visitors show up…

I only had remnants of the last Colorado package, and though I wasn't planning to go back, showbusiness was taking longer than anticipated, so I needed some more inventory to keep me afloat— just a tiny bit longer. But I hadn't been able to leave Renée for even a second, let alone to go to Colorado to meet My Grower for more weed cause, well… then she'd just be, I don't know… in my apartment wondering what to do. So, as my supply began to dwindle, I got more and more stressed about everything we bought, *and* not only that, but my clients got harder to handle cause the last of a package was nothing but that shake from the bottom of the bag and people hated buying that shit. That's why I'd mix all the weed I had left, all the different strains, I'd mix them together, give it a different name, and simply re-sell it as a different product. But people saw through that shit.

"This is Jumbo Kush. It's perfect joint-rolling weed," I'd say.

"It chlook like last but meexed," the Chicken-farming Jew would say in response.

There was no pulling one over on that guy, and it woulda been bad business if I tried. So I told him the truth: "Okay look… It's the best of the best, all mixed together. A healthy salad I cooked especially for you. That's why it's a bit cheaper: It's not pure. But I know you like good and cheap, am I right?"

"Not wrong, but not right."

So anyway, all I knew was I had pot, cash, and a stripper—dancer—in my tiny studio in Park Slope, an off-duty lesbian cop as my bottom neighbor, and a Doberman that was now nearly six-feet tall when she stood on her hind legs. Let's just say it was a tight squeeze.

Eventually, Renée found a job at some café down on Wall Street. Her *first day* on the job, she says to me, "How do I get there? Will you come with me?"

"To Wall Street then come right back? That's crazy! Just take the subway!"

I guess the nicer thing to do woulda been to go with her, after all, she was from Nevada and knew nothing about New York. Anyhow, I told her hell no and gave her directions on how to get there… But I fucked up. I gave her the wrong route and she called me from Bedford and Nostrand Avenue from a fuckin payphone. Basically, at that time, it was one of the worst intersections of Brooklyn. It's where Biggie and Jay-Z are from. I think. Who knows a specificity like that? Anyway, she was PISSED THE FUCK OFF—rightly so.

That fight carried into the evening, and I knew she was gonna be mad when she came home from work, so I poured myself some scotch before she walked in and put on *Mad Men*. That show always made me feel like it was okay to drink scotch. I mean, I was a hard-working man. I deserved a drink. Or seven. But was I hard-working? I wasn't sure. But I made a lot of money, that's what matters. Though I'm not even sure I made that much money. It just looked like a lot all in cash, stacked up like that.

When Renée got home, she threw her shit down and paraded around the studio, which wasn't a far parade, and got all pissy. I went up to her and kissed her.

"Stop it!" she shouted. She was always shouting.

"Do you… wanna have sex?" I asked.

Oh man how could I say that to her right now? She slapped me in the face five times till I fell on the couch, which morphed into a bed at night, like I told you, other than the times it stayed out all day. But since Renée moved in, I tried to keep it tidy, and at that time, the bed was a couch. So yeah, she slapped me in the face five times and I remember that shit vividly cause I was so proud of myself that I didn't lose my temper and sock her in the jaw. I just fell back on the couch and took a deep breath. Then she slapped me again and I got up and chucked her off me. Dammit. I almost made it. Then came the words—bad words:

"YOU FUCKING SLUT STOP HITTING ME!"

"YOU FUCKING ASSHOLE! YOU SAID YOU WOULD TAKE CARE OF ME!"

"I AAAMMMMMMMM YYYOOOUUUU FUUCCK KINGGGG—CAN'T YOU SEE HOW MUCH I'M DOING FOR YOU?!!?"

"ALL YOU DO IS DRINK!"

I tried to get away from her psychosis, but when I went outside on the porch to smoke in peace, the lesbian cop neighbor was outside with her lover and said:

"Sorry to bring it up again, but… Always smells like marijuana up there."

"Yeah well, I like to smoke. Too much maybe, I know."

"I know that, but it smells pretty strong… How much marijuana *do you have* up there anyway?"

"I buy an ounce at a time."

"Huh."

And that was that. It was a rough day all around, but at least that was the last we spoke of my weed habit, well, until she came up with her gun ready to chuck my ass in jail… But that came later.

Point is I knew how loud Renée and I were getting when we argued, and I was scared she was gonna rat me out; she knew everything. So whenever the fights got too loud, I'd grab a duffle bag—cliché-sounding I know, but it really *was* a duffle bag, from American Apparel actually, and I'd shove all my money and all my pot in the bag and call the local car service. It usually showed up within three minutes. Then I'd escape to my brothers till she calmed down.

"36ᵗʰ and Second please."

"Brrewklin?"

"No, Manhattan."

"You go to Mahatt'n?"

He was like Hispanic maybe. Anyway, no cabbies liked to drive to the city, so I always had to convince them that it was a good idea:

"That's right. And there's *always* someone there that needs to go to Park Slope, always. It'll be good money for you—and a quick ride too, plus I'll leave you a nice tip. Thank you so much." I always thanked them before they actually agreed to drive me. In fact, I went overboard. "I really REALLY appreciate it man." That way they felt obligated to drive me there.

But after a night of hiding out at my brother's, sleeping on his slippery leather couch, waking up with my face glued to the armrest, I knew I had to come back home—which was a shitty feeling knowing I *had* to come back. After all, now there was someone depending on me. And usually, I'd escape for one night, come back, apologize, and try to get her back in a good mood so I could exist somewhat peacefully for another twenty-four hours, but on that particular day, when I got back to Brooklyn, Renée delivered some life-shattering news…

CHAPTER 36: SCRAM!

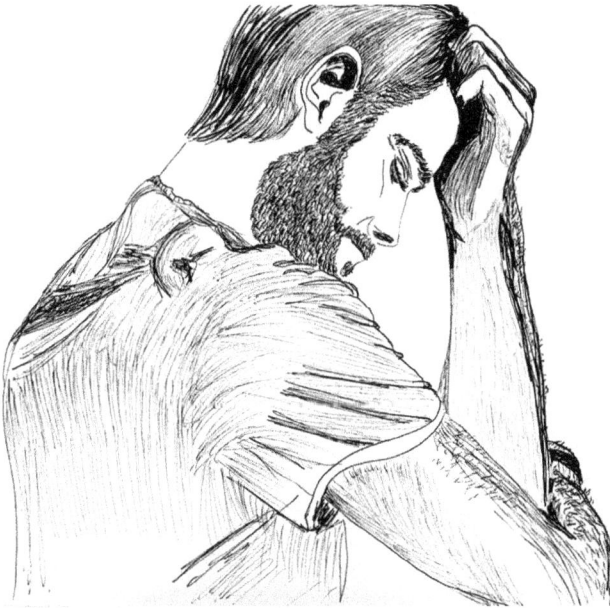

First, it started with our average fight.

"WHY'D YOU LEAVE ME? I HAD TO TAKE CARE OF OOLI! I THOUGHT YOU WEREN'T COMING BACK!"

She was crying. I felt pitifully vile. "I'm sorry." But what more could I possibly say to make our situation better? I fucked up. Again. I wanted to kiss her spirit and make everything all better. I wanted to be a better man. I just didn't know how. Then she told me.

"The neighbor came up."

"Which one?" I got scared.

"She came up with her gun."

"WHAT?! WHO?! THE COP?"

"Yeah."

Renée was sitting on the bed, the bed was pulled out, and she looked down and spoke softly as if she'd done something wrong.

"What'd she say?"

"She asked if everything was okay."

"What'd you say?"

"I said you took off right after you got violent with me."

WWWWHHHHHHHAAAAAATTTTTT?!

I freaked out in my head but kept my cool and said, "I gotta go to a café to do some work. I'll be back later."

"You're leaving again?"

"Yes. I am. Bye," and I left.

I went to the Red Horse Café on 6th avenue, a few blocks away, and went on Craigslist. I found an apartment down by Coney Island... In a part of Brooklyn I'd never heard of called Midwood. I called the agent's number and asked, "Can I see the place?"

He talked with a very think Orthodox Jewish accent.

"Chyes. Chwhat time?"

"Now. I'm on my way."

So I took a cab down there. I had four grand in my pocket. I arrived thirty minutes later at this all-Russian neighborhood. Nothing was in English. It was the most depressed looking building I'd ever seen on Kings Highway and Avenue P on East 19th Street.

I met the Orthodox Jew real estate agent on the sidewalk by the front door and he said, "Chjust you?"

Did he think I was married? "Yeah why?" I say to him.

"Chit's beeg."

"Big is fine, let me see it."

So he took me up to the apartment. It was enormous. Like sixteen-hundred square feet. About ten times the size of the Park Slope studio. Without even looking around I said, "I'll take it."

"Chyou cannot rent."

"What?"

"No chsublet."

"What do you mean? Rent it to other people? It's just me."

"Thees chvery beeg for chjust you."

This fuck didn't believe me… "IT'S JUST ME!"

"Why you need such beeg apartment? You cannot work office from out here."

What a fuckin—"I work alone, just me. There's no boiler room I'm building here, I just like the apartment." I took out a stack of cash. "How much?"

He looked at the money for a second. He musta been thinking: This isn't kosher. HAHA! I said this wasn't kosher while telling you about an orthodox Jew! That's kinda funny. Anyway, what I was doin looked shady for sure, with good reason. I was shady in general.

"Chyou have gewd credit?"

"I have the best credit." I pulled out my phone and showed him my credit score. "I need this place today. I need it now. I'll sign the lease."

He thought for a moment. "If I hear you renting or office, lease done."

"Deal."

So I went back to the Red Horse Café and opened up my computer. It was a Sunday, so they didn't have the air conditioning on. It was like early October or something, and it was hot out that day, and I was sweating in the humidity of the coffee shop, but all the cafes in Park Slope didn't use electricity on the weekends... Some hippie contract all the businessowners made with each other—part of the reason I loved the neighborhood so much: the culture. But anyway, I was hot in that fuckin place as I navigated my way back to Craigslist on my laptop and found a moving company. I called.

The guy who picked up was Russian, I could tell by his accent. Everyone in Brooklyn seems to be Russian.

"I need to move right away," I told him. We ironed out a time for he and his crew to bolt my belongings from Park Slope to Midwood. Then I went back down to Midwood when the orthodox Jewish real estate agent said my key was ready. This is all confusing, I know, but I had to do something drastic to straighten this situation out. At any moment I could be prosecuted and thrown in prison for domestic abuse. Then they'd find my money and weed when clearing out my apartment, at which point they'd call the DA and up my charges. Then I'd have to go *back* to court and have a *new* trial, where the jury would deem that *more* time was needed to rectify my soul. It'd be a catastrophe. I'm not sure if that's actually what would happen, but who cares? Point is, at *that point* Renée would be alone with all my things, steal all my shit, and render me completely impoverished. I'd be ten times worse off than I was before I met her. Something had to happen and happen fast.

So I went *back* to the Red Horse Café for a *third* time after I had the key and got word the movers were a few hours away to call my cop neighbor and make sure I was safe…

I met up with her at some local bar. She drank as much as I did, or close to it.

The first thing she said was: "So I heard your ruffle tussle with your girlfriend last night. Did she tell you?"

"She said you came up, yeah." I took a swig.

"So what happened?" She asked, eyeing me like I was a piece of garbage.

I had to right this wrong and disappear without disclosing too much, but enough so that she wouldn't look further into the incident…

"She hit me. And I threw her off me," I told her.

WHOA! I TOLD THE TRUTH! IT JUST CAME OUT!

"Did you call the police?"

"You mean you?"

"I work in the city. I mean the local precinct. Did you file a report?"

"No, she's tiny. I just didn't know what to do. She's like five feet tall. I couldn't call the cops on *her*."

"Well, if you don't file a report on her, I will."

I took a swig. This was going bizarrely. "I'll do it tomorrow morning, first thing. Are you working tonight?" But I knew she was working that night cause she always worked on Tuesdays.

"Yes, I have to leave but wanted to talk to you about this. I was going to come over anyway if you hadn't called."

"I'm glad you came, I'll grab your drink. Have a good night at work, be safe."

She left. The movers had been calling me, but I didn't pick up. Finally I called them back.

"WHAT FUCKIN SHEET MAN?!" they screamed with an accent.

They were mad. "Sorry sorry, I was with a client. Are you on the way?"

"HERE!"

I ran back to the apartment and there was a huge moving truck blocking the entire road, cause in Park Slope, well, in Brooklyn, if there's a truck on the road, you can't get around it. So traffic had been stopped on 10th street.

The movers were two scary Russian guys. I went up to them and said, "Look. This might be hard. There's a girl in there. She's not going to know what you're doing. She might throw things at you. She'll be loud. Just get in and out as quick as possible."

Look, I was *not* about to go to prison. I *had* to do this. Every time I thought about getting caught, about not being able to drink in prison and detoxing off Xanax and getting the jitters and the shakes, about being alone in my head in a metal room without booze, sweating and going mad, I shivered in horror. No way. I knew what I was doing might equal years in prison, right? I don't know, but I had no attorney. Renée ratted me out. Who knows what else she'll say to her? I had to get out before anyone found me. I kept tellin the movers:

"I'll tip you well. Just get this done and meet me by the new address."

Renée was lying down when I let them in. The Russians were efficient, grabbing all the shit, all the furniture, and moving it into the truck, all the while communicating in Russian and ironing out their strategy as if this was just another job.

"What the FUCK ARE YOU DOING GREG?!"

"I'm sorry Renée. I have to do this. I'm sorry I let you down."

"YOU'RE LEAVING?!"

"I'm sorry." Then I looked at the movers, who had started throwing loose articles in boxes and rearranging them so they didn't break inside the box. "DON'T WORRY ABOUT HOW THEY'RE PACKED! JUST GET IT OUT!"

"WHERE AM I SUPPOSED TO GO?!" Renée screamed at me.

I took out a few hundred dollars and handed it to her.

"I'm sorry. Go wherever you want."

"BUT I HAVE NOWHERE TO GO!"

"I'm sorry. I have to leave." The movers were looking at the sofa bed. "Sorry Renée, can you stand up? They need the bed."

"NO!"

"RENÉE STAND UP!!" She wouldn't move at first, but she acquiesced eventually, stood up and cried. What have I gotten myself into? The Russians put the couch in the truck. Before I left, I told her: "The wifi still works. The computer is yours. Here's a suitcase. The rent is paid. There's some more money in the front pocket. I'm sorry." And I left with Ooli.

We disappeared to south Brooklyn and never came back…

CHAPTER 37: THE EDGE OF EARTH

It was just me and Ooli in a big-ass, ugly-as-fuck apartment at the edge of Earth.

The sound of loud trucks unloading Russian sodas into the Russian supermarket below the apartment went all night long. The hallway smelled of musk and there were six doors right next to each other on my floor—the second floor. Without knowing better, you'd think you'd walk right into your adjacent neighbor's bathroom after opening the front door, but no. Open the door and you enter sixteen-hundred square feet.

Entering the apartment was a sad feeling; everything about it was depressing. A narrow foyer dumped you into a colossal living room, which spider-webbed into three other rooms, all far too big to furnish. Even after spending thousands of dollars on furniture, the apartment still looked empty. There was nothing on the walls. No décor at all. In the living room I had a larger-than-life flat-screen TV, which I paid for in cash, sitting on a basic Ikea TV table—the same Ikea TV table the entire world also had—and then my black leather sofa bed from Park Slope. It looked sad and sparse.

Plus, I was so far south that none of my friends—or clients— would even come to visit me.

Wait.

Do I even have any friends? I guess Wally was my friend. Wally was this guy I met one day when I was hanging out with this shitty band from Brooklyn's manager. They were a shitty band but knew how to promote a show, so I always booked them. Their manager was a bit sleazy but knew everyone. We did coke together often. Anyway, he's the one who introduced me to Wally. He had Wally doing some bullshit intern work for him. Eventually Wally quit. He was just out of college and looking to take over the world—Wally was, so people often take advantage of guys like that. He was tall and wore a suit when he didn't have to. Trying too hard maybe. He had a lot to learn. But after he quit the internship, he and I hung out regularly. Maybe we can work together? I told him all about everything I'd built. All that I'd won, and all that I'd lost. I tried to impress him cause he was younger than me, and if I can't even impress younger dudes, then what the fuck am I doing, right? I should be an idol. But yeah, he wanted to take over the world like I did and we often pondered how to do so together. We hadn't figured it out yet. Only thing that bothered me was the fact that he had an advantage over me: he was younger. I was already twenty-six by the time I met him. But anyway, he mighta been my friend, though he had lots of friends so it's hard to tell. Point is, he was the only one who came over. And Joey Landlord… he came over too. I'll tell ya about Joey Landlord after this…

But yeah, the loneliness crept in. I worked on Black Apple solo. What exactly *was* Black Apple now that it's just me?, I wondered. Nothing really. Just a name.

Minnie must be some porn star by now. Or model. Or whatever. I still jerked off to her. Jessica. Don't think about her right now. And now Renée. Fuckin shit. No more. I'm done dating.

I had just gotten back from Colorado, again. I always said it'd be my last trip, and it never was. At least I could finally go now that I was alone again. I had seven pounds of pot in my dresser—a smaller amount than normal cause seven pounds was the exact amount I needed to sell to get to eighty grand in cash, and I swore to myself (again) that this was the *last* trip. After all the product is gone, I'm done. Out. So, till then I set up my pot office in my second bedroom. In that bedroom, center stage, was this Godfather-like desk. I sat behind it whenever clients would come over, which like I said, wasn't very often given how far away I was. I had to take hundred-dollar roundtrips to North Brooklyn and Manhattan to meet people, but whatever.

I had my two biggest concerts to date scheduled on January 28th and 29th at The Music Hall of Williamsburg and The Mercury Lounge. I figured these would be my last two shows. I was tired of everything. But at least I had Wally to help me out with those. I had to prove to myself—and to him, that I could do a *great* show, at least once. But you *have* done great shows Greg. No, I mean a HUGE show. Why does everything need to be bigger and better? Shhh…. Be quiet. My head was loud. It always was nowadays.

Anyway, the room I slept in had a California King-sized bed and a smaller dresser to the side. I looked at it. There was nothing but sticky glasses with remnants of scotch all over. Empty bags of coke. The bed wasn't made. Clothes were all over. Joint roaches in every home-made ashtray. My closet door was open and stuffed full of still-packed bags from the move. Beneath all the clothes was my safe.

Fuck I forgot to feed Ooli.

Maybe I should give her away... Yeah. It's what's best for her. I didn't realize how much work all this would be. All I wanted was a friend and Ooli was too much work to keep happy. Plus, every time I walked her around the neighborhood the Russians all looked at me like I was a Nazi. I'm a Jew, just like you... pieces of Russian shit. But still I wasn't a Jew like *they were* Jews. They were serious Jews—Russian Jews.

Then my doorbell rang.

It was some burnout who was referred to me, you know, one of those guys that does nothing but smoke his bong and go to music festivals... Broke, no direction in life, uncombed, wavy hair with no hygienic care in years: a burnout. I can't believe I was taking on shitty clients again.

Anyway, he came in and I had to keep Ooli from jumping all over him with all my might. I couldn't tell if he was scared of her, or if he didn't realize she was there, or forgot every now and then, then remembered again and got startled. He was in his own world. Total bum. But still, I shared my entire head of thoughts and sorrows with him on that day as he stared at my whiteboard, opposite my Godfather desk, with writings so mad only an insane asylum veteran would be able to decode it.

"What's that?" he asked me.

"Oh, see, that's an idea I have for a festival. See that's the middle, it's like a village, and those are like... I dunno, huts kinda. The idea is everyone walks out of their hut and is forced to meet in the middle. It encourages friendship, cause why do people go to festivals, right? To make friends."

"Well... I've been to quite a few festivals, eh hah ha," he had this stoner laugh. "And there're more reasons to go than that I think."

He might be right. Maybe I didn't think this through? I had never been to one music festival my entire life, and here I was criticizing why they were all doing it wrong. "Okay, well, all that can be worked on, but the general idea is to create a utopia of life in one place—a new town, a city in the middle of nowhere—"

"—like Burning Man?"

"Uhh... I don't know, I've never been there."

"Sounds like Burning Man eh hah ha."

"I don't know. But look, the idea is—the real idea, is the *promotion* of the festival—not the festival itself, which can be curated however, but what is something all festival-goers do?"

"Uhh..."

"—They smoke weed! So I promote the festival with rolling papers! Like you know, flyers but they're rolling papers. People would HAVE to look at it like thirty times, all day, every time they rolled a joint, so they'd be reminded about the festival all week while smoking—and people that smoke, they smoke all the time, right?"

But that was it. He lost interest. He didn't have the vision I had. I gave him the weed and he left. I cleared space on my seventy-inch whiteboard, careful not to erase some of the genius still comprehensible in my memory. I was *always* comin up with ideas like this, and so I needed a really big whiteboard to write it all down on—but thing is, lots of it made no sense an hour later, let alone *two days* later. Complete nonsense by then. So that's why I needed an enormous whiteboard, so I could leave the old ideas on there—graphs, charts, pictures and all, till I remembered what the hell I was thinkin about at the time. Actually I just wanted the biggest everything and this was the biggest whiteboard I could find. So I got it.

I re-drew the pic of the insane music festival that was just in my head. It was in the shape of a circle, right? A circle is what I was thinking of... yeah. A circle. And the people—a bunch people, they'll be sleeping in teepees and huts—which surround the circle right here, yeah, okay cool and then... ummm, fuck. What was it? All surrounding a circle so that—so that what? Oh right! So they wake up in the morning and *have* to walk past each other. They'll have no choice but to communicate. That's all I ever wanted... People to talk to. And this festival will solve that problem.

What to call it? I'll call it Wonderland, cause that was probably my biggest success to date... Man that was a while ago. But this will be the Wonderland *Music* Festival. It had a nice ring to it. Of course that name has been used a billion times by now, but when I came up with the idea, I thought it was innovative. But who knows? I'd never been to a music festival. I heard they were fun though. I called up Wally and tried to get him psyched...

"DUDE! I GOT A BRILLIANT IDEA!" I said to him.

"I'm on my way my dude!"

He was always so excited to make money. So was I. Maybe that's why we got along. He was the only friend willing to come to Midwood to see me. He got over and I showed him my whiteboard.

"Dude what the—," and he started laughing—"What the *fuck* is that? It looks... *AWESOME!*"

"It *is* man."

"The Wonderland Music Festival?"

I had written the name of it on the whiteboard, of course.

"Yeah dude, it's gonna work, but here's the brilliant idea... WE DON'T USE FLYERS! WE MAKE CUSTOM WONDERLAND ROLLING PAPERS TO PROMOTE IT!"

"Holy shit. My mind is blown." He was always so excitable. Maybe *that's* why we liked each other. "So how do we make rolling papers?"

"I don't know."

And that was the end of that discussion... Until I reached out to that kid came back over a week later—the stoner festival kid—for more weed. I kept having to spot him a hundred bucks here and there. He *never* had the entire amount he owed me, but I liked talking to him, plus he was my festival consultant, so I just gave him discounts. And it was worth it, cause on that day everything came to a turn when he offered to put me in touch with his friend, the heiress of ██████████ rolling papers: Judy (not her real name). Obviously.

But I kinda veered off track from the actual festival when I started crunching the numbers on how much it would cost to buy the promotional rolling papers, and how much we *could make* if we were to actually *sell them*.

I called up Wally immediately, "WALLY! Fuck the music festival! LET'S JUST SELL ROLLING PAPERS! *TWEED* ROLLING PAPERS!!"

"NICE! What's Tweed Rolling Papers?"

He was confused... OH WAIT—You must be confused too... I never told you about Tweed. It's another BRILLIANT idea! Okay, so, one day, years ago, my brother, Eric, came home from his art college that he was goin to... Fuck, he's out of college already? Anyway, he was in school and came back to his apartment with an idea for an advertising campaign for a medicinal marijuana dispensary. He was studying graphic design and advertising and so this was one of his projects. He drafted up an entire look-book. The dispensary had these old-school Tweed vibes. The budtenders *wore* Tweed. The grinders looked like Tweed. The merchandise *was* Tweed. Lastly, the custom-designed rolling papers had this Tweed pattern. It was fucking awesome. Every person that came over his apartment raved about how amazing the concept was, cause his look-book was always just chillin out on his living room table with a prototype right next to it. But he had no idea how to do anything with it. So I called Eric, "YO! WE'RE GONNA BRING TWEED TO LIFE!" Wally was right next to me. I had Eric on speaker.

And one month later...

Me, Eric, Wally, and our friend Elly Belly had 35,000 Tweed booklets on a cargo ship sailing across the Pacific Ocean towards the port in Long Beach, California.

The plan was to travel to music festivals all over the country— you know, so I could finally experience them, and sell Tweed, one-by-one, out of our car—or Wally's mom's car—while *simultaneously filming a movie about it*. This was SURE to work. I would do it all at once: Start a business *not related to music or theatre,* travel the country, meet chicks at music festivals, get me out of the weed game, *and produce my first feature-length film!* It couldn't fail.

Till then, I just had to liquidate this weed. Then, well, then I'd be on my way to my last, greatest, and final idea, the idea that would shape my life forever. And it did.

But first... Joey Landlord.

CHAPTER 38: JOEY LANDLORD

Joey Landlord and I were almost friends.

It was some time around five in the evening when he came over—and I remember that it was around that time because I was on my second glass of scotch. I generally never drank before the sun went down. But since it was the winter and the sun kept setting earlier, the time of day I poured my first drink was creeping up on me.

The buzzer went off and Ooli immediately started barking. I loved her but she kept me prisoner in my own apartment. I couldn't leave without her tearing all my throw rugs to shreds. Everything I owned, which wasn't much, had to be elevated out of her reach any time I left—and elevated really high by the way, given her giraffe-like legs and kangaroo jumping ability. But I was tellin you that Joey Landlord and I were almost friends. He was the only original client still willing to visit me down here in south Brooklyn, even with the scary dog. That's what I liked about him so much: his loyalty and his temperament. I wonder if he liked me too?

I buzzed him in, listening for his footsteps to get closer to my door so I'd know precisely when to open it, so Ooli wouldn't make a great escape into the hallway and let the building know that I was housing an attack dog. I did that while rapidly rounding up all the toys on the floor that we'd need to keep Ooli distracted till business had concluded—and that was no easy task. She needed about as much attention as I did.

He knocked on the door and Ooli barked like someone was hopping a barbed-wire fence. What had I gotten myself into? I opened the door fast, holding her back with every fiber of bicep, lateral, and whatever other muscles were required to keep the goddam dog from ripping my arm off.

"Yo man! Come in!"

"Dooooddddd! —Hii Ooli!—**DOWN!**" and he kneed his way down my hall, knocking her down with his knee every time she jumped to lick his face. She was friendly but goddam annoying. She was ninety pounds of pure adrenaline. I handed him the tug-of-war toy that she loved—or hated—as soon as he made it to my living room. I was embarrassed about it all but tried to play it off, though playing it off is super tiring, I can assure you that.

I kept thinking Ooli might cure my emotional despair after me and Jessica's tumultuous departure. Trouble is, as I then knew it, was I had no idea how to take care of a large and dominant dog. It was clear my brilliant idea was now a burdensome terror that kept me trapped in my own home.

He followed me through my astronomically large-for-no-reason apartment, still with barely any furniture in it, to my Godfather white desk in my office. Office for what? I don't know. To prove to myself that I had a real job; that I wasn't damaged; that I was no more behind in life than any other twenty-six-year-old dude; that I had earned what I had; that I was loved; that my legacy was coming to fruition in just the way I had planned it when I was kicked out of my parent's home at fourteen. Nevertheless, the desk served no purpose. Still it sat in the center of an empty room, in its Godfather-like fashion, with nothing else to accompany it other than an adult-like dresser. But there were no clothes in the dresser. There were six pounds in the dresser. My clothes were on the floor of my closet. The place was too damn big to furnish every square foot. I had a hard enough time buying groceries at the Russian supermarket. I could never tell if I was buying rice or couscous. All the pictures on the boxes were ambiguous illustrations.

But the craziest part about my office were the crazy ideas written in different colored dry-erase board markers and all the insane concepts that made *no sense* to anyone other than me—and even to me, they hurt my brain to try and reconnect how I was thinking when I scribbled the damn picture of teepees with arrows pointing to a baseball field and stick figure people conversing in a town square. Was that a town square? What the fuck did I draw that for again? Anyway, to try and then re-explain what it was to anyone other than Wally was a nightmare. It simply made no sense.

I snapped out of it when I noticed Ooli jumping all over Joey Landlord. I wandered through my mind far more often since winter crept in—most of the day I was in a daze. Sometimes I felt like everything was on stilts and my sanity may come crashing down at any moment.

I snapped out of it again.

"SIT THE FUCK DOWN!" I screamed, trying to take responsibility for my fucked-up dog. Maybe I was the fucked-up owner? That's a better bet. What a dumb decision it was getting her. I was trying my hardest at life.

"All good dude. OOLI!" And Joey Landlord looked her in the eyes till she looked like she might cry and sat down. Jeez, what a nightmare this was. Then he looked at me, "YOOooo!!" and he came in for a big, weighted hug. He was a big guy. I wasn't. He squeezed me like he was my older brother. "I like what you got goin on here!" It was the first time he had seen my new place. "So what happened to your girl?"

"Jessica? The one with the dog?"

"Nahh... The redhead—the stripper from uhh—Elko?"

"Ohh... Renée," I said to him, trying not to seem like a total failure, "I left her three-hundred dollars, a suitcase, my computer, a month's paid rent, and took off. No idea where she is."

"Oh shit. Wherez she gunna go?"

Oh no, that sounded really bad. I'm not a bad guy. I'M FUCKING TRYING GOD! HOW DO I DO THIS?!

"I had no choice, she was gonna rat me out. My fuckin neighbor—the cop—"

"I remember—"

"She came up with a loaded gun and asked me what the fuck was goin on? I found this apartment on Craigslist in literally one hour, took a cab down here—the orthodox Jewish real-estate dude almost didn't even rent it to me cause he thought I was gonna sublet it out or whatever—"

"Right, yeah—It's a big place for one person."

"Right. That's what he told me, but I just gave him all the cash and told him I needed the fuckin goddam apartment ASAP. Then I found some Russian movers on Craigslist and had them move all my shit, and Ooli, within one hour while Renée was crying. It was fucking terrible."

I found myself explaining my life—why I did the things I did—*all the time*. Was I doing something wrong? Was that whole situation my fault?

"The Craigslist mover-and-fuckin-shaker! Well, I'm glad, ya know—I don't know. Got outa that situation I guess, right? I mean, you had to—fuckin shit dude. No more dating strippers."

"She wasn't a stripper though—I mean, she was, but she was a dancer. Super talented. Fuck. I don't know man." I was always defending her.

"Well, don't worry about it now, right? It's in the past. You gonna call her? Where will she go?"

"I don't know. Colorado maybe? Back to Nevada possibly? I don't want to talk about it man. It's been a hard week."

"You're good dude! Look, it was as much of her decision to hop in the car with you as it was for you to invite her, right?"

"Right. Yeah—I don't know." Ooli jumped. "OOLI! SIT THE FUCK DOWN! FUCK!" I really had no idea how to handle her.

"So don't be so hahrd on yourself dude. You're good! Hey—goin fishin next weekend, you should come."

"I will. Maybe."

He always asked me to come fishing with him—even in the winter. But I never did. He looked at my screenplay. I always kept it out so people knew my bigger purpose: to become a renowned filmmaker, though that ship had sailed. Honestly I just forgot it was out.

He picked it up while Ooli was busy gnawing at the rubber tug-of-war ball like it was a long-lost villain from her puppyhood. He started reading the first page, which really bothered me. I hated first drafts—and even though I had re-written it seven times, it was still a first draft in my head.

"You *wrote* this?" he asked as if it had already been made into some fabulous Hollywood blockbuster.

"Well, yeah, who else woulda written it?"

"What's it about?"

This was my chance to prove how interesting my life—and the people in it, truly were. Eh hem… "It's about this girl I met in rehab when I was in Louisiana—when I was fourteen. She told me she witnessed a murder when she was younger that went unsolved, and that it was the Sheriff's son who committed the crime. So I met up with her when I found her on Myspace like ten years later and she flew up here from Lake Charles—some rich guy she fucked from the casino flew her out here, and when she got here— she looks like a porn star by the way—she proceeded to tell me at ten in the morning over two martinis that her boyfriend had been spying on her for two years to find out how much she remembered about the murder—they actually made a *Cold Case Files* episode about it I think. Anyway, she told me that her boyfriend was trying to kill her now that he realized she remembered too much about the murder because he was actually the gay lover of the Sheriff's son—the one who did the murder—and that he had only been with her for two years to find out how much she knew. She might be crazy, but I've been researching it all, and everything checks out.

She and I fucked a bunch too, so I know her well. So yeah, what she's told me seems to add up."

I totally fucked that elevator pitch up. That was like an hour-long explanation that practically made no sense.

"Brooooooo."

I tried to redeem myself. "So now I'm writing this screenplay trying to figure out what happened."

"So it's like some kinda fuckin psychological coping method or whateva."

"Exactly. Anyway, so that's what it's about." I was feeling not so strong about my delivery, so I just went over to my dresser and did what I did best: sold pot. "So I got three. All insane."

"Bro, why the fuck you think I travel from fuckin Jehrsey at rush hour to get here?" He rubbed his hands together in anticipation. "Aiight, whattaya got?"

I opened the bottom drawer of my dresser and took out three jars. I began my pitch: "Sweet Island is probably the worst I've got, and it's still the best pot in the city." Ooli got up from her momentary state of calmness and the tension began building once she realized I hadn't pet her in five minutes. The hourglass of insane barking had been flipped and time was of the essence before she freaked out that I was ignoring her, but if I pet her now, she'd expect me to keep going and then I wouldn't be able to stop and this deal would be extremely difficult to complete. I had to get this damn deal done soon. What a needy dog she was. "Then I got Northern Lights, which is like smoking Aspen."

"Smokin Aspen?"

I was getting nervous. "Give her the toy." It did no good if *I* held the toy. She wasn't interested in me when other people were over—it was pretty bad actually. She was a good dog, but the situation was quite dire.

"Don't worry bro, I got this. Two pitties at home. Lemme see that shit."

"Look at these nugs, like fuckin pine trees." I took out a big ol' fella. "It's expensive, but worth every nickel. You'll be the talk of the Irish pub with this shit. Smokes smooth and tastes like Aspen." I put the nug back in its jar. "Check this shit out…" and I picked up the last jar. This was the climax of my presentation.

I opened the lid and turned the jar upside down and let him gawk as none of the weed fell to the ground. For once, something worked out as planned. I'm not tryin to be a downer here, lots of good shit was in my life. Like Ooli, I loved her. Anyway, I stood there holding the jar upside down like a damn magician. I really *did* have the greatest weed in the city—maybe the world. I was so proud of myself. "See that?"

"Holy shit bro."

"Not one nug. That's how sticky this shit is—sticky as *fuck*."

"What is it?"

"Silver Haze."

His eyes lit up, "Duuuuuudddeee! I fuckin want *that* one!" Then he reached into his pocket and pulled out a Jersey wad of cash. "How much for a fuckin"—he was counting his cash. Ooli began taunting him with sharp miniature growls. He kept losing his train of thought. Goddam dog. "How much for a fuckin—uhh, gimme a fuckin… half pound. How much for the sticky shit? Tha silver?"

"Well, no real price breaks. I'm selling ounces for $450—but I can do $3,400 for a half, but I don't owe my grower as much for the Sweet Island. I can sell that to you for less, like $2,800 for a half." I always *loved* explaining why the weed was so astronomically pricey. That was my time to brag about what a risky entrepreneur I was for transporting it across state lines. But Joey Landlord was never concerned about money. Maybe being a landlord was a good job? Should I get into real estate? That's a respectable outlet, right? I could invest in a rental maybe… The truth is, I had no idea what to do with my cash, but I pretended like I did.

"Aiight my dude. One Sweet Island, one Silver."

"So one pound in total, yeah?"

"Yeah, and how much for that one Northern Lights nug?"

"The one I showed you? The pine tree nug?"

"Yeah, *that one.*"

"That's my display nug. I can't sell it."

"BBRROOOOO," and he lowered his voice, "*brrrooooooo,* you got a *display nug?*"

"I do."

"Fuckin gangsta bro. Aiight playa—keep your display nug. Just one Silver and one Sweet Island. I'll slang this shit and be back next week so keep some of that Aspen saved for me." He gave me the money—$6,200 total. "So you gonna come fishin this weekend? We're goin, don't forget."

"Yeah, maybe." Like I said—we were almost friends.

Ooli let out her first real bark, indicating this better wrap up now. Her barks were so sharp they cut holes through my eardrum, especially that first one. It always came outa nowhere. This better be done soon, I thought. And I still had to package it all up. "Just keep her busy for another minute."

"Bro, I told you, ain't no thing my dude. I got two pits back home. I told you that, right?"

"Oh, yeah. Right." But I didn't remember.

I took out all my packaging materials from their respective drawers in my Godfather desk: scale, Tupperware bowl, vacuum-sealable bags, and FedEx envelopes. I placed just the right mixture of fluffy nugs and dense nugs into the Tupperware and weighed it all out on my shitty scale. I really had a bizarre way of spending money. Expensive pot, big TVs, lofty apartments, Godfather desks, expensive jars, a pure-bred Doberman—but a shitty scale? Tupperware? Tools I used every day for my budding career? (no pun intended) I never understood myself in that way. But the scale worked, so why buy a new one, right? Plus, nobody was judging me off my scale.

I weighed out a half pound of both strains, put them in the vacuum-sealable bags, then went over to my kitchen and vacuum-sealed them, careful not to crush the buds. I kept the vacuum sealer in my kitchen in case the feds busted in. Then I could explain to them the vacuum sealer was for food, just like it was sold for. Not sure what I would say when they found thirty grand of pot in the dresser though...

Anyway, then I put each vacuum-sealed bag of pot into a separate FedEx envelope. I stole those on the regular from the

FedEx store. Well, they were free, but I took like fifty at a time. Then I gently placed both FedEx envelopes in a Banana Republic shopping bag, which I had to the right of my fridge. I had shopping bags from all kinds of different stores from all over the city and always gave the right bag to each client. I thought it was an impressive strategy since Joey Landlord would *definitely* buy a shitty sweater from Banana Republic. He wore these baggy jeans and crumby sneakers with these preppy sweaters, which is dumb if you ask me, but what do I know about fashion? I was wearing valor sweatpants with no underwear. Anyway, I kept those next to my fridge, right next to two gigantic black garbage bags completely full of empty scotch bottles. I waited till nighttime to throw those out so none of my neighbors thought I was an alcoholic.

I handed him the final product and locked the door behind him. I waited till I heard the sound of the front door closing on the first floor and finally let out a powerful: "SHUT THE FUCK UP OOLI!" that I had been holding in for quite some time. I just hated her sometimes, but she was all I had. Maybe I *should* go fishing with him this weekend.

But it was nearly New Year's eve, and my chapter in Brooklyn was at an end...

PART 3: A WHOLE NEW WORLD

CHAPTER 39: CUTTING LOOSE ENDS

Winter got cold. Life even chillier. I gave Ooli away. Luckily it was to my parents. Finally, I got what I wanted: peace and quiet. I was all alone, but all alone is anything but peaceful or quiet. My head was loud. My mind was a terrible neighborhood. Getting stuck there was dangerous. Roll up the windows, don't stop for red lights. You've been on a long journey with me. I've taken you through sorrowful meadows with bleak intersections. A chuckle here and there, maybe an adventure around every corner, but it's time we shoot this beast dead. After all, this way of life wasn't working. It took me twelve years to figure it out, but alas, I'm ready for something different.

It was 4AM in late February. I twisted and turned in my California king-sized bed trying to keep sane. I went from room to room in my apartment all night. Finally I was in my bed. Maybe I'll sleep. No way I'd be able to sleep with all the scotch and coke I did—alone. Whatever movie I'd put on was still playing. Perhaps on repeat... who knows. I could hear the TV. Silence was deadly, there always had to be ambient noise. The TV did the trick. Not one movie I saw in the last five years has been retained in my memory. No idea what I watched in my twenties. Many movies. No idea how the plots were structured. My room was gross. Empty scotch. Sticky glasses. Licked-clean coke bags. Joint roaches. Random dollars. Dirty underwear. Huge bed. I lay and all I could hear was that damn sixteen-wheeler truck unloading whatever dry goods it was unloading into the Russian supermarket below my apartment. Beep.

Beep.

Beep.

It wouldn't stop.

Beep.

Honk.

Beep.

Out the window were dirty tarps and boring buildings with dull colors and smoggy air. The icy wind beat the windowpane. Brooklyn seemed so ugly that night. I got up to look out the window, down onto the truck unloading its bland cereal and cheap soup. I tried to see the subway—it was above ground in my part of Brooklyn—but the angle of the window never let me see it. Still I always tried. I don't know why. People were outside living sub-par lives. I went to my closet and chucked clothes out of the way till I found my backpack and my journal and my video camera. I shoved it all inside my bag and zipped it up. I opened my safe and grabbed a few stacks of cash: three thousand dollars. I left three pounds of weed in my office and walked out the apartment and onto the street. I waited the amount of time it took for a yellow cab to wander its way down King's Highway, which was quite a bit of time sometimes. People in this neighborhood didn't leave. They stayed here till they dropped dead. They were born and died on the same lot of land in the same six-person family house. I had to get out.

Finally, I got a cab.

"JFK"

Where was I going?

"Aeirpwert?"

It was some weird accent…

"Yeah."

"Whewt fliyght unda eirline?"

"I don't know yet. Just drop me off wherever."

I got to the airport. It was maybe the Delta terminal. Any terminal would work. I bought a one-way ticket to San Diego, no idea why. I was tired of not having seen California. Maybe Cali would solve my problems. I had so many…

So I hopped on a plane. There were two god awful layovers somewhere, who knows where. It was nearly 10PM by the time I landed, but I can't remember exactly. It was the longest flight of my life, longer than going to Argentina or Hawaii. I walked outa the San Diego airport and the warm air rid the chills from my veins immediately. I looked around. Where to go? What's that? I saw a green shuttle bus parked by some pick-up station. I walked over. The driver asked me where I was goin.

"Can you take me to the cool part of San Diego?" I asked.

He dropped me off in the middle of The Gaslamp District. I put my backpack on the ground and looked at the chaos. I went inside some bar and ordered a drink. Scotch. Any brand'll do. Doesn't matter. I pondered life as I normally do at moments such as these. What should I do? Why am I here? Where do I sleep? What do I fear? I had always been scared of hostels, not sure why. What's a hostel anyway? I don't know, but I always wanted to try one. Just never had the balls. I googled "hostel san diego." I was determined to make this my first night staying in a hostel. Up popped *USA Hostels San Diego.* It was only a few blocks away.

The bar was now closing. I was the only person there. In fact, I had been the only person there since the second I walked in. This felt like something I had to do. I stumbled over to 5th Ave and G Street and knocked on the hostel door. Someone came through on the buzzer

"Yeah?"

"I got a reservation."

"A bed?"

"I made a reservation online. Just now. might not be in. it in?" I was so drunk. "Just got here from NY. I'm from NY. I just got here."

They buzzed me in, they checked my ID, they gave me a receipt, which was to be magnetized to the side of my bed, and a towel, and key. I walked over to room five.

It felt odd. My life was so different already. Eight hours ago I was staring out my Brooklyn window with a nose caked up with coke, listening to the sound of that damn truck hauling in shitty Russian food. Now I'm in a hostel in San Diego.

I opened the door to my room and flipped the lights on. There were eight people asleep in their beds. Oh shit! Fuck. I hit the light switch again and found the flashlight app on my phone. I no longer had a Blackberry. Now I had an iPhone. I stumbled around the small room like a dipshit, aiming my light in peoples' faces. I found an empty bed. My head was dizzy as I made myself comfortable. I fell drunkenly asleep. The noise of "The Party Room" down the hall made me feel like I was missing out on youth as I drifted off.

And then… My world was jolted awake.

CHAPTER 40: HOSTEL EXPERIENCE

"EY!"

I woke up. It was like fuckin 4AM. "Thehs someone een me fucken BID!" Some drunk-as-fuck British dude starts screaming at me. Sweat crowded my brow immediately. What was goin on? "THEHS SOMEONE IN MA FUCKIN BID!" the idiot kept screaming, then he marched outa the room to the front desk. I could hear him from down the hallway: "AH NEED ANOTHA FUCKIN BID! THEHS SOMEONE IN MA BID!"

I looked around me. There were clothes all over the bed I was in. Dammit, I *was* in his bed. Fuck. Hostels suck. I got up—nervous as shit—and hopped in another bed at the other side of the room hoping all this would disappear.

I woke up startled as hell in the morning and remembered everything. I was petrified to leave my room. What if this guy kicks the shit outa me? Should I check out? I looked over at his bed and he wasn't there. Did he end up coming back in? Was he still drunk? Or was he awake and wandering around? How will I know who to dodge? I looked at his stuff and his stuff was not there. Fuck... he could be anywhere.

I didn't see his face last night; it was too hazy, and I was sleepy as fuck. He coulda been anyone, but I'd remember that accent forever. I had no idea what to do or where to leave my bag or if any of my belongings were safe in the room, so at 10AM or whatever, I opened the door slowly, backpack on back, looked both ways before crossing the hall to make sure the British dude who nearly pummeled my face in five hours earlier was nowhere to be seen, and tip-toed my way past the front desk to the room referred to as "The Party Room." I wasn't ready to leave just yet. No, I needed to find clarity in my life and this British fuck wasn't about to ruin my agenda.

It was a two-floor hostel. On the walls were trippy murals painted with purple and gold accents. It kinda felt like I was at a hippie Moroccan slumber party. Anyway, I walked covertly into "The Party Room"—a room with a wrap-around couch, beer pong table still dirty from the night before, and a TV that was off. That's where I bumped into Rico Suave, some Latino of some sort, talkin with some white chick who coulda been from anywhere European. Rico Suave looked like he was about to start nibbling her ear before breakfast. I interrupted cause I needed to make friends ASAP. I had to try something different with my life…

"Hey! What are you two doing today? I'm Greg."

"Rodrigo," said Rico Suave. His English was nearly accent-less.

"Hey thehr. I'm Allison."

"Hey."

"Hi," they collectively said, waiting for me to say something more substantial.

I didn't know how to talk to people. So I just spoke as fluently as possible, projecting as much confidence as I could muster. Actually, I think I was just being myself. "So uhh… I almost got my ass kicked last night."

"What?" Rico Suave says. "In a fight?"

"Not really… Some angry British dude woke me up cause I was in his bed at like 5am and he flipped his shit."

"No wayyy, thas crazy. Here? What's he look like?" Rico Suave asked.

"I dunno. I was half asleep."

"Well, maybe he was only drunk," the white chick said, maybe in some kinda Scandinavian accent—not that I know what an accent like that sounds like or anything.

"I don't know. But now it's all weird."

"No no my friend. Just a mistake I am sure," Rico Suave said.

"Yeah. So what are you two doin today? Are you from… Spain?"

"Brazil."

"Oh. And you?" I asked the girl.

"I'm from Romania." Romania? Where the fuck is that I thought quickly.

"I'm from New York."

"Cool."

This is awkward Greg, fix this. "So what are you two doin?"

"Ehhhh I theenk we go to the Whale Watching, yeah?" and Rico Suave looks at his prey. She nods. I wait. "Ehhhh you want to come with us?" he finally asks.

"YES!" I said enthusiastically. I mean, I *really* didn't wanna see that British dude but I wasn't about to leave without experiencing this hostel. So I spent the day whale watching, cock-blocking, and somewhere along the way I met an Irish girl named Maggie. I fell in love with her in about ten minutes and made plans to visit her in New Zealand, where she was planning to relocate. By the end of the day, not only did I have friends galore and a potential new love interest, but I had told everyone about the British dude. I was building an army.

THEN…

A door opens. It's like 6pm. Some dude walks up the stairs to where we're all congregating on the second floor and says:

"Ey me fahkin hayd! It's fahked!"

I recognized the voice right away. "IT WAS YOU!"

"What's thayt mate?"

"YOU WOKE ME UP AT 5AM AND FLIPPED OUT AND SCARED THE SHIT OUTA ME! IT WAS YOU!"

"Oh thayts raight (remembering through a fuzzy blur), eye'z sorry bout thayt mate. I was fahked last night," and he extended his hand.

"Aim Maytt. From Sydney, whehr you from mayte?"

Ohh… He's Australian. And so that's how I met my new best friend. We spent three weeks wandering around the city together, dicking around, smoking weed, and genuinely having fun. It was the first time I laughed since I was ten. I still remember smoking in the park with him somewhere in the Gaslamp District saying: "Man, Ima get you back for that one." And I did. With carrots. Let me explain…

Ya see, it all started when he told me that if you eat twelve carrots you get a disease called Carotitus (or some shit) and you turn orange. I told him that was the dumbest thing I ever heard. He told me he knew what he was talkin about. I told him he was drunk. He said, "I'm sober. YOU'RE drunk." He mighta been right. So we made a bet:

"Aright, if this idiotic disease actually exists, then I'll eat twelve carrots and get Carotitus, which doesn't exist—"

"—MAYT! EET DUZ EXIS—"

"—But if I win, and this disease does not even come close to existing, then YOU have to eat twelve carrots and we'll see if *you* turn orange."

"Eets uh bet mayt."

"Good."

Anyway, he heads out of the hostel to some place with somebody and I start frantically googling Carotitus with Maggie from the common area of the hostel. Nothing came up. See? I knew I was smarter than he was. Oh wait. I was spelling it wrong. *Keratitis*. Shit. It *does* exist! So, I came up with an idea to ensure I wouldn't lose this bet. I mean, fuck… I don't wanna get fuckin

Keratitis... shit sounds terrible. So, I made up a fake Wikipedia page. I even found a fun picture of carrots and formatted it all like this:

Carrotitus (car-it-tie-tis)

From Wikipedia, the free encyclopedia

This article is about the myth of the cultivated vegetable disease known as Carrotitus. For other uses, see Carrotundria (disambiguation).

Carrotitus is a fictional fairy tale myth created 78 years ago in 1933 by an American plumber named Buck Hoolahan.

The wide spread myth carried across seas when an Irish petroleum importer by the name of McCarthy Mundalo fell off a third story port pier into a cargo container of full of carrot extract. McCarthy Mundalo, in a fit of outrage, then declared war on all carrot farmers. In 1934 he ran a NY Times ad campaign about the fictional disease of Carrotitus and it's affects on skin pigmentation.

It was the cause of an international carrot panic that later became referred to International Carrot Panic.

Through extensive scientific research, it was later concluded by the American Institute of Vegetation and Agriculture that no such pigmentation alteration could occur by carrot consumption.

Other

Carrotitus¹ is a search results clustering engine and an open source project
Carrotitus Search, a commercial spin-off of the Carrot² project
Pikpik Carrots, in the game series Pikmin

[edit] Idioms

Carrot and stick

[edit] See also

Carat (disambiguation)
Caret (disambiguation)

This disambiguation page lists articles associated with the same title.
If an internal link led you here, you may wish to change the link to point directly to the intended article.

"Hey, can you maybe print out a couple pages if I email them to you?" I ask the vagabond chick at the front desk, some girl who didn't seem to give a fuck about anything other than "experiencing life" and "going with the flow."

"Obsolutely nao probelum," she says in some Euro trash accent, and printed it out for me. Then I ran downstairs and posted it with scotch tape on the front door of the hostel and called him up. We had exchanged numbers and everything, we really were friends.

"Dude. Come back to the hostel, I gotta surprise for ya..." I tell him.

I see him reading the fake Wikipedia print-out from outside before opening the door. I couldn't contain my laughter as he ripped the taped page off the glass and walked up the stairs shaking his head going: "Aiight mayt. You ween."

That's when I saw my chance…

"I'll be right back," I tell him with victory.

I ran off to the supermarket to buy the biggest twelve carrots I could possibly find—monstrous ones—and brought them back to hostel. We were scheduled to drive up to Los Angeles—to the airport, where Matt and Maggie were both departing from to go back home—Matt to Australia and Maggie to Ireland (before she headed to New Zealand). So, I prepped the carrots on a plate and we got in the rental car I had rented and began our drive to LA, where my life would change forever… But first, the carrots.

Maggie drove while I recorded Matt on my video camera in the backseat eating carrot after carrot. And just as he's getting sick as fuck and he says to me: "Me stomach mayte…"

I tell him: "Hey dude. Don't eat that last carrot."

"Why's thayt?"

"Cause I don't want you to get Keratitis," and I hand him the *real* Wikipedia page all about the actual disease, the one that really does exist... pretty nasty shit actually. "Told ya I'd get you back."

"Well played mayt, well played."

And that was that. I dropped them both off at the airport and it was the last time I saw either of them. I was beginning to feel much less depressed. I had to keep going. I had to keep this happy-momentum up. So, since I was in Los Angeles, I thought maybe I should give Jerrod the Agent a call. I mean, we worked together for like a year and I had never met him. So, I called the motherfucker up and said:

"JERROD! I'M IN LA!"

He told me to meet him at an address later that night.

"Oh and... no offense, but I've been tracking your life on Facebook. Wear something a bit... nicer."

I looked at myself. I was in a bandana, ripped jean shorts, flip flops, and a tight, dirty white tee shirt. So I checked into a hostel in Santa Monica, dropped my shit off on my bed—the right bed— and ran to Zara.

"Give me the best outfit you can put together," I told the pretty gay guy in his early twenties who was working there. He picked out a spectacular arrangement. Then I arrived at the address just in time. It was a fancy house on Sunset. I called Jerrod the Agent. "Are you here?"

"Oh shit. Running late. Just go in and ask for Lauren."

Oh man... I *hate* doing shit like this. But fuck it, I was on a mission to build a new life, and a new life I got, cause it was at that party that everything changed...

CHAPTER 41: DOWN THE HOLLYWOOD HOLE I GO

I walked between the trimmed hedges of the stone walkway to the heavy door of a Hollywood home and gave a knock. Nobody opened. I knocked again. Nothing. I could hear piano music from inside. The door wasn't locked, so I just walked in.

Wow, now *this* was a fuckin party. I got a few stares from a few glamorous people as I closed the door behind me, avoiding any eye contact as I choreographed a gameplan in my head, but I had none. Do I look nervous? How do I act calm?

All around me the traffic was constant. Everyone was attractive. The ages ranged from twenty to sixty. There were gray-haired curls and straightened, bleached porn hair all over. There were crop tops and skirts, flowy dresses with wood earrings. There were white people and black people and Asian people, but everyone's race evaporated with glamour and reduced to elegant. There was a band in the room to the right: a pianist, a guitar player, and a drummer. But they weren't a band. They were simply guests who decided to "jam out" for a bit. To my left was a kitchen with plenty of prepared foods going in and out of the oven. In front of me was a long oval table set for about forty people. Everyone had eaten, but still a few lingered in their seats. Glass doors were in the back of the dining room. Through the glass doors was a plethora of people lounging and smoking and drinking by a pool on the patio furniture. I was dressed appropriately: tight button-down shirt—checkered, and blue chinos with a crease running down to the Zara shoes I bought. I truly fit in, but I was screaming with panic inside my chest. I'd never felt less comfortable in my life.

A girl walked by me. She was strawberry blonde and not necessarily so attractive, but fancy nonetheless. Her facial expression read: *don't, just don't*. But I stopped her anyway.

"Hey, do you know where Lauren is?"

She looked at me, eyes open, mouth agape. "Oh! Are you Greg?"

Holy goddam shit. This chick knew my name? I was in love. "Yes! It's me!"

"I'm Lauren! Come!"

I met thirty people a second for the next hour. I was given a punch-filled vodka mix. Many people were friendly, and only a few standoffish. Still, it was better than anything I'd ever experienced. Lauren left my side once I was in a conversation on the patio, explaining my journey to some curly-locked man. The man I spoke to was a film editor.

"Do you know who owns the house?" I asked him.

"Sure do, helluvaguy! It's maigh house," he said in a toned-down British accent.

"Oh shit! You're the host! What a party!"

"Thanks mate, come by any time."

"You do this often?"

"Every Tuesday."

"Oh wow."

"Come by whenever. Enjoy!!" and he walked away.

Not too long after that, a girl who looked too hot to stand came up to me. She was my height—5'9"—and had short, dyed blonde hair that barely passed her earlobes. She looked dumb. I don't know why, she just did.

"Isn't the pie amazing?"

"Oh, I haven't eaten anything," I told her.

"Wait." She got me a slice and fed it to me. "Mmm, so good. I *love* pie."

"It's good. Yeah. Do you come here often?"

"This is my second week, but I definitely love it. *Love it.* I'll come back next week if you do."

I was awestruck. This fuckin chick—a stranger, is saying she'll only come back if I do? "Oh, I'm not sure. I don't live here."

"Me neither!" she said. "I live in Newport Beach."

"Oh, where's that?"

"It's in the OC."

"Sorry, I'm from New York. What the fuck is the OC?"

"Orange County. Oh my gosh, you have to come. Maybe next weekend?"

"Hmm… I'm not sure I'll be here."

"Here, text me."

I couldn't believe my luck. I pulled out my phone. "Okay what's your number?" and I texted her. She replied immediately.

"So nice meeting you!" and poof, she left. I didn't even get her name.

Just then, a guy, movie star-looking, came up to me. "Not a bad flock, eh?"

"Dude. These chicks are awesome," I told him.

"Seriously awesome indeed. Cheers," and the movie star left.

I didn't even take more than three streps before Lauren found me: "Get ready, we're leaving."

"Oh, is Jerrod here?"

"He's meeting us. We'll take Ace's car."

"Okay, well I don't know if I can leave my car—"

"—meet me by the front in a sec," and she left on a mission, assumably to find the rest of her crew. Am I part of her crew?

"Don't stay out too late," an older ex-model-looking woman said to me. Then she continued… "I'm Silvia. I've never seen you."

"Oh, I'm new. I live in Brooklyn."

"Oh, Brooklyn. I spent *many occasions* in Brooklyn. Back then it was a wild place. Is it still so wild?"

"It can be. Some parts."

"I've seen it all. I used to model a bit…"—I later found out she was a supermodel—"so times moved fast in those days. What's your name?"

"I'm Greg. Do you come here every week?"

"I sleep here."

"Oh. With uhh… what's his name…"

"What's his name indeed," and she winked. "Enjoy the party."

She walked away. I went inside and had to actually *dodge conversation,* something I've never had to do, to get to the front door where I was to meet Lauren. She was waiting impatiently.

"Come! Let's go!"

"Where we goin?"

"To a club."

"I hate clubs."

"You'll like this one."

We got in the backseat of a car and Lauren sat on my lap. There were seven of us in the sedan. The driver was some guy—no idea who, but he looked similar to many of the other guys at that house, another guy and some girl in the front passenger seat, and then a couple of chicks next to Lauren and I. Lauren pulled out a bag of coke. She did a bump and passed it to me. Her ass was grinding on my dick, which I was sure she could feel. I swear she was rubbing her ass cheeks on my cock but I couldn't be sure. I was getting hard. I was nervous about that. I did the coke. It was high-quality coke.

"Damn, it's good."

"The best."

We got to some club. No idea where we were. The club was red and empty. We went to a table and Lauren kissed and hugged everyone at the table in exactly the same way. A short white guy with a Kangal hat and thick-framed glasses came up to me. He was skinny, a few inches shorter than me, and looked like a skater with a good job. He opened his arms.

"Finally we meet!"

"Jerrod?"

"Welcome my man. Hey, sorry I didn't make it to the dinner party, but this is where the fun starts. You like champagne?"

"I love it, yeah."

"Great. Going to an after-hours champagne spot later on. Crazy place. You'll see…" and then he pulled some hipster black dude duo to me, "my newest artists. We're gonna do big shows with these guys."

"Sup," said one, offering me a fist-bump.

"What's good," said the other, offering me the same fist-bump.

"I'm Greg."

"Biggest promoter in New York," Jerrod told his new artists.

"Well, maybe…" I said.

Jerrod whispered in my ear: "Never downplay yourself."

"Got it."

Then Lauren grabbed my hand and said: "Let's go."

"We're going already?"

"See ya later man," Jerrod said.

"You're not coming?"

"Lauren'll take good care of you man. Welcome to LA."

Lauren pulled me out of the club and into another car with another crew of people. We sat in the back again and she pulled out more coke. We got to another spot, but it wasn't a club. It was a loungey type bar with light music and wood everything. The acoustics were fire—even I could tell that. Fire? Do I talk like that now? I don't know. But there were disco dancers on the rafters. The bar was quiet and it was easy to order a scotch. And after an hour there, Lauren pulled me out of that place and again took me somewhere else.

By 2AM, when apparently all the bars and clubs closed, I was so gakked out on coke and drunk on whatever that I didn't think I could continue, but we did and showed up to the side of some building in a not-so-good area. Jerrod met us outside.

"Just stand here," he told me.

A door opened on the side of the building and Lauren and her fancy girlfriend were let in. She didn't bother paying any attention to the fact that I was still outside.

"Are we getting in?" I asked Jerrod.

Jerrod shouted to the guy who opened the door for Lauren, "D-Rock! It's Jerrod." D-Rock looked at him, then me, then closed the door. "Don't worry, we'll get in," Jerrod told me. But it was quite a while waiting, though Jerrod didn't make much noise about it. He just talked my ear off about music.

"You're so coked out," I told him after one of his long monologues that I'd already grown accustomed to.

"Me? No, I don't do coke."

"No?"

"Sometimes."

"Tonight?"

"A little."

Then the door opened and we were let in.

Inside was intimate. Maybe fifty people in a cozy black and gold room. The décor was homey. The bar was to my left. They only served champagne in small bottles. The bartenders were all attractive Asian chicks, and one dude—who was, I suppose, attractive also.

In the back was a DJ with dudes and chicks laying on couches, which were scattered throughout the room. I rubbed against every single person in the joint, but not aggressively; softly. Everything was moving slow, and sex-appeal was the theme. Sexy everything. When I went to the bathroom—there was only one bathroom—dudes and chicks peed next to each other and blew coke by the mirror. I was given a bump by some slick couple in black.

An hour or so later Lauren found me: "I want to leave."

"Okay, umm… how do we get back to where my car is?"

"You can't drive, don't be silly. We'll take a cab—they're always outside. You can come back to my place."

We walked outside without saying bye to anyone and got in a discreet black car and she gave the driver her address. Forty minutes later we got to a bungalow in West Hollywood. Inside the bungalow were books about Japan and Buddhist chachkies.

"I study Japanese," she told me. "I have class in the morning."

"It's like… almost five. You have class?"

"At nine. Let's go to bed." We got in bed and she wrapped her arm around me. "Can I have a kiss?" she asked. So I kissed her.

She took her dress off while under the covers. "Do you have a condom?"

"I don't."

"I'm okay if you are."

"I'm good."

"You swear?"

"I think so."

"You think?"

I mean what was I gonna do, go get checked for herpes right there on the spot? I had to fuck this girl. So I said what everyone woulda said: "I swear." My heart wasn't even racing with anxiety the way it normally was. I slid inside her hard, and once I'm in, the hardness stays. So it was no problem after the first few pumps.

I woke up a few hours later with Lauren looking like an entirely new person, in school clothes and shit. "Off to Westwood" she told me.

"Where?"

"UCLA. Will you be here when I get back?"

"Umm…"

"Cause it's okay if you are."

So I stayed and just hung out in her bungalow. In fact, I stayed there for a week until I was like: "I gotta go back to San Diego and return this car."

But just as I said that I got a text:

Come to Newport!

It was that girl from the dinner party. So I finally picked up my car, rife with parking tickets, and drove to Newport Beach and saw signs for boat rentals. So I rented a boat and texted her back:

Come meet me by the boat rental place.

She showed up with her friend. Lauren came with me. Me and three chicks on a boat. The weather was perfect. The girls were lovely.

"I think I may move here," I said.

"You're totally invited."

And so I drove back to San Diego, flew back to New York, and gathered my belongings to relocate to Los Angeles. And that's how I met Savannah.

CHAPTER 42: BANISHED FROM BROOKLYN

Look there's a lot of sex in this chapter, but it's in here for a reason. I was addicted, and it led to some chaotic incidents. So, I'll tell you a bit about how it shaped my life then we'll get to my last couple of romances before The Final Debacle got me sober. We'll start with Savannah, shall we?

Savannah was my new LA roommate. She was eighteen studying fashion at the Fashion Institute of Design & Merchandising. I met her on Roommates.com. She told me she had $800 to spend.

So, a $1600 apt we should look for? I sent her via email.

$800 total. I only have $400 per month. She wrote back.

So, I found a joint on craigslist for $1,200—as close as we could get to $800—and told her I'd cover most of it. I flew into LAX at 3PM in April of 2011, picked her up in a rental car at FIDM after class sometime around 4:30PM, and had the apartment rented by 5:15PM. We got to the apartment to look at it and there was a couple in there looking before us. I heard one of them say:

"Ugh, the carpet is *gross.*"

So as soon as they left, I told the agent: "Here's $2,400 cash. We'll take it. And you know what I love most? The carpet."

The paperwork was drawn, my credit was approved, and Savannah and I sat in our new treehouse-looking apartment, which was really an attic converted into a loft. You could barely walk around with the angle of the ceiling. The windows were never closed because the weather was so perfect. We didn't even get an AC. The entrance of the apartment—a door down a creaky flight of stairs—was never locked, nor closed for that matter.

For months, Savannah and I had nothing but a mattress pad—not a mattress, a mattress pad—and a thirty-dollar desk from Ikea. By then, I was twenty-six and a full-blown sex addict... not a great combo for a freshman chick roommate who gave the greatest blow jobs known to mankind (except for my wife). She'd stick her finger in my ass while rubbing my balls and I could last about two minutes. It was very convenient, especially if I was in a rush, which I always was, to somewhere sincerely unimportant. I found out about her love for oral sex on the first day in our new apartment. It was right off Melrose and Fuller in West Hollywood.

"If you ever want a blow job, just ask," she told me while we sat in the unfinished part of the attic, a creepy but adventurous place to explore on the first day of our new home. It was like our own little clubhouse. She was so giving, seriously she was. I wasted no time.

"Well, I'll take a blow job then I guess."

And so she blew me—not with the finger in the ass yet, she didn't discover I liked that till fifty blow jobs later... actually, I had no idea it would feel good till she did it. Anyway, on that first night, she gave me four blow jobs and we had sex once. That's not an exaggeration.

I bought a bottle of champagne for us to celebrate our new life in LA. She was from North Dakota, but she didn't drink, so it was just me drinking and smoking, and every hour or so, she'd get up and walk around in her thong, and I'd get horny all over again, and finally ask for yet another blow job. It was fairly ideal.

I had no car, so I kept extending my airport car rental one month at a time. I was rarely in LA, even though I moved there. I was always on the road, especially when Tweed arrived, but even before that, I was now completely addicted to hostels. I mean, they changed my life and I was determined to use them as a vessel to better my existence. I even stayed at USA Hostels Hollywood while living in Hollywood just for a chance to meet foreign chicks and maybe get laid. But anyway, point is me and this chick Savannah did nothing but lay around and fuck for months. I barely left the apartment when I was in town. The only place I went to were those dinner parties on Tuesday. I built up a repertoire of acquaintances at those parties, like Crystal.

Crystal was from Australia but was going to college in Claremont. I met her at the dinner party and woke up in her bed the next morning. I couldn't remember sleeping with her, nor could I remember where I put my car, but she wanted to get together the next night, so I told Savannah I'd be with a chick.

"That's cool, I have a project to work on anyway."

She really didn't give a shit about anything, it was amazing. So when Crystal came over and we had sex, Savannah was in the other room on the floor on her computer designing steampunk lingerie or whatever it was. But Crystal, boy… she nearly killed me. I was choking her out while fucking, you know, the way you're supposed to do it, and she enjoyed it. All was pristine. Then she got on top of me and started choking me.

"I can't—(gasp)—breathe."

"No?"

She squeezed harder. "No, get (gasping) off." I tried to use my legs to push her off me but she was too strong. I headbutt her in the face and elbowed her jaw and kicked her off me.

"What? We were just role playing, no?" she said grimly.

"You gotta leave."

"Oh, but I live in Claremont."

"I'll drive you."

"It's far."

"I'll drive you."

After I got back home I saw on Facebook that I had gotten a message from Mimi, a girl I knew from childhood when I used to make out with her older sister in eighth grade. At the time, Mimi was like seven, her sister was my age, like thirteen, but when we bumped into each other all grown up at Nassau Community College five years ago when I was taking acting classes, I swapped sisters since we were now better suited in age proximity. I was thrilled to hear from her.

So you followed me to LA, yea? she wrote.

Mimi! You live in LA now too?? What's ur number?

And so I went to her place in Burbank and an unhealthy romance started. We slept together for a few months until she got into a lesbian relationship with a girl named Molly from San Francisco. Molly was the best lesbian ever. She was a tiny Asian chick with a minor affinity for men.

"Do you think maybe we should have a threesome?" I asked them both one day.

"Of coouuurrseee you want to fuck my girlfriend already Mr. Cayea," Mimi said. "Wow. You really are… I can't. Just… Stop."

But Molly was actually into it, so we arranged a threesome at my apartment in Brooklyn, which I was still paying rent for. See, they both decided to move back to New York after they fell in lesbian love in California and I offered to sublet them my apartment in Midwood for half the rent—exactly what the Orthodox Jewish real estate agent asked me not to do a million times, the exact thing I thought he was *insane* for suggesting I might do. That's where the threesome was scheduled to take place…

But it was totally ruined in Brooklyn a month later when I kissed Molly after doin a buncha coke with Mimi in the bathroom at some trendy bar in Williamsburg. I thought we were all on the same page, so when Mimi left us for a moment to smoke a cigarette outside, I gave Molly a kiss, but then she ran outside to tell Mimi about what had happened and a jealousy war broke out. Turns out Molly was a manipulative self-homewrecker who was *not* as into a threesome as she led me to believe she was. All she did was use the kiss as a way to get back at Mimi for some arbitrary resentment she had against her. I was getting involved in shit I wanted nothing to do with. But even after that kiss debacle in Williamsburg, I patched shit up and was still determined to make this work, so we all went back to my ex-apartment together. Whatever I had to do to somehow finagle my way into this love triangle, I was prepared to execute… but I fucked it up even more when we got into bed together.

"No threesome," I said to them both. "I'm just tired. Let's just go to sleep."

But while we were in bed, not having a threesome, in my massive California King, I was trying to get my dick out've its coma of coke. You must be sick of hearing about this shit, am I right? This is just *always* a problem. Imagine how *I* feel about it. But anyhow, the best way to solve dick coma problems is to go where you're comfortable, and that meant Mimi.

"GREG! NO!" Mimi shouted as I snuggled my soft dick inside the crack of her ass, trying to think of the good ol'times in LA when I rammed her pussy so hard it nearly fell off.

"Holy fuck. Fine. Okay. Goodnight," I said. What a different girl she'd become since she used to ask me to choke her so hard she may pass out. I remember once at her place in Burbank, I was fucking her on her bed, and she barked at me to choke her, which I did, gladly. I love that shit. But then her face started turning purple.

"You… you, okay?" I asked trying not to sour the moment.

"HARDER! CHOKE ME HARDER!"

"I don't want you to… you look," and I softened my grip, "like you're gonna—"

"CHOKE ME TILL I PASS OUT! FUCK THAT PUSSY FUCK IT FUCKKKKK"—

But I was seriously nervous she may die, so I finished up ASAP cause it was starting to turn me off. This girl has a serious problem, I thought to myself. But so remembering that night—oh wait, day, it happened at like 4PM—but yeah… remembering that day of sex and lookin at the situation I was now in: not even being able to caress my dick inside the crease of her ass, I mean what the fuck? It was heartbreaking. What had I done? Where'd I fuck all this up? So I tried once more, but with Molly.

Quietly, Molly whispered: "No, we can't."

"Are you *actually* trying to fuck my girlfriend right next to me after I told you no?"

"Uhh…"

"Get out."

"But—"

"GET THE FUCK OUT! WE PAY RENT HERE!"

"But only half of it!"

"THAT'S NOT MY FUCKING PROBLEM!" Mimi shouted.

Point is my sex life was a mess. But anyhow, that's not important, cause it was time to meet Woody for our final business meeting before Tweed arrived. I hopped on the road to meet him in DC, where he was living at the time.

Along my way to New York on that road trip I slept at any hostel I passed, in fact, I specifically drove to them desperate to meet more girls. I was now addicted to drugs, alcohol, sex, money, and hostels.

I met a musician at The Lazy Lizard Hostel in Moab who burned down a forest. He had started some major forest fire and was now hiding out in Utah. Oh, and I was nearly *denied entrance* at BonPaul and Sharky's hostel in Asheville when I asked:

"Can I get a bed?"

The dorky fuckdick at the shitty-ass front desk looked me over and said: "We have parking spots in the back for $5."

"No beds inside?"

"You have a car?"

"Yeah, how you think I got here?"

"Just you?" and he looked at me sideways. For the first time I realized I was being judged by my alcoholic hippie appearance.

"Yeah, it's just me."

"No drugs, right?"

"No no, nothing. Just tired."

Finally he let me in, but it became clear I had to shower. My hygiene was really deteriorating. Anyway, the last stop before I got to Wally in DC was Virginia.

It had been years and I missed her, so I decided to check in on Poe to see how she was doing. All I can say is, surprisingly, she was still alive...

CHAPTER 43: LAST TRIP TO POE

Visiting Poe was terrifying.

Her three children were bouncing off the walls of her middle-class home in shitty, rural Virginia when I arrived. The living room wasn't nearly as messy as you'd think an ex-hooker junkie homeless runaway chick's house might be. There was some beer on the table—whack cans of hick beer, but that's about it. Her freezer was full of frozen chicken nuggets and shit, but overall she actually seemed kinda… well, normal. Miraculously she hadn't touched heroin since her first kid, Tay, was born.

Tay's dad was a gangster Poe used to fuck in Providence. I stayed at his place once. He was about thirty years older than she was. Poe's middle kid was from some random dude she was no longer with, and the third kid—now she has five—but the third kid was from her then-partner, a guy she'd been hiding me from the entire time I was there, which wasn't comforting.

Poe kept getting hotter. From hippie to hooker she now rested somewhere in the middle, like a reformed slut with whimsical viewpoints. A smile never left her face and this chick laughed as if her past never existed. You never woulda known she was a sixteen-year-old hooker strung out on dope with nowhere to live ten years ago. She really seemed normal. It was odd. Except for the insane children and possibly abusive boyfriend who may ice pick me to death at any moment—at least that's how she was making me feel, and except for the trailer park—which I'll tell ya about in a second—all seemed fairly normal for a broken family in the center of nowhere.

"So this is where you live now, huh? No more Providence?"

"Not so much anymore Greggy, ya know? Papo doesn't want me there anymore. It's a bit complicated. He always wants Tay, but never wants me. I told him you can have Tay, he's so much work, ya know? And he loves his dad. He speaks Spanish. I don't know Greggy, but I'm so glad you're here! I wanna introduce ya to my family! They all live at the trailer park. It's a bit run down but we all really love it there. I really missed ya so much ya know? I wanna hear everything! How have you been, where is KC? Are ya'll two married yet? Where do you live? Come! We'll go see my nephew! Oh, will you drive? So tell me! What's your life??"

And we got into my car.

"Are the kids okay alone?"

"Oh we'll be back! They're okay, it's fine. Baby Dee will come by. There's always someone here. So tell me, are ya'll two getting married? You and KC? Am I invited to the wedding?"

"Nah I mean. We broke up years ago."

"Oh so you're single huh Greggy?"

"I guess so, yeah. You?"

"I wish I was, but I never will be…"

The entire visit was confusing. She was adopted into a wealthy family, who gave her money, yet she chose to live near her biological family, who all lived in one trailer park—a scary place to say the least. I was about to find that out…

We drove out of her suburban neighborhood full of basic homes with overgrown lawns and out into the country and through a field to where there were a bunch of trailers scattered all over. I drove over the lumpy grass to her biological sister's trailer, and in the uncut grass, next to a dinky barbecue that cost probably no more than ten dollars to buy at a broken-down gas station, was a group of three kids next to a shotgun, all of them wearing Dallas Cowboys hats. One of the kids was black, and the other two were white hicks. They were probably like fourteen, and their race is important, which you'll find out about in a moment, which is the reason I brought it up.

"Should I just, park here?" I asked Poe.

"Anywhere! Yay, I'm so glad you're here! That's my nephew!" and she opened the door and ran over.

I was forced to walk over alone and as I got closer to their circle around the dump bbq, nobody looked at me except for brief glances out of the corner of their eye. I was being publicly ignored and Poe didn't say shit about it. The three kids actually laughed when I said:

"What's up?"

"Oh shit," the black kid said. "Ya'll come from The Gap?"

The Gap? You believe this shit? This dumb fuck thinks I shop at The Gap? I was wearing a goddam tee-shirt with jean shorts and Birkenstocks. This fuckin moron… Desperate piece of trash. Dumpy-ass hicks. And they're laughing at me? A successful drug dealer? Eat a dick.

"Ya'll be nice! This is Greggy! He's from New York!" Poe said.

Ah. Why did she have to bring up the fact that I'm from New York? Obviously this wasn't my audience. Goddam idiot Poe is. Actually, I can be from wherever the fuck I wanna be from. I'm not scared of these toddlers. That's when something weird happened…

One of the white hicks said:

"Look like some nigger car."

He was talking about my rental. It was an Impala—they always give me Impalas. But the weird thing is the *black* kid laughed and then said:

"Ahh he nigger!"

I had to pause. Did the black kid think he was white? I kept thinkin about Chappelle. That skit he did. You know the one

I mean? Doesn't matter. I was just thrown off guard. I mean, I was used to racism, that's old news. But a black kid hating black people? And he kept goin… N-word this, n-word that. And not a "niggA" with a soft "uh," no. These n-words had dramatic "ers" at the end. It was aggressive. Does this kid know he's black? What in the fuck? I felt like I was surrounded by Nazis, and one of them was black—which was a mindfuck. I really felt like these kids might shoot me. I was afraid to turn around. I could feel the bullet ripping through my spine. I'd drop half-dead just before I got back to the car.

"Right on. Well, riveting to meet you all. Poe, let's go."

"You don't tell my aunt when or where to go motherfucker, aright?" The black kid said.

"Raymond! Stop acting like that. Well, ya'll are in a bad mood so we're gonna leave," Poe said as she grabbed my hand.

"Don't be touchin her cuz!" he yelled at my back. The *fuck* is goin on here?

When we got in the car I was like, "Poe, what was that about?"

"I'm sorry Greggy they're usually not like that. Ray ray just sometimes gets in a bad mood, that's all. He's got personality problems, ya know?"

"Which one was that?"

"The half black half white one, ya know?"

"Who is he?"

"He's my nephew! He's really nice an all, ya know? Just—"

"—How is he black?"

"Well, this one time, Polly, ya know? My sister, the real one, she slept with a vagrant. He still hangs outside the liquor store.

We pass him all the time. She slept with him, ya know? And got pregnant. He was a black guy, but we don't talk about it, and so she had Raymond and yeah, it's sometimes weird, ya know? But Greggy I'm so sorry he was bein a bit mean to ya."

"Wait, your sister fucked a homeless black guy, had a kid, and that's him?"

"Yeah dude, crazy right? And we see him all the time! His dad! But Polly don't want nothin to do with him no more. So... and my cousins won't let her talk to him anyways, ya know? So, we just ignore it kinda. I wish it wasn't so hidden, ya know, the truth an all."

"And he never even says hi to him? His dad?"

"Oh no, we never talk about him. Definitely don't talk to him."

"So is that why he doesn't like black people?"

"Well, see, that's the thing. None of my family are very smart. So, they hate anyone different."

"But... *he's* black. He's not different."

"Yeah, but everyone in the trailer park is okay with it, ya know?"

"This makes no sense."

"Haha I know! It's all so confusing. I dunno but nobody gives him crap about it cause they know it wasn't his fault, ya know? We all consider him family. They do too, my cousins."

"But he *is* family."

"I know, right?!"

The whole situation was baffling, uncomfortable, and completely insane. And I hadn't even met Baby Dee yet...

"Well, whatever you're crazy family situation is, they don't like me."

"Nooo! They just take some time. But they'll like ya, they'll love ya like everyone loves you Greggy. They're comin over later, so ya'll all can talk."

"Poe please, no. No way. I am *not hanging out* with them later. No fucking way, I'll leave."

"Nooo Greggy, okay okay, we can get outa town for a bit. I'll call Baby Dee and maybe she can watch the kids, ya know?"

"Baby Dee?"

"Ya! She's my cousin. We all call her Baby Dee. Her brother's in prison for murder, my Uncle. It's nuts! His girlfriend cheated on him, then for his birthday she told him which guy it was and they kidnapped him and drove him out into a field and beat him with a bat till he died. It's a terrible story. They put him in the trunk but had to break his legs to make him fit, ya know? But then they got pulled over three days later and now he's in jail forever. So all the guys from the other trailer park give her respect an all. He's a powerful figure around here. So everyone's safe when we're with Baby Dee. Everyone still looks up to her brother. He controls a lot. He writes all the time."

"Yeah that uh… sounds pretty fuckin, well. Terrifying."

"I know! Right? My family is *crazy!* Come! I'll call Baby Dee and I'll take ya to Williamsburg! Ever been there? It's out of town and safe! You'll love it! It's really a beautiful place! Oh Greggy I'm so excited you're here!"

So we drove down to Colonial Williamsburg, to the historical downtown, and went to the only restaurant that was open. We sat outside in the back of the americana restaurant in the moonlight. I'd never gotten over this girl, even when she was such a whore. I just loved her so much but everything in the world was wrong with her. Still, I had to save her from this place.

"So... how do we get you out of this place?" I asked, worriedly.

"Away from the family? I know. I need to. It's hard though. My parents gave me the money for the house, my adopted ones. Ya know? Oh! They live here! We can go to their house! And my brother is here too, adopted brother. He's okay. We get along but he's embarrassed to be seen with me. But he'll like you. Can we say you went to college? Just so everyone knows you're a good influence an all, ya know? Raymond and all them... They once found out I had a friend who went to college and everyone liked him cause of that. So we can say the same thing!"

After dinner she took me to where her adopted brother lived— and I say lived because now he's in prison for rape, for raping his girlfriend, who I was about to meet...

She was a beautiful Icelandic chick—probably still is, and her brother was a blond kid, good looking I guess, and he had a buzz-cut that made me a bit frightened of him. I was scarred by military cuts. I could sorta see how he might rape a chick. But at the time he was a decent dude, though you could tell he was mortified to be Poe's brother. I mean, he made us wait outside his apartment complex by the pool and then came from some odd roundabout way to bring us beer, almost as if he'd do anything to keep us comfortable enough to not ask to see his apartment.

We talked for about ten minutes before he and his girlfriend left us alone at the pool with the beer. The entire exchange was brief and curt. Thinking back on it, totally makes sense their relationship was havoc behind closed doors. He just seemed so secretive. There wasn't much to say after he left…

"Sorry Greggy, he's ashamed of me. But he loved you! Could ya tell? Everyone loves you! Remember on Thayer? All the girls thought you were so handsome. Especially Kiki. Oh, come! Let's go to my adopted parent's house! It's real big! They're away!"

"Poe, no more family. Definitely not your fucking adopted parents."

"Please Greggy! They're not even there. I want ya to see their house! It's so big and fancy, you'll like it."

Okay okay, so I drive us over there to a suburban neighborhood outside with colonial houses all over. We pull up to a home of about five thousand square-feet. The front yard was kempt, upscale, and completely dull. The lights inside the home were off. I was horrified they might show up at any moment. Meeting those people would be terrible. I knew all about her past and I couldn't stomach lying to adults I found atrocious.

We parked the car and went in through the front door.

"Poe, I get it. It's a nice house. Can we leave?"

Just then…

"Elizabeth?"

A somber woman with stiff creases walked down the stairs.

"Mom I thought you weren't here."

"Is that why you showed up?" She looked at me. "A friend?"

"Yes! This is my friend from New York. We met at Hidden Lake! Remember? I told ya all about him and his poetry! He's the wonderful writer remember?"

"Hmm."

"You don't remember?"

"I'm sure I do. But your father and I… we're just about to leave, so…"

"Where ya'll goin again? I always forget. Ya'll take so many vacations!"

"Well you could've had the same opportunities to do just that Elizabeth, but you blew it. And now that's impossible for you. With that said, I think you should leave."

"Don't be silly mom! I was just gonna show Greggy my room an stuff and where we all used to play ya know? Baby Dee's watchin the kids so… But then we'll leave, yeah?"

"I think it's better if you leave now."

I stood there in the middle of a situation I needed out of. I hated being in parents' houses. All parents hate me. Even now. That's not true. My in-laws love me. But you know, sometimes my mind is all fucked in the head, see what I mean? Whatever. Point is Poe's mom was an old skank and definitely not my greatest fan.

"Sorry to bother, let's go," I told Poe.

So we ducked out the front door as fast as we entered.

"Drive around the corner and just wait a bit, ya know?" Poe said to me.

So I did that, and we waited till we saw her parents leave, then we pulled back around to their house. At first I wanted to leave, now I was mad and wanted to fuck their house up. They really did suck.

Poe entered the code by the garage.

"I'm surprised they gave you the code," I told her.

"Oh they didn't. My brother told it to me."

We went up to her childhood room, which had been converted to a guest room, even though the house probably already had ten others.

"Is there anything to drink?" I asked. "Your shitty parents must have something."

"Oh Greggy, you drink too much!"

"Me? You're the heroin addict!"

"But I haven't touched that stuff in almost nine years. Aren't ya proud of me Greggy? Hold on, let me find you something."

I heard my heart beat in my eardrums. I was panicking. I don't know why. She came back and opened some sparkling wine. I poured it in my mouth. It came bubbling out. I poured more. I drank half the bottle until my nerves settled. Poe grabbed the bottle from me and drank some herself. I grabbed it back. We tumbled on her bed. I tickled her. That's a way to engage in sex—a trick I picked up along my sex addiction. She hugged me to stop the tickles, like a boxer when he's getting hit too much. We fell on the floor. She got on top of me...

"Greggy, we can't."

She said that with her lips an inch away from mine. I grabbed her ass. She let me. I grabbed her tits. She let me. I tried to kiss her. She stopped me. We woke up the next morning in a cheap motel.

"What happened? How'd we get here?" I asked.

"Greggy you don't remember filming me?"

Huh? Filming her? What's she talking about?

"Filming you? I don't remember..."

"You don't remember showing me Autumn? Hmmm?"

It all sounded crazy to me. "Autumn? You know Autumn? Fuck I don't remember. Is that bad? Should I be worried? Am I dying?"

"Greggy you're not dying. You're alive!"

I watched the footage she showed me on my video camera. It was a mishmash of angry questions about her horrific past as a junkie and teenage hooker, clearly resentments boiling to the surface which were now, apparently, all on video. How embarrassing. I had to leave.

We drove back to her house in rural Virginia, pulled into her driveway, and when she opened the door, I stayed put.

"I'm leaving," I told her.

"No Greggy, please! Stay one more night! Please don't leave me so soon, okay?"

"No. I don't like it here. Your family is crazy."

Just then Baby Dee pulled up in a brand-new, tricked-out white Jeep, the kinda car only dirty money buys. The car was far too nice for her attire—or life. Her hair was blonde and stringy and a bit ratty. Her tee shirt didn't cover her belly button. Her jeans were tight. Her makeup was dark. She had piercings, but not too many. She was about five feet tall and looked like she was headed for prison in the not-so-far future.

"Ya'll bitches ran away! Look'it yew, wit some fancy man. You know they gon give you shit."

The kids ran out of the car and into the house. All three of them.

"Greggy this is Baby Dee. Tay! Not so fast!" And Poe ran after one of her million kids. I don't like kids. They make me uncomfortable. I had to get out. Baby Dee was staring at me.

"Hey, I'm Greg."

"Yeah ah knew who you are. Fancy New Yorker."

"Not sure about fancy."

"Ahm just playin. You gon be here layter? We throwin a party."

"Nah, I gotta leave."

"Bullshit you do." Poe came back outside. "Poe they all comin in a bit. Figir we throw a party fer yer fren."

"Greggy will you stay? They'll be nice, I swear!"

"I didn't say they wouldn't be!" I couldn't believe she said that. "Nah, it's not about that Poe, I gotta get back. I got work."

But Baby Dee grilled me… "Oh work huh? What kinna work?"

"He's an actor! He went to college an everything!" Poe said.

"You some sorta Hollywood?"

Jesus fucking christ, I thought. "No, not yet." I said and gave Poe a hug. "See ya soon."

Another truck pulled up. Raymond got out.

"Oh shit. Ya'll two left huh? Where ya'll go?"

The scene felt a bit intimidating all of a sudden.

"Down to see my parents! Ya know, Williamsburg!"

I kept trying to leave. "Okay Poe, bye! Nice to meet everyone."

One of Poe's cousins got out of Raymond's truck—one of the white hicks. He was carrying a case of beer. Shitty beer. Hick beer. Teenage beer.

"Yo, he's leaving. You don't want a beer?" Raymond angrily asked.

"Ya'll don't drink beer up North?" said the cousin hick.

"Shut up ya'll. Ya'll know they be drinkin appletinis and shit," Baby Dee said. She was about fifteen if I had to take a guess.

"Nah, I drink scotch mostly," I said, now getting a bit irritated.

Raymond didn't like that. "Scotch? Fuck you so convoluted for?"

He definitely used the wrong word there, but I didn't say anything about it.

"Ray-ray! Be nice!" Poe said.

"It's all good," I told her. "Yo, I gotta leave. Have fun."

Another car showed up. Holy shit. I felt like I was being attacked. I got in my car, put it in reverse and tried to leave the driveway, but I was being blocked in. I stayed in my car thinking. I could hear Poe screaming at them to move. Nobody listened. Finally, Baby Dee said: "Ya'll move," and she said it casually. And just like that, the cars moved.

I drove to DC and never came back again.

In DC Wally and I formulated our Tweed strategy, then we both drove up to Brooklyn to sell the rest of the weed in my dresser at a discount, give away all my furniture, sell my electronics—which Wally took a small commission of, and then I told the landlord I was done with the apartment and that I was breaking my lease—sue me.

Wally stayed in Brooklyn to squat with one of his ten trillion friends while I scrambled my way back to LA where 35,000 booklets of Tweed Rolling Papers would be arriving at the port of Long Beach in just a month or so. And it was on that final drive back to LA that the cartel nearly got me.

It all started when I met Lina, who *constantly* told me everything was safe…

CHAPTER 44: CRIME SCENE

The hostel was draped in pastel led paint, chipping its way off the side of the ex-colonial home. In the backyard was where my room was. It was next to a stage for budding musicians who couldn't lock down any real music venue to play at, an outdoor kitchen, which had seen better days, and a swimming pool that was actually in decent condition. My first night there I was told to not leave at night due to rising crime, so I just hung out in the living area and met a girl from Germany with gristly brown hair and an English vocabulary better mine. She spoke with a British accent and her features were angular and very German.

"What's your name?" I asked when the last person up at that hour left the common room. It was like 1AM.

"Lina, and you?"

"I'm Greg." I was out of scotch, so I asked her: "Is there anything to drink here?"

"Ehmmmm… Maybe de kitchen?"

I went into the kitchen filled with parcels of leftovers from backpackers over the last decade and rummaged through the fridge—probably last cleaned out in 1997. Nothing.

"I can't find anything, where else can I look you think?"

"Ehhmmm maybe de Dutch guys in the back?"

"They're gone."

"Ders a store maybe?"

"The hostel said not to leave after dark cause of crime."

"De crime? Oh come on. Ders no crime."

What's this bitch talkin about? "This is New Orleans," I told her. "There's a ton of crime."

"Oh come on, ders nothing too bad."

"Where are you from?"

"Berlin. Have you been?"

"No, is there crime in Berlin?"

"Not really, no. Some."

"Okay well here there's a lot of crime."

"Are you scared?"

"Of getting shot? Yeah. I just need a fucking drink. Is there any leftover beer?"

"Well, I don't know. I can help you check?" We both went back into the kitchen, but it was useless. I was starting to panic.

"Fuck. I need something."

"Come here and relax." She put her hand on me. We kissed. That took my mind off drinking till the morning. I woke up so impressed with myself that I'd made it a night without drinking it almost felt like I was healthy. Of course I had drank earlier in the day yesterday, so not like I made it a *full day,* but still, progress.

I asked Lina at breakfast: "So, where you heading to next?"

"After here I think I'm going to Austin."

"Me too!" And I was. "Then El Paso," I told her.

"Get out! I am also!" She said. "And after der, LA."

"That's where I live! You wanna ride with me? I got a car!" And so that's how we ended up at the motel run by the cartel in El Paso.

"I was in jail here once," I told her right when we got into the city limits of El Paso on I-10.

"You've been to jail?" she asked ignorantly. Of course I have woman, of course I have.

"Yea, there's a border patrol stop seventy miles ahead. They caught me with me weed and threw me in jail."

"Oh wow. Dats a story, yeah?"

"I guess. Look at this place," and I looked at the El Paso city line. "This whole city is crawling with cartel," I said, unsure if that was true.

"Why is der cartel? Who says dat?"

"*I* do, look," and I point to Juarez, the most dangerous city in the world, right over the border about ten feet that way, right over the wall. It was so close you could touch it. And I mean that. We drove downtown and in the middle of the city is the border fence. You could slide as much coke through that thing as you wanted to, if that was something you actually wanted to do, which it's not for me, but for you, I don't know. Just saying, it was close. The houses were built right behind it, touching it even. It's a bizarre setup, and so that's how you know if there're a buncha Mexican hooligans sellin drugs on the corner—they're fuckin cartel. It's goddam Juarez, that's just how shit is.

"Still you don't know der cartel," Lina says like a total amateur.

"Fine, don't believe me. Just saying it's not fuckin Disney world here like you think it is." She was getting on my nerves. "Let's just find a place to sleep."

So we found this random motel.

"How bout der?"

"It looks shady," I told her.

"But everywhere is shady to you," Lina said to me.

Find you bitch. We'll stay at the shitty motel if that's what you want. It actually seemed decent at first, but when we paid for our room and got the key and headed to the second floor, there was caution tape all around the side entrance. "See?" I told her as we ducked under the yellow caution tape and found our room.

"Doesn't mean ders cartel," Lina interjected, just to be combative.

Fuck this bitch. Anyway, inside our room everything was five feet tall. It was a motel for short people—dwarfs, little people, midgets, whatever. The entire interior was low. So bizarre. The doorknob, the bathroom sink, the toilet, ceiling, the mirror on the wall; all of it. "Mexicans must be short," I declare to Lina.

"Not all of dem," she replied.

UGH! This fucking girl. "Let's go get some food," I said, and by food, I meant a drink.

"Sounds good."

Finally, something the girl agreed with me on. So we leave the room, and on our way out, we see this Mexican kid, maybe fifteen years old, at the end of the hallway by the caution tape.

"What's that kid doing?" I asked her.

"I don't know, but it is a bit odd, isn't it?"

As soon as the kid saw us leave the room, he threw a stone down to the parking lot.

"Should we keep going?"

"Yes, we need to eat," Lina says.

So we walk towards the kid. I hide the fact he's making me nervous. He moves outa the way as if he's my butler when we got to him. Something felt off. We walked down the stairs, again ducking the caution tape, and at the bottom of the stairs was a Mexican chick waiting by the shitty pool thirty feet away from the stairs, but it was clear she was waiting for us to leave. Were we interrupting a drug deal? Was this some kinda cartel-owned territory? What the fuck is going on?

"Did that not feel sketchy to you?" I asked Lina as we crossed the street towards some adobe-styled restaurant.

"Well, yeah. A bit."

We walked inside the restaurant and immediately I felt like I was on the set of a western film. Inside the adobe hut of a restaurant felt like a mob hangout. There was only one table filled with porn star-looking Mexican chicks in hooker boots and tiny skirts sitting with outa shape, well-eaten, big-bellied Mexican men, double their age, wearing cowboy hats and cowboy boots with bold belt buckles encrusted with diamonds and drinking cervezas. The room quieted when we entered.

"Oh wow, look at dis," Lina said as she showed me her phone. "De last review says de place is on de news every morning and to never stay there. Look, eh murder. Wow. Shocking right?" and she showed me the reviews of the motel we were staying at.

"See? I fuckin told you. Shit is dangerous…"

"Yes but you think everything is dangerous."

I wanted to kill her, and the side-stares from the gangsters at the table to our left weren't helping. We gotta get the fuck outa here, I thought. But Lina was *never* scared, even in horrifying neighborhoods. I was always terrified of bad neighborhoods. I don't know why. Probably cause they're dangerous, but even not-so-dangerous neighborhoods made me paranoid. I was just sure life would kill me at some point, which it will, 100%, but like… I don't know. Maybe in some gruesome before-my-time kinda way.

I leaned close to Lina and said, "Can we please just get outa here and go back to the room and get our shit and start driving?"

"It's late though."

"We can stop somewhere. Ever been to Vegas?"

So, finally, I got her in the car with me. I patted myself down ten times before we got to the border patrol checkpoint where I was thrown in jail not too long ago. The checkpoint was in a different town since we were heading west, but still it jarred all my nerves loose when we went through it. I was sweating.

In Vegas, Lina and I tried to have sex, but she wasn't perfect-looking and if a chick wasn't perfect-looking by then, at that time of my dysfunctional sexual appetite, if she wasn't barbie-doll plastic or at least troubled in the soul in some way, I was turned off and couldn't perform. It was only getting worse, but I never had a problem when it was clear I was meaningless to whichever girl I was with. If I didn't matter to them, I was good. If I was special in any way, I couldn't do it. I don't know why. I'm flawed maybe. I like weird shit. I couldn't get hard at all no matter how hard I tried (no pun intended) with Lina, and I can only imagine it's cause she saw something special in me, and like I said, that wasn't my style. And so I embarrassingly drove in silence from Vegas to our final destination, LA and asked her: "Where do you want me to drop you? You wanna come back to my place?" But I only asked that to be polite. I wanted to erase this road trip from my memory. Not cause of her, she was awesome. We had a ton of fun together. In fact, this one time, when we first met, right after we had left the hostel in New Orleans, when we were connecting with each other on Facebook, I typed her name in: Lina Weber, and two people came up: her, and some fat dude with goofy hair also named Lina Weber. His profile pic was him holding a big container of Walmart-brand cheese puffs.

"Look, this guy has your name! OMG, I have such a great idea," I told her.

So we went to the local Walmart wherever we were, somewhere in Louisiana at that time, and we found the same Walmart cheese puffs.

"Der deese ones!"

She grabbed the container of shitty cheese puffs and held them in the same position the goofy dude with her name held the container in, I snapped a photo, we made it her profile pic, and then she friended him! HAHAHAHA! How confused he musta been!

Anyway, those were the good ol' days. Now I was inviting her back to my place out of sheer guilt, but she just looked at me and said:

"What's de use? Just drop me at de Greyhound."

But when I brought her to the station, a crew of dudes were shooting dice and playing cards under a tarp. Four gangs of dudes and chicks were on each corner of the four-corner intersection by the station. Homeless people had taken over the parking lot. It looked like the shitty parts of Buenos Aires.

"No way am I leaving you here."

"What? It's fine. Just drop me."

"No, stop saying everything is safe. It's not. Not everything is safe. I'll take you to another station."

So we drove to San Diego, two and a half hours away, just so I could leave her in peace. It was an insane thing to do maybe.

When I got back to LA, I told Savannah about what happened, but all she focused on was the sex part:

"You've never had a problem with me," she said. "I know what you like." And she was right. She did. Am I in love with my roommate? And just as that thought came into my mind, I got an email that Tweed was on its way. YES! Here we go…

I called Wally and within twelve hours he was at my front door and together we waited with six months of anticipation under our skin. And when the shipment arrived, it was like god delivered the pallet herself.

And before we realized our rolling papers were actually *not* the rice papers we were advertising them as, before we got a cease-and-desist letter from one of the biggest rolling paper companies out there, before we realized we had been swindled…

We had quite an adventure.

CHAPTER 45: TWEED

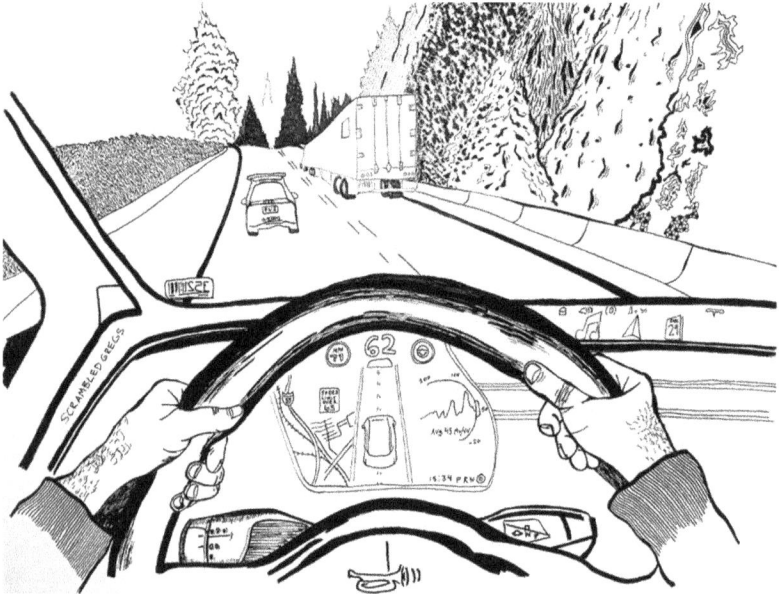

Wally's mom's car immediately got stuck in the mud as we drove onto the field of our first stop: The KahBang Music and Arts Festival in Bangor, Maine. Luckily, some dudes in a truck lugged us the fuck out. We gave them some Tweed as a thank you gift then went around pitching our rolling papers to the high school kids in raver outfits after setting up our tent. It was my first music festival and I hated it. I couldn't stand the large amounts of strangers all in one place. I felt like everyone knew each other except for me.

Paranoia crept in fast.

I became obsessed with being accepted by everyone I saw, even if it meant giving away more free Tweed to let them know I was a good dude. Our second day there, me and Wally were invited to a campfire and given food inside someone's VW bus, and I couldn't try and sell these people something after how kind they were to allow us into their circle, so again we gave out free Tweed as a thank you gift. By the end of the festival, we had sold zero Tweed and given out a thousand dollars' worth of product. Well, maybe not a thousand dollars' worth of product, that'd be a dickload of rolling papers. But still, we gave out a lot.

"This isn't working man. We can't keep giving this thing away. We need to sell this shit," I told Wally.

"But everyone loves them! It's so hard to not make them happy!"

"I know but like, we gotta sell the shit, right? Okay, maybe sellin em at this festival isn't a great idea."

"But it's our *only* idea."

He had a point. "What if... we go to town and find all the smoke shops and sell it directly to stores?"

"Dude, that's what I initially said!"

"I know! And it's a good idea! So let's go, right?"

So we went to town and walked into the first head shop we saw. The nag champa tickled my nostrils as the door beads clanked together upon entering the store. The clerk waited for whatever we were selling, cause it was obvious we weren't consumers.

"Great news," I said to the guy. "We have the world's greatest rolling papers and now so will you. Check them out," and I placed an unopened, beautifully packaged box of Tweed on the counter.

Silence.

Oh man, this is *not going to work.* What have I done with my life? This was such a silly fuckin dumbass idea.

"Whaht makes these any different than all tha othas I already sell?" the owner of the smoke shop asked. And then, I don't know, but I just got… mad.

"Yo, we literally came here from LA to your shop here in Maine. How many other traveling rolling paper salesmen have you met in the last ten years? This never happens. People like us don't just show up every day. We drove here from California to bring these to you—custom made, by us. And here's the thing… worst case scenario is it takes you a while to sell them all—but they *will* eventually all sell, and you'll be tripling your money. There's no way you won't triple your money. It's impossible. Just *might*—worst case scenario—take longer than expected. But think of it this way: If they sell right away and they're gone in a week, I'll give you our number and you can just call us up and ask for more and since you're the first store we've gone into, we'll have this special relationship that we won't have with anyone other than you. It's a win-win. You can't lose on this. That's what makes them so different: us!"

I kinda lost it for a moment. I was less angry after the pitch, but a bit worn out. We stared each other down for a moment till he looked up and said:

"How mahch?"

Oh my god. He wants them? Wally and I had decided on thirty dollars per box beforehand, but before I could price them out for the guy, Wally chimed in with: "hundred bucks for three boxes. That's two hundred in profit you'll make. Sound good?"

Then we waited.

"Only cauhse I like youz guys."

And that was how we made our first sale.

My vision of life as an entrepreneur solidified. We cockily walked into every smoke shop in Bangor and continued our sales pitch. We were a huge success. We got in the car and went to every surrounding town and were hitting up like ten stores a day, sometimes more. Nothing stopped us, especially not the weather.

In Portland it started raining and my flip flop broke off. I walked the entire city barefoot while slanging Tweed and didn't even bother buying another pair of flip flops till later in the day cause we were so on fire and I didn't wanna stop the flow. The sales trip kept garnering more and more momentum. There was this other site called Twitter. So, we started a Twitter account and people started following us, retweeting our photos, and sending us messages. Flea, the bassist from 311 retweeted us. That was our first celebrity endorsement, but there were more. It felt too good to be true. We were worn out by the time we got to Camden, this fancy ocean town on the coast of Maine. We stayed with a family friend of some kid we met at the festival.

"If you guys needa place to stay, I got an aunt in Camden!" some random kid by the campfire said on our second day of the music festival. He actually gave us his number, and we *actually* called him when we got to Camden, and he *actually* got his Aunt to let us stay with her. It was crazy. And when we showed up, she was *clearly* hitting on Wally. Wally was tall and had good hair. Maybe that's why.

"Do you two drink? I just opened some wine," she said as she took us into some outdoor patio room with candles lit. "Make yourselves comfortable."

Her husband was in the kitchen and gave us a nod. We nodded back. Sup. We walked inside the screened-in, lightly decorated room, packed with homy tchotchkes and a tinge of candlelight. We sat on an expensive couch and looked at each other like what the fuck? She came in with a smile and three glasses of wine. I was so happy she had wine. It was getting to be seriously exhausting having to make up excuses as to why we had to pull off the highway and go to a supermarket before nightfall...

"Oh shit! I gotta get something at the supermarket," I told Wally this one time.

"Like what? There's food at Billy's."

We were going to his friend Billy's when we were driving through New Hampshire to Burlington, Vermont and I noticed some of the towns had strict alcohol restrictions. That terrified me.

"Yeah but I just wanna get some snacks and shit," I told him. But when we parked in the parking lot, I ran to the other side of the shopping center to a liquor store and bought a bottle of scotch that I knew no one would be interested in drinking other than me, then ran to the supermarket to buy potato chips. "Picked up a bottle cause, hey, why not, right?" I said when I got back. I always made sure it was smoked scotch cause people hate that shit and I hated when other people drank my booze. That's why I stopped buying wine.

I'd buy the shit but then four friends who weren't really my friends, just some random kids in New Haven who invited us to crash on their couch or something along those lines, they'd each pour a glass from my bottle and then I'd have to race two glasses down my throat and hope to catch a buzz. That's no fun. Plus, to have a buzz and not have any more alcohol was like getting half a blow job—torture. Beer was also a bad beverage to buy cause I couldn't buy too many or else people'd think I was an alcoholic. So, I'd buy a medium amount, like twenty-four, then drink five beers immediately just to make sure I got enough to get me drunk—or at least heavily buzzed, which again, is not a fun feeling. Buzzed is only the beginning, and if you gotta stop at the start, why go to begin with, right?

And if I *didn't* make up some bullshit excuse about why we had to pull over, and if I *didn't* stop at the store before we crashed for the night, I ended up in very troublesome evenings where I'd have to scour the guests' house to find extra booze. Even worse than that, sometimes *Wally* would wanna do the shopping to bring wine to whoever's house and he'd buy *one bottle*... ONE BOTTLE!

Are you goddam kidding me?

For FOUR people!?

Holy shit, no. Drinking two glasses of wine was like peeing for ten seconds then holding it for the rest of the night—who can live like that?

Anyhow, that's why I'd continuously have to make up reasons to pull off the highway and find a shopping center. It was especially annoying to Wally when I couldn't find anywhere on the pull-off...

"Just get back on the road man."

"Wait, I just need to—one sec. One more minute. There's gotta be somewhere around here."

Finally we'd arrive like ten miles away from the highway and I'd park, jet to the liquor store, buy scotch, then run to the supermarket to get some Pringles, and come back to the car like no big deal with my signature throwaway line:

"Saw this and thought: why not?" Then I'd chuck the scotch in the back and pretend I'd already forgotten about it. "You ready?"

And so yeah, that actually became my life for the duration of the sales trip. I started to hate it. It was tiring too cause I insisted on doing all the driving so it'd be easier to pull off the road to grab more alcohol.

Anyway, I was telling you we were in Camden with that sexy aunt who was flirting with Wally in a buzzed-milfy kinda way. After the wine, when it appeared she'd had her fix of flirtation, she encouraged us to walk down to main street and explore the bar. She *really* wanted us drunk, which I loved… unfortunately she wanted to fuck Wally.

We went to the bar and played darts next to country club-lookin folk. It wasn't long before we felt a bit outa place. We were covered in accessories and hippie jewelry by then. We really looked the part of traveling rolling paper salesmen. Anyway, I was drunk enough to fall asleep, so we left the bar and walked back to the milfy aunt's house and crashed out.

And so life went…

Crashing with strangers who we met two towns ago, forming a following on Twitter, taking millions of photos, buying more and more tie-dye everything, fighting with Wally, hightailing it to the liquor store but pretending to be at the deli… I mean, it was goddam tiring.

After a couple months on the road, I was ready for vacation. We had sold Tweed to about a hundred stores in the Northeast, and so I told Wally I was gonna go visit my parents. They *really* had no idea what my life was. I loved them, but whenever we saw each other, I felt way too uncomfortable to sleep in my bedroom—old bedroom I should say, so I'd sleep downstairs in the basement on the couch. Plus, I had to be somewhere where I could drink in peace, and the basement was perfect cause I could sneak out the garage to smoke a joint when I needed to, which was often.

But what I was most excited about was The Mayweather fight. I *never* missed a pay-per-view fight. I loved the feeling of watching two dudes possibly kill each other. Anything could happen, just like my life. It was comforting to see such chaos. It was the only activity I truly enjoyed: a good fight with a bottle of scotch all to myself, and some weed rolled up in a joint. But the real trick of it all was to time the alcohol and drug consumption perfectly so that I was slightly buzzed by the start of the main event, which normally started at around 11PM eastern time. But to do all that took some planning…

Anyway, Mayweather was fighting Ortiz. It was September 17th of 2011, five days before my mom's fifty-seventh birthday, and twelve days before my twenty-seventh birthday. It was the perfect night. Truly it was.

Then I got a text from Chloe, who was having a much rougher night than I was… So, I invited her over, and that's how the start of the final debacle came to be…

CHAPTER 46: THE FINAL DEBACLE

Ah, and so we arrive close to the beginning of where this story began, about three months before that tension-filled trip to Vail, our not-so-romantic ski trip, and where I would conclude my last drug deal of my life… But as you know, I was sober during that trip, and I wouldn'ta gotten sober had it not been for the terrible evening Chloe and I shared at Crazy Girls, the strip club on Sunset and La Brea in Hollywood. But how the fuck did we get from my parent's basement in Long Island to Los Angeles to the strip club that ended it all?

Let's back it up a bit…

My buzz had just kicked in—perfect timing, and I was ready for the main event through careful preparation of tapered intoxication until the very last moment, when the buzz was released into a minor drunk by 11PM. That's when my phone buzzed.

"Hi!" I said to Chloe. "Can I call you back?"

But she was upset about some fucked up shit that happened in Miami… "Will you come pick me up from the train station?" she asked with complete disregard for how important a night it was for me.

It was at that moment I knew I had to make a decision: miss the fight I had been carefully pacing myself to enjoy—the fight I'd been waiting months for, or go and pick Chloe up—my only friend left in life, and miss the opening of the fight—the best part—when she could *easily* take a goddam cab from the station and be here in a few minutes. It was an easy decision:

"I can't Chloe, the fight is just about to start… Take a cab."

"Are you serious? A *fight?* You are so inconsiderate, seriously. I'm *astonished* you would make me take a cab. I would *never* leave you without a ride, ever. Ugh. You are unbelievable."

"Okay okay… What if I pay? I'll pay for it. You'll be here in five minutes, just—I'll meet you outside. Text me when you're in the driveway."

"Greg. You *have* to be kidding me."

Goddammit… So in a fluster—and drunk, mind you, which I never bothered to bring up to her as a reason I couldn't drive, I rushed to pick her up and was in a horrible mood by the time I got back since the fight had already started. By then my buzz had been killed, and she was upset about the entire scenario—despite the fact that I risked missing a first-round knock-out on her. Whatever, at least I didn't crash the car… I guess.

But that's not the point. The point is, that's how Chloe came back into my life in a big way, and it matters little why she came back to LA with me—though I'll tell you: her career had taken a pitfall. But like I said, that's not so important. What's important is the first thing she said when she walked into my unfurnished apartment after we landed at LAX and drove to Hollywood in the yellow Fiat the Hertz dickhead fucked me with after I told him the first car they tried to rent me was a piece of shit was this:

"Wait. Where's the bed? You don't have a bed?"

I had never thought of it that way: I don't have a bed. Hmm. She's right. Savannah and I had been sleeping on top of a mattress pad for nearly six months by then, transactionally fucking like crazy. She had a boyfriend actually—Savannah did, so it worked out well that I was still dating, but boy, she really was a country chick who gave zero fucks about anything and that alone was incredibly rewarding to have in my life. Like the first time we did anal.

"You can cum in my ass," she told me after I pulled out.

"Yeah?"

She looked back at me with her ass still up in the air... "Yes silly, you don't need to pull out, you can cum in my ass."

So I stuck my dick back in her ass and came a bucketload. But look, that's not the point either. The point is I let Savannah and Chloe get acquainted while I ran out and bought a mattress and a big TV to keep Chloe happy. After all, she was the only *real friend* I actually had. We'd known each other our whole lives. She meant more to me than anyone in the world.

We met in special ed in seventh grade. We were both losers with learning disabilities. Then we stayed friends when we both became popular in eighth grade, when we both grew out of ugly and into desirable. I got handsome and she grew wonderful tits, a priceless asset in middle school. She was the only person to write me while I was locked up in rehabs and juvie. Nobody really kept track of my life except for her. So, she was pretty special. I *had* to keep her happier than she'd ever been, but that proved to be harder than anticipated when it dawned on her that I had a serious drinking problem...

Every night I began cooking at like 5PM so I could fill up my scotch glass in the kitchen and hide it in the empty cupboard, the cupboard I never had any food in—not once. The only thing in there were empty canisters from medical marijuana joints. I never realized how much I smoked until I had to start buying it—shit is expensive. Anyway, I'd take a swig, then stash the glass back in the empty pantry and continue whistling while I cooked some mediocre meal, but I generally fell asleep while the food was still on the stove. I'd wake up and see the peppers burnt to a crisp.

"Don't worry, I turned the stove off," Savannah would say.

"Oh. Shit. I musta…"

"Yeah. It's okay."

And then I'd repeat the behavior later that night, every night of my life.

But Chloe was special. I really thought if I were to get married, it should probably be to her. She was fuckin hot and had these demonically green eyes with tiny pupils, like black dots swimming in a sea of kryptonite. Nevertheless, I fingered her for the first time in the front seat of that damn yellow Fiat that everyone laughed at when we got to the used car dealership in Oxford… When I decided it was time for me to finally buy a car instead of renting them every month from the airport.

I felt so accomplished—not about the car.

My entire life I had wanted her, but I never said anything… and finally I had fingered her. What a wonderful feeling. But the sex got weird. I couldn't perform—not that I wanna get into that again. I mean shit, it's nearly the end of the story… last thing I need to write more about is my incompetent dick. It got to a point, actually, that when I *could* perform, it was like the luckiest night of my life. What a shitty condition I have. But what's important to note here is the Chloe-finger-bang blossomed into a short-lived romance that fizzled out as fast as it ignited.

Still I stayed faithful during its short tenure, even when Savannah asked if she could blow me real quick while Chloe was in the shower. I actually ended up telling Chloe about that for some reason, I guess to prove I was wanted, and from that point on, whenever she had to go somewhere, Chloe made either me or Savannah go with her. She never left Savannah alone with me ever again, with good reason I suppose. Another thing is Savannah never had any clothes on either. She walked around in a thong and this stretched-out, white V-neck tee shirt about as thin as tissue paper. It was phenomenal. I always wanted to fuck her, and she wasn't even that hot, but I was so addicted to our transactional relationship… It was everything I'd ever wanted. So, when I turned down her generous offer to blow me while Chloe was in the shower and said:

"I can't, I'm actually together with Chloe now."

Savannah acted surprised: "Oh wow, I had no idea. Okay… But… Maybe… Just a little?"

"I can't. I want to, but I can't."

It hurt my soul to decline that, and even though I'd already had so many, it was never enough. But anyhow, I stayed faithful and patted myself on the back about it.

The relationship between me, Chloe, and Savannah was like a reality TV show: toxically stable. Chloe and I would try and fuck and behind the curtain, one foot away, was Savannah Skyping with her boyfriend.

And then came the day of my twenty-seventh birthday. It was supposed to be my greatest birthday yet. I had made it to twenty-seven and was still alive. What an accomplishment…

But I passed out at 8PM after drinking a bottle of scotch while pretending to cook, so it went minimally celebrated. That's why the *real* celebration took place two weeks later, on October 14th of 2011, the night of The Final Debacle.

But before we get there, I should let you know something… And this might feel weird to hear such a detail all the way at the end of this book, but it's important that it comes up now and not at any other time… Throughout this entire story, I had been going to see a therapist.

Yes, that's right.

All these internal battles were actually fought, not only between my ears and in the crevasses of my mind, but also in the serene setting of a wonky therapist's office in Long Island.

And truthfully, the only reason I didn't tell you about that till now is cause it genuinely slipped my mind. That's how goddam ineffective these visits were. I was only going cause my parents offered to pay for it years ago, and maybe I felt like I owed it to them to try and work on myself or whatever, but this therapist… he was in Long Island, right? And I went once a week to this fucker's house-office, though I showed up later and later into our appointments as life went by. In the beginning, right after KC and I had broken up, I'd get there at 11:30AM, right on time. By the end, I was arriving at 12:45PM—fifteen minutes *after* my appointment had ended. I mean, I didn't wanna hurt his feelings—I wanted him to know I did my best to get there.

The entire relationship was basically me telling him why I was running late.

"I have Tourette's," I told him after a year of seeing him. It took me everything to work up the courage to tell him that.

"Are you sure?" he asked me.

"Am I sure? Uhhh, yeah, I'm pretty fuckin sure Doc."

"You don't seem like you have it."

I was furious. I stopped talking to him about it.

And see the reason I'm bringing this up now is cause I was *still seeing him* even in LA—we'd Skype in my car so Savannah—and now Chloe—wouldn't hear anything. The only reason I still saw him was cause I was too much of a pussy to break up with him.

"Why don't you stop seeing him?" Chloe asked me right after one of my visits.

"You think I should?"

"You're supposed to feel better after you talk to your therapist. This guy makes you feel worse."

She had a point. She was especially pissed when I told her he didn't believe me I had Tourette's.

"Yeah, he doesn't think I have it," I told her. And I didn't even tell Chloe I had it up until a few days before that. I pulled over on Ventura Boulevard while we were driving through the valley and said—cause I couldn't keep it a secret any longer, I said: "I gotta tell you something." But I couldn't get the words out. Then I started hyperventilating.

"What is it? You can tell me anything. I'll always love you. You know that."

We stayed parked in that parking lot for like an hour before I pushed the words through my lips:

"I have. I uhh. I'm, I have." Then I started crying. Finally, through the fast breathing and tears, I managed to say: "I have Tourette's."

"That's it?" she asked me. "That's what you thought I would judge you about?"

I was so happy *someone finally knew about it.* Anyway, when I told her that my shrink didn't think I was telling him the truth, she erupted into fury:

"ARE YOU FUCKING SERIOUS? That's like... *emotional* abuse. You NEED to break up with him."

And so that's what I did. I broke up with him right after my twenty-seventh birthday. I had always said to myself if my life was still a mess by the time I turned twenty-seven that I would make a drastic change... so, this was it. The change I was drastically making was to break up with my shrink. After all, I had been lying to him about selling drugs for like six years by then. It didn't start like that though. In the beginning, I told him everything, how much I was selling, all that. But when he began to tell me I had to stop, I just started lying to him.

"I'm not stopping."

"Well, you really should."

"Look, I just won't talk about it with you then."

"But I'm your therapist!"

"Okay, I'll stop."

"Are you lying?"

"I'm not lying."

"We'll see…"

And so from that day forth, I lied to him every single week. It was goddam exhausting. So, already I felt like a new man— no therapist, time to start anew. I realized I could take my life wherever I wanted it to go. Chloe really was a wonderful influence. That's why I wanted to remember my birthday with her by doing something special…

It all started at a restaurant on Hollywood Blvd.

"Let's go to a strip club," I suggested. "You want to? We'll re-celebrate my birthday. I won't pass out this time."

"Fine, but *no drinking,*" Chloe made me promise.

"Oh come on. Two drinks. It's my fuckin birthday."

"You passed out on your birthday."

"But this is my new birthday."

"Fine, two drinks but no driving."

"Deal."

"Promise me. Say you promise."

"Of course I promise. You think I would drive drunk?"

But at the end of the night, I handed the valet parker my ticket and got in the car as soon as he pulled it around…

Chloe didn't move.

"C'mon lezzgOoo!" I told her. She stayed put right next to the bouncer. "Fuck'r'you DOING?"

"No Greg, no! You PROMISED!"

She turned her back to me and said something to bouncer, not sure what. Was she hitting on him in front of me? That's when I lost it.

"What'in the'*fuck'r* you doin? Huh?! CHLOE! Fuggin bitch'r you doin?! Flirting withuhh FUGGIN bounZer?"

"STOP! No! I'm not talking to you. Get out of the car!"

"OH, YOU'LLRUH FUCKIN THE BOUNCER HUH?"

I could hear my voice saying words I detested, words I would never voluntarily say, but I couldn't stop them from leaking outa my throat...

"You SAID you wouldn't drive!"

"FUCK! FUCKIN SHIT you think I'm doin?? Mm'NOT! I'm... I'm fuckin... I'm PARKIN'IT the fuggin, fuck... the goddam CAR! Dumb piece've fuck'n slut BITCH! Iz jus'like I told'jyou! So I don't gotta drive it! FUCKIN DUMB CUNT BITCH!" The anger kept building. I couldn't tame it down. "I'muh gonna fuggin PARK IT! THERE! LOOK! And thez get us a fucking cab for us! WHY'RZU STILL STANDING!? HUH?!"

"No. I'm not coming. GET OUT OF THE CAR!"

These weren't her words; there'd be no way to know for sure how she said what she said, but these mis-quoted replicas of the sentences she actually said will do just fine. How she worded her phrases isn't so important. The idea is she was terrified of the monster I had become. It was infuriating. Me? A monster? I'll show you you goddam bitch...

"FUCKING SLUT!"

I got in the car and slammed my foot against the pedal until it could go no further. The RPMs redlined and the engine sounded like it may fall out. I couldn't see straight, but it was important she know how I felt, and it was dire I go fast. The faster I drove the more serious I appeared, and I was serious I tell you. I was so upset. I had to show it. I had to put myself in enough danger to scare her. I was doing this for her. Where am I?

I was back by the valet parker.

Wait. Had I not left? No. I did leave—I was sure of it, but I was now back in front of the strip club. How did I get back so fast?

"You're SUCH AN IDIOT! Get out!!"

I opened the door and the car slipped forward. Fuck. I forgot to put the car in park. I hopped back in and jolted it to park. Then I got out and screamed: "FINE! I'M UH NOT WON'T FUGGIN DRIVE!" But then I saw her walking away. Was that her? She was down the street. "CHLOEEEEEEEEE!!!" I shrieked. The cars looked. The people saw me as the gargantuan tarantula that I had become. "Where'in the FUCKIN SHIT are you going!?" I belted like a mad man.

"Go away! I'm going to a hotel!"

"FUCK'YOUR BITCH AN FUCK'N—FINEEEE!"

And then…

Blackness.

Thump. Thump. Thump.

[GASP]

I shot up, sweaty, out of breath. What's going on?

I was in my apartment. It was light out. I was on the mattress. I looked at my phone. It was 5:45AM. There was an unread text from my neighbor:

Sorry couldn't get the coke mate.

Coke? What coke? I looked around the room. Chloe was on the futon. Right, we had a futon. A gross one. And Chloe was on it. Chloe? I thought she was… wait a minute. What? It all came back to me. Some of it. The part at the strip club came back to me. Wait, did I have more than two drinks? I saw myself saying I would only have two drinks. I was saying it to Chloe. Did I not do that? I logged into my bank app and looked at my credit card bill. I spent $254 at the club. Wait, on what? I remember paying cash for a girl to dance for Chloe. Was the rest spent on drinks? How much is a drink there? Probably expensive, that's why. But even if it was $15 a drink, which is a lot, and even if Chloe had three drinks, which she didn't, I remembered that. That means I drank... Fuck. Way more than two drinks.

But she was serious about that? Of course I wouldn't just have *two drinks*.

I saw the look on Chloe's face as she slept miserably. Even while sleeping her eyes were filled with disgust. How'd she get here? Did I drive? I looked out the window and there was no car there. How could this happen? I lost my car? What happened? I crawled to Chloe on my knees and put my face right near hers. It was then I saw that she wasn't even sleeping.

"I'm uh... I'm sorry," I said from the lowest part of my ego.

"Of course you are." I let that sink in. What could I say to make this better? Nothing. So I just stayed silent. Savannah was asleep behind the curtain she put up. Was she sleeping? Was she listening? "You're an alcoholic Greg, and I'm going back to New York today."

Everything in my life fell to shit with that one line. If I lost her, I'd have no one left.

"No, please. I'm sorry. Please, don't leave me. Please. Please stay, Chloe, please."

"No. Stop. Don't talk to me."

"I'll never drink again."

"So go to an AA meeting."

There was nothing left to say. I left the apartment and walked a few miles, staring at the cracks in the sidewalk, hoping a truck would swerve onto the curb and blow me to smithereens, and let my feet drag me all the way to the strip club. My car *must* be somewhere around there. It was the saddest walk of my life. I had burned my last bridge. There was nothing left to live for. Maybe I'll kill myself? But how?

I walked and walked. Finally I got to the strip club. A strip club at six in the morning is a very sad view. Next to the unlit neon lights screaming at oncoming traffic that there were "sexy girls" and "topless women" inside, next to the closed strip club was a gas station. There were no cars anywhere. Nobody was outside. And amidst the silence and morning desperation was my new Nissan. My white Nissan Sentra I had bought after I fingered Chloe for the first time in the parking lot in that shitty yellow Fiat. There it was. It was in the gas station.

How'd it even get there? Where are the keys?

I walked over to it and the keys were on the front seat. The door was open. Wow. Someone coulda stolen this shit. I drove it home. Maybe I should drive it off a cliff? But which cliff?

I don't fuckin know. Nothing works out. Nothing has amounted to anything. I was even out of money. How'd that happen? I had eighty grand a year ago. What the fuck? I give up. But something inside me said:

At least go to ONE meeting... after that, kill yourself.

So I went to the first AA meeting I could find near my apartment. It was October 15th of 2011. The meeting was at a library. I walked all around lookin for the room but couldn't find it. Then I went upstairs and saw a room with the door closed. That must be it. So, I went closer to see. I peeped inside the small window of the door and saw three people sitting around a circular table. Abort! Leave! And I ran out.

So much for going to a meeting...

No.

I have to go to at least one before I kill myself.

So I sat in my car and looked up another meeting. I found one. It was in a long room by a parking garage in West Hollywood. It was full of gay meth heads. I walked in, shriveled and small, and sat in the back of the flavorless room, then ran out as soon as the meeting ended. One guy stopped me and asked for my number. Is he gay? Yes, he is. But does he think *I'm* gay? Why does he want my number? I gave it to him anyway. Chloe stayed another night, still intent on leaving, just later on in the week perhaps.

I sweat and convulsed with tremors that night, my first full day sober in ten years. I had to hold my eyes shut with all my strength. They kept springing back open. I laid there, begging god to let me somehow get to sleep without a drink. I prayed my head off, uncertain if god was real. He's not, but maybe he is? And then...

I woke up.

I did it! My first twenty-four hours sober since I was sixteen. I went to another meeting that night, and after four months, Chloe was still with me and I hadn't yet killed myself. But it was getting harder and harder. I was barely able to maintain a conversation. And I was bored. I was *so* bored with my new sober life that I decided to write down my entire life story, everything that had happened to me and try and make sense of it all. I called the book No Direction Home.

Should I write it all in one book? Nah, that's too much shit. It'll probably take three books to write all this shit down.

And still there was Tweed, which had been slowly fizzling out after we got a cease-and-desist letter from a competitor telling us we couldn't advertise our papers as "rice papers" anymore. Yeah. The chick from the big rolling paper company had swindled us and sold us wood pulp paper. Fucking cunt. Our competitor apparently ran a lab test on our papers and emailed us saying we were full of shit, that they were *not* rice papers at all...

Not only that, but now that I was sober, I ignored all of Wally's calls. I told him we had to stop Tweed, that we would get arrested if we kept going for false advertising. I don't know if that's true, but he didn't care and wasn't willing to quit. Really I just couldn't think of weed for too long before feeling like I was going absolutely insane. So when Wally invited me to a weed convention to promote our business, I told him I was out. I offered Wally the CEO position and gave him more stake in the company. Just leave me alone, I was thinking. I didn't wanna deal with it. I was too busy trying to survive without scotch and coke and weed and wine and fuck. Why am I alive? I need a meeting. But I stopped going to meetings after only a few. I told Chloe they just weren't working for me, but I was sober and that's all that mattered.

Then one day Chloe was finally ready to go back to New York. I had nothing left for me in LA, so I sold my car for a few thousand dollars and flew back with her...

But before that happened, I begged her to come with me to Colorado. I just had to do *one more deal*, just one more deal to fund my sobriety. And it was on that trip to Colorado that I bought and sold my last ten pounds, at four months sober. Five pounds to Joey Landlord, and the other five pounds to my Harlem Guy. I picked it up from My Grower, shipped half to Jersey, the other half to Harlem, and got the checks in the mail. It was the quickest flip I'd ever done. And can you believe I got away with it? Doesn't make sense, I know.

But right around that time, when we got back to New York, Chloe left me for greener pastures. I realized there was nobody left to keep sober for anymore. So, after I pulled up to my parent's house—I was driving my parent's car—it was right after Chloe admitted she had been secretly dating other guys, I sat in the car in front of their big blue house in the driveway, now painted a dull shade of gray, and decided to call it quits. It was time to drink. I tried; it didn't work.

Wait.

Just go to *one more meeting* and *then* drink, I said to myself, back in my parent's basement at twenty-seven years old.

My entire extended family was upstairs having Sunday dinner. I was in the basement hiding. I stood up, mechanically walked up the stairs to the main floor, and looked at everyone enjoying their dessert in the kitchen. My mom looked at me as I sat down at the table, the one everyone had already dispersed from now that coffee had been served, when suddenly, I stood up again.

"I'm going to an AA meeting," I told her.

She smiled. "That's the best news I've heard since you were fourteen."

I got back in my parent's car and drove to a meeting in Glen Cove, one that I had found on some AA website. I sat down, angry at the world, and waited for the meeting to start. It was at the bottom of some church filled with blue-collar workers. Firefighters and cops and construction workers maybe. Finally, the meeting started… only one more hour till I can drink again. After this meeting, I'm getting drunk.

My mouth watered.

I imagined the scotch touching my lips, burning down my throat, relieving all my troubles. Just *share* before you leave, Greg. Don't just sit here quietly. Tell the world your pain.

"My name is Greg. I'm an alcoholic. I've been sober four months and I don't like it. It's been no fun at all. Tonight I'm going to drink. Just thought I'd share once more, just to prove to myself that I tried everything I could, but it was useless. I hate everyone here. Thanks."

"Thanks for sharing, Greg," the group said as methodically as they woulda said regardless of what I shared. Fuck this room.

The meeting ended. I was ready to leave, ready to drink. Again, my mouth was watering. I opened the door—

"Got a cigarette?" some old guy asked me on the way out.

"Uhh… yeah," and I handed him one. I had started smoking like a chimney since I stopped drinking, it was the only thing that made me happy.

"Nice night out tonight, eh?" he says. "Know what the wife said to me today?..." I really didn't care what his wife had said to him that day or any day, but I didn't know what to do with my hands so I pulled out a cigarette and lit it up. I didn't even hear what he said as the cigarette I gave him dangled from his lips. "Got a light?" he asked after saying whatever it was that he said.

"Uhh yeah."

And I gave him a light. Another guy joined us, so I pulled out another cigarette cause all these people made me nervous. I had no idea how to act. I finished that second cigarette and had no idea what to do, so I pulled out another cigarette. I smoked the entire pack. I could barely see straight an hour later when everyone was finally done talkin my ear off.

I stumbled back to my car, drove to my parents, head banging with pain, skull about to break. I opened the garage and collapsed on the couch in their basement and fell asleep. I had never felt so sick. I woke up the next day and again said to myself: I'm drinking tonight...

BUT...

I'll go to one more meeting, just to prove I did all I could, then I'll pour myself the greatest drink of my life. So, I went to a meeting later that day after a full twelve hours of depression, and walked into some Baptist church, already excited for the meeting to end though it hadn't yet started. I walked in and the room got quiet. What the fuck?

"Would you like to share?" the guy chairing the meeting asked.

This isn't how meetings are supposed to be, I thought. I been to millions of meetings, and they're not supposed to ask you to share. What the fuck is up with this guy, I wondered. But I started talkin anyway—I spoke for an hour. The meeting ended and some

Indian guy bombarded me and told me about some Ponzi scheme he had started as a drunk. I lit a cigarette cause I had no idea what to do. After the first Ponzi scheme he told me about, which I cared nothing for, he told me about the second and even his *third* Ponzi scheme he had started. And somewhere along his story about his path to sobriety, I began feeling sick from all the cigarettes again. I drove home and got inside and again collapsed on my parent's couch in the basement without a drink.

That was ten years ago. I've been sober ever since. I now go to meetings weekly, and I haven't stopped since those blue-collar workers talked my ear off at that Glen Cove meeting. Sometimes new people ask me for help, so I tell them what I did and how I stopped. My family and I have reconciled. I'll be getting married in May 2022 to a sober chick with a fat ass and colorful hair. It couldn't be a better fit...

And all I can say is, whoa. What a ride.

But before you leave, I wanna say thank you. Thanks for reading all this shit, and perhaps I'll tell you about how I became a world-famous roadtripper when I was five years sober when I broke the Guinness World Record for Longest Journey by Car in a Single Country with my ex-girlfriend, or perhaps I'll tell you about the time I circumnavigated South America by bus, or the time I met a man dying of cancer at a hostel in Fairbanks, Alaska— maybe even the time I almost died in the Grand Canyon, or was jumped on Hollywood Boulevard and ended up in the ER next to gunshot victims... or what about the time the LAPD helicopters chased after my U-Haul? So many tales to tell you now that I've been sober… but I suppose that'll have to wait for another book, after all, it's been over 400 pages. So, for now, I bid you farewell.

Oh, one more thing…

I love you.

xo,

Greg

KEEP IN TOUCH:

ScrambledGregs.com